P9-CFP-604

Operation Broken Reed

Operation Broken Reed

Truman's Secret North Korean Spy Mission that Averted World War III

Lt. Col. Arthur L. Boyd (Ret.)

DA CAPO PRESS
A Member of the Perseus Books Group

Originally published in 2007 by Carroll & Graf Publishers

Designed by Bettina Wilhelm

ISBN-13: 978-0-7867-2086-6

Published by Da Capo Press
A Member of the Perseus Books Group

It is to honor the dead and their sacrifice that this book is written.

"Not knowing a damn thing about the enemy is the worst damn pile of dung that any commander will ever fall into."

—General George S. Patton

Contents

Prologue

"For the want of a nail," begins Benjamin Franklin's refrain on the loss of a shoe, a horse, a rider, and, eventually—the battle. Yet in war, it is not nails but intelligence that decides battles. Indeed, it is accurate, correctly interpreted intelligence, *or the lack thereof,* that leads to war.

Tragically, the often quoted phrase "history repeats itself" couldn't be closer to the truth with respect to world leaders' blatant, wanton disregard of the need for intelligence that has led to tens of thousands of battle deaths. The strange paradox is that lessons learned have been lessons forgotten.

From June 1950 until July 1953 the United States waged war in Korea; though there were 33,686 battle deaths and over 100,000 wounded, it is America's forgotten war, a war so forgotten that 8,100 U.S. servicemen from that time are still unaccounted for.

It took fifty years for a monument to be erected to honor those who fought and died.

After the war, Korea existed on the periphery of American politics until only recently. Today it moves relentlessly closer to center stage, though for Americans its history remains obscure, riddled with misunderstanding. More than a million American soldiers served in Korea, and billions of dollars have been spent occupying South Korea over the last five decades, but most Americans know nothing of a country where so many of its youth died, and where many more might die someday.

The Vietnam War is vivid in the collective memory, but the Korean War era is shrouded. When people today think of the United States during the early 1950s, they conjure up a time of peace and prosperity, one long before war protests, and certainly before the threat of international terrorism, of which North Korea is a significant part. The early fifties evoke a slumberous period of tranquillity, roller rinks, and drive-in movies, yet the reality was very different: during those years, the United States, China, and the Soviet Union teetered on the brink of World War III; atomic war threatened annihilation.

The Korean War era was one of fear and suspicion—possibly greater than at any other time in American history. The cold war dominated all events; it was a period of atomic terror, the Red Scare, and blacklists. Americans were afraid during those years, and their fear was real—the world *did* teeter on the verge of atomic war.

Few Americans knew then, or realize now, that a hair-trigger nuclear scenario played out in Washington and Moscow during this time. In 1951, President Harry S. Truman faced a fearful decision: should he follow the advice of those who wanted to escalate the Korean War and defeat the Communist threat, or should he accept a stalemate, with the United States not winning a war for the first time since 1812?

Truman had undergone one of the most stressful presidencies in history. He himself would have started his litany of troubles on April 12, 1945, when President Franklin Delano Roosevelt died, thrusting the weight of a world at war on Truman's shoulders. The most improbable of vice presidents was not prepared. Roosevelt had been president for twelve years, longer than anyone, winning a fourth term even while desperately sick—collapsing the very day of his nomination, caught by his son at the convention, the event hushed up.

Truman, picked at the last moment from near obscurity in the U.S. Senate to be the vice presidential candidate, after a career as a haberdasher and ward politician, had been as surprised as anyone. In eighty-three days as vice president, the shortest of anyone ascending the presidency, he had met with Roosevelt exactly twice, and those were photo ops. He was virtually clueless about the course of the war in Europe and the Pacific, and had never even heard about the atomic bomb until a few months before he ordered it dropped on Hiroshima and Nagasaki, ushering the world into the atomic age and an arms race of which Albert Einstein and others had forewarned him. Nevertheless, he had no regrets or second thoughts about the decision to drop the bombs.

In March 1947, Truman proposed a new foreign policy for the United States: the country would intervene wherever necessary to prevent the subjugation of free peoples by communist totalitarian regimes, beginning with those in Greece and Turkey. His target was the Soviet Union, which he felt was undermining the foundations of world peace, threatening the security of the United States, and violating the Yalta Agreement in Poland, Romania, Hungary, and Bulgaria.

This new foreign policy placed the United States on a collision course with Russia that culminated in Korea in 1950.

For Truman, 1948 was his only good year. He'd won election to the presidency in his own right, defeating the heavily favored Republican Thomas Dewey; FDR's former vice president Henry Wallace (the man Truman replaced) running as a Progressive; and Senator Strom Thurmond, who bolted the Democratic Party because of its civil rights plank to run as a Dixiecrat.

Before that, there had been other great accomplishments—the United Nations, the European Recovery Program—named the

Marshall Plan after Secretary of State George C. Marshall—the North Atlantic Treaty Organization, the Berlin airlift, integration of the armed services, and the formation of Israel.

But those halcyon days were over by 1951, when newspapers blared awful stories of Americans dying in Korea, spies in government, and corruption at the door of the Oval Office (seven members of Truman's administration, including some of his closest aides, would eventually go to jail).

Everything soured after 1948. The following year brought terrifying news that the Soviet Union had developed the atomic bomb, a full decade earlier than expected. A month before that, a State Department white paper revealed that China, the world's most populous country, had fallen to the communists. On October 1, 1949, Mao stood on the Tian An Men—the Gate of Heavenly Peace in Beijing—to proclaim the People's Republic of China, warning that "The Chinese people have stood up . . . nobody will insult us again."

The words were prophetic, and should have been heeded by General Douglas MacArthur and Truman.

Republicans scored 52 percent of the vote in the 1950 congressional elections; Truman's own party had gotten a mere 42 percent and saw its majority in the Senate cut from twelve to two, and in the House from seventeen to twelve. Just two weeks before the election, Puerto Rican nationalists stormed Blair House, where Truman was living while the White House was being renovated. The assassination attempt failed, but a White House policeman stationed outside was murdered and another wounded in a fusillade that engulfed the Blair House lobby. Had the assassins waited another twenty minutes, they would have killed the thirty-third president of the United States.

The year had started with the conviction of Alger Hiss for passing secrets to the communists and Senator Joseph McCarthy brandishing a list of 205 "known communists" in the State

Department during a speech in West Virginia; everything since had been downhill.

Then came Korea, a country with a history dating back to 2000 BC.

Three kingdoms—Silla, Koguryo, and Paekche—existed on a peninsula in East Asia (what is now Korea) long before the birth of Christ. They fought among themselves for centuries. Silla became dominant in the late seventh century, but Koguryo fought back and unified the peninsula in 936 AD. The Mongols invaded in 1259 and ruled until the Koguryo empire returned to establish the Yi Dynasty in 1392, a hundred years before Columbus landed in America. The Yi Dynasty lasted until 1910, when the Japanese invaded and subjugated Korea. Their domination was complete and brutal.

After the Japanese defeat in 1945, Korea was split into two countries at the thirty-eighth parallel—North Korea, the Democratic People's Republic of Korea, under Kim Il Sung, whose capital was Pyongyang; and South Korea, the Republic of Korea, under Syngman Rhee—its capital was Seoul.

Kim Il Sung, a communist trained in Moscow, had fought Japanese rule. Rhee had been a leader of the provisional government that had resisted the Japanese since 1919.

The Soviet Union and Red China backed North Korea; the United States supported South Korea. On June 25, 1950, North Korea invaded South Korea to unite the country under communist rule. The United States militarily backed South Korea. A civil war led by opposing patriots took on the overtones of a conflict between major powers and ideologies.

The United States voted in the United Nations to stop the Communist invasion and sent troops, but its forces were driven back relentlessly. By August 1950, poorly trained and ill-equipped UN soldiers had been rolled south to the end of the peninsula only thirty miles from Pusan. Allied forces were facing another

Dunkirk, but General Douglas MacArthur, against the objections and advice of even the Joint Chiefs of Staff, launched the brilliant Inchon landing on September 15, relieving the pressure. In October, the U.S. Eighth Army pressed beyond the thirty-eighth parallel and attacked north, reaching the Yalu River, which separated Korea from Manchuria, by October 24, 1950.

It was here that MacArthur made a disastrous mistake. Believing the Chinese could not muster more than 60,000 troops along the border, assuring Truman there was little risk of Chinese involvement, MacArthur pushed forward.

A month later, the Chinese counterattacked in force: 260,000 troops of the Sixty-third Chinese Army swept across the Yalu and drove the UN forces back seventy miles south of the thirty-eighth parallel. UN forces rallied, and after a year of vicious and bloody battles, attacks, and counterattacks, the conflict was at a stalemate. Unwilling to accept this situation, many in Congress and many military leaders pressed Truman to launch a massive offensive to include the use of tactical nuclear weapons.

Believing he had been duped by MacArthur, whom he relieved in April 1951, and without clear knowledge of Communist Chinese intentions or capabilities, Truman felt boxed in—he did not want to lose the war, but neither did he want to expand it. Hovering above it all was the Red Scare, the palpable fear of communist conquest of the world. Yet hovering alongside that fear was the specter of nuclear war.

In 1951, the world was more imperiled than at any time in recent memory.

Any decision Truman made risked major global consequences. Acquiescence to the communist attack would not only enrage political foes at home, but possibly feed Soviet and Chinese aggression. Expansion of the war risked nuclear escalation. Compounding Truman's problem was his belief that he did not possess sufficient intelligence on enemy capabilities and intentions to make a proper assessment for a course of action.

Feeling he had only months to make a decision that would determine the future for decades to come and the lives of millions, Truman authorized Operation Broken Reed.

This is the true story of that mission and how close the United States came to global nuclear war.

It is a story of daring, heroics, sacrifice, and death, a story of ten men who went behind enemy lines in January 1952 to collect, process, and transmit military intelligence concerning the North Korean and Communist Chinese armies. Their mission, called Operation Broken Reed, originated in the White House with Truman's full backing; it discovered that China's resolve and military forces were far greater than anyone had suspected. Pressing the war would incite China and the Soviet Union. The mission convinced Truman that disaster would result.

Broken Reed (1951–1952) was what today would be called a Special Access Program (SAP), or "black" operation similar to the Iran-Contra operation run through the National Security Council (1983–1986), and the current war on terrorism, primarily directed through the Defense Department, but with the unofficial authorization of the NSC.

Broken Reed was conceived and implemented at the highest level of government by President Harry S. Truman, Secretary of State Dean Acheson, Secretary of Defense George C. Marshall—the only permanent and voting members of the NSC—along with CIA director Walter Bedell Smith, White House Counsel Clark Clifford, W. Averell Harriman, chairman of the Joint Chiefs of Staff Omar Bradley, and a very few others.

President Truman, in the midst of his first elected term, contemplating reelection in 1952, faced rabid criticism at home, both for his administration's failure to foresee the war and for his failure to deal with Soviet espionage, a public perception known as the Red Scare fueled by McCarthyism, a hysterical national response to the threat of communism.

Worst of all for Truman, a larger war loomed—atomic and catastrophic.

Broken Reed's conception and execution were a result of what Truman felt to be a breakdown in intelligence gathering: essentially, how could the Central Intelligence Agency (CIA), responsible for human intelligence (HUMINT), the Armed Forces Security Agency (AFSA), responsible for communications intelligence (COMINT), and the military have so badly miscalculated? How could they have missed a *war?*

Worse, they collectively knew almost nothing of the enemy or of Korea's allies—China and the Soviet Union. Would China, with its million-man army, jump in to help North Korea? Would the Soviet Union use nuclear weapons? These were critical questions; indeed, millions of lives and the course of history depended upon the answers and upon Truman's response. The correct answers and proper response rested on intelligence, and it was this that Truman felt he lacked.

Compounding Truman's distrust and concern were almost daily revelations about communist infiltration of the U.S. and British intelligence communities, along with the defection of agents, such as Donald Maclean and Guy Burgess, and the release of atomic secrets to the Soviet Union. Klaus Fuchs, Julius and Ethel Rosenberg, and others were arrested by the FBI in 1950. A dark canopy of suspicion hung over the government.

To appreciate Truman's desperation for an operation such as Broken Reed, one has to understand the confusing state of U.S. intelligence in 1950, a morass that impelled him to take extreme measures. Broken Reed was not the first, and certainly not the last, cloak-and-dagger "black" operation run out of the White House.

Indeed, Truman's predecessor, Franklin D. Roosevelt, reveled in such secret operations, especially before Pearl Harbor, when he personally nudged the United States to closer ties and cooperation with Britain. Every president since Truman has conducted SAPs from the Oval Office.

After World War II, U.S. intelligence gathering devolved into such disarray that at Truman's instigation, and mostly through the work of Dean Acheson, the National Security Act of 1947 was passed. In addition to creating the NSC, which would oversee all national security issues, a council with only three permanent and voting members—the president and the secretaries of state and defense—it chartered the CIA. The CIA was charged with the collection, evaluation, and interpretation of "foreign intelligence information originating outside the continental limits of the United States by any and all means deemed effective." Essentially this is termed HUMINT—human intelligence gathering, as opposed to COMINT, communications intelligence gathering.

For COMINT, a 1948 NSC directive gave formal power to the United States Communications Intelligence Board (USCIB) "to effect the authoritative coordination of Communications Intelligence activities of the Government." In addition, the directive stated that "the special nature of Communications Intelligence activities requires that they be treated in all aspects as being outside the framework of other or general intelligence activities."

In essence, COMINT was singled out for unique status in the government—it operated in an autonomous vacuum answerable in the end only to the NSC—the president, the secretary of defense, and the secretary of state.

The following year, in 1949, the AFSA emerged under the direction and control of the Joint Chiefs of Staff. In 1952, the AFSA became the National Security Agency (NSA), the most secret agency in the government; its control was taken from the military and placed directly under the NSC.

In 1950, intelligence gathering was a churning cauldron of problems; untested remedies were still in the future.

The forerunner of the CIA, the Office of Strategic Services (OSS) under the legendary William Donovan, had been disbanded in 1945 and its agents dispersed among various government departments—State, War, Navy, and Treasury. There was no central agency for the collection of HUMINT until late 1947. There was no "home" for spies until the CIA was created. It was still a fledging organization when the Korean War broke out. Most of its operatives were in Europe fighting the enemy, the KGB; for all practical purposes, there was no HUMINT coming in from the Far East, especially in regard to Korea.

The collection of COMINT was in even worse shape.

COMINT is a specialized and highly technical field generally called cryptology—code and work in all its aspects: creating codes, breaking codes, and analyzing and evaluating intelligence from codes no matter how they are transmitted.

Secrets are usually encoded so that intelligence is passed in a secure manner. It does no good for a spy to seize a document or to record or intercept a coded transmission if the code in which it is transmitted can't be broken. Espionage requires both effective HUMINT and COMINT.

Modern U.S. COMINT dates to World War I and two men: Herbert Yardley and William Friedman. Yardley was the father of American cryptology and in 1917 was put in charge of the War Department's MI-8, responsible for all code and cipher work. For added secrecy, MI-8 was not in Washington, D.C., but had an office in New York City with a Grand Central Station post office box. During World War I, Yardley went to Paris to develop closer ties with France's secret Cabinet Noir. His work during the Paris peace talks was so important that MI-8 was continued after the armistice with fifty-one employees and an annual budget of $100,000, split between the War and State departments. MI-8 was the United States' Black Chamber.

At the same time, Friedman and his sole assistant comprised the Army Signal Corps' Code and Cipher Section.

In World War I, MI-8 created its own code to transmit secret material and deciphered nearly eleven thousand foreign messages. World War I also saw the first use of Native American code talkers—Choctaw Indians.

In 1919, Yardley broke the Japanese secret code, giving the United States an almost complete and uninterrupted ability to decipher Japanese radio traffic throughout World War II. The order to attack Pearl Harbor had been decoded many hours before the first bombs were dropped. The long delay in transmitting the warning to Hawaii was the result of human error; for a long period of time, the chairman of the Joint Chiefs of Staff could not be found—General George C. Marshall was horseback riding in northern Virginia. COMINT did, however, have a decisive role in the Battle of Midway, and was crucial in defeating the Nazis. Without Ultra, the code name for Britain's greatest secret, and the cipher machine Enigma, which broke Germany's code, Hitler might not have been defeated.

So, for quite some time, cryptology's importance had been appreciated, yet the Black Chamber's fortunes declined in the 1920s because intercept traffic diminished drastically and the MI-8's budget was cut by 75 percent.

MI-8's end came in 1929, when Secretary of State Henry L. Stimson discovered with horror that the United States was spying on foreign governments. He uttered the legendary words: "Gentlemen, do not read each other's mail," and terminated all funding for MI-8.

Nevertheless, more secretive minds prevailed, and MI-8's activities were transferred to the Army Signal Corps under

William Freidman. The new organization was called the Signal Intelligence Service (SIS) and placed under the control of the secretary of war. The SIS grew from a staff of 331 at the time of Pearl Harbor to over 10,000 by World War II's end. The Navy, a separate department equal to the War Department (the two merged in 1947 to become the Department of Defense) also did cryptology, but on a smaller scale and limited to ships at sea.

Once the United States was at war, Stimson, now the secretary of war, had changed his mind about reading other gentlemen's mail. Indeed, he actively promoted COMINT. In 1943 the SSI became the Signal Security Agency, then the Army Security Agency. After the war, in 1949, it became the Armed Forces Security Agency under the direction and control of the Joint Chiefs of Staff.

It was the failure of the AFSA to foresee the Korean War that incurred Truman's wrath, and largely brought about Broken Reed.

The governing body of COMINT was also in constant flux, from the informal Army–Navy–Communications Intelligence Coordinating Board to a formal State–Army–Navy Communications Intelligence Board, to a 1946 U.S. Communications Intelligence Board (USCIB), then in 1949 to the Armed Forces Security Agency Council (AFSAC), under the USCIB. The changes were reflected in the quality of COMINT; the product mirrored the disarray, a result in large part of the constant squabbling for control among the various players—State and Defense departments, the Joint Chiefs of Staff, and the CIA.

The chaos and confusion are evident in the AFSAC's selection of intelligence targets for the AFSA to concentrate on. In the seven months prior to North Korea's attack on South Korea, Korea was listed last among the top twelve target areas of concern. North Korea was not considered a threat. Korea was likewise not a concern for the CIA, which listed it fifth in potential danger.

Three weeks after North Korea's invasion of South Korea, the USCIB stated that "The present scale of communications intelligence effort falls far short of meeting total requirements or even enabling the U.S. to exploit available communications information to its full potential."

In the midst of a sudden and unexpected war, Truman was told his intelligence community was unprepared and unable to provide adequate intelligence, despite the AFSA's 8,500 personnel and $60 million budget, and despite the CIA's vast resources. Truman was so disgusted that he directed his defense secretary to create a committee to evaluate American COMINT and take corrective action. In June 1952, the committee issued a 239-page report that blamed the intelligence failure primarily on the military services and the Joint Chiefs. The committee also recommended that the AFSAC be disbanded and replaced by the NSC. As a result, the AFSA became the National Security Agency, and control was taken from the military and given to three men—the president and the secretaries of state and defense, meeting as the NSC.

This transfer of control, however, took place more than two years *after* the Korean War began, two years of military failure and stalemate, and even more years of bureaucratic lumbering to remedy and stabilize COMINT.

In the meantime, Truman was losing the Korean War. Men were dying. He needed immediate intelligence; he could not wait. HUMINT, COMINT, and the military had failed him, and it might be years before the intelligence community could provide him with the information he desperately needed on the strength, capabilities, and intentions of North Korea, China, and the Soviet Union.

Truman was a decisive leader who had not hesitated to drop atomic bombs on Hiroshima and Nagasaki; nor had he hesitated when North Korea attacked—he immediately sent in his armies. He did not hesitate when faced with an intelligence breakdown that threatened to lead to a larger and more destructive war—he ordered Broken Reed. He gathered with Acheson, Marshall, and a very few others to solve his most pressing problem—lack of knowledge about the enemy. He did this because he wisely feared plunging humanity into World War III and annihilation.

He also did this because he believed he had implicit and de facto power under the National Security Act of 1947, and NSC Intelligence Directive No. 9, which placed COMINT "outside the framework of other or general intelligence activities" and ultimately in the hands of the NSC—himself and his secretaries of state and defense.

In essence, Truman sliced through the bureaucracy and red tape to do what he felt he had the power to do. For the sake of secrecy and the national interest, he cut out layers of middlemen on boards and committees.

He was dealing directly with Secretary of State Dean Acheson; Secretary of Defense George C. Marshall, the architect of military victory in World War II; CIA Director Walter Bedell Smith, Eisenhower's chief of staff; and Chairman of the Joint Chiefs of Staff Omar N. Bradley, Eisenhower's field commander in Europe. With these men, the victors in World War II, three men with fourteen stars among them, two generals of the U.S. Army, how could he go wrong?

Broken Reed was a transdepartmental, interagency operation involving State, Defense, the military, AFSA, and the CIA, along with Chiang Kai-shek and the British Admiralty, all under the auspices and direction of the president of the United States.

Because Broken Reed was also a Special Access Program (SAP) reporting unofficially to NSC members, there were no records, transcripts, or evidence. The operation itself was micromanaged by one man with direct access to the White House—George Brown. Whether he was military or CIA or AFSA has never been determined—nor has his real name.

Operation Broken Reed is a first-person account of this harrowing mission behind enemy lines, and of the ten men who undertook it over fifty years ago. Seven of the men perished on a frozen road in North Korea during the final hours of the mission; I saw them die. Two others may have died from wounds afterward.

My national security oath forced me to live with memories of Operation Broken Reed for more than forty-six years, never able to share them with anyone. The story you are about to read has haunted me throughout most of my lifetime. I have relived scenes of death and destruction again and again and again through hundreds of flashbacks and nightmares. Those thoughts and dreams have kept memories of a hellish intelligence mission alive—as if Broken Reed had taken place only a few days ago.

I have been diagnosed with combat-related post-traumatic stress disorder (PTSD). Those who live with the horror of combat memories will readily identify with my unsuccessful attempt to forget the dreadful events that are embedded in my mind. The more effort I made to forget, the fresher in my mind every moment returned. Every dialogue, each scene of my Broken Reed odyssey, I have replayed endlessly.

Following the mission, I made every effort to avoid anything and everything that had to do with Korea. I declined to read, discuss, or view anything about the war there—or those who had a vital part in its outcome, such as President Truman and General MacArthur.

Even so, only six years following Broken Reed, I was assigned to the United States Seventh Infantry Division in South Korea. Other than while serving as a team member on Broken Reed, that period was the most troubling time of my life.

When Operation Broken Reed was declassified in 1998, I began receiving psychiatric care and Veterans Center counseling in order to restore peace to a troubled mind. It was during that time that I recalled a promise I had made during the mission debriefing to tell the story of Broken Reed in order to pay homage to those who had died.

It has required seven years and five difficult rewrites to finalize the story of Broken Reed. Hour upon hour has been spent in research that helped to provide details that otherwise would have been left out. Archive maps were reviewed in order to pinpoint locations, retrace the armored-convoy route, and mentally walk once again over a thirty-mile frozen mountain trail that provided three survivors an escape route to the Yellow Sea. Historical military archives provided valuable information that confirmed and reinforced my memory of twenty intelligence reports that were transmitted to President Truman.

Everything concerning the mission is described in as much detail as I am able to recall.

Conclusions were made based upon historical facts. Conversations that took place between intelligence team members have been re-created and remain crystal clear in my mind.

What I have written is recounted in honesty. After fifty-five years, there is no way that I could recite verbatim what was said and by whom, but the substance of the conversations stands as faithful.

During my spiritual journey, I graduated from Bethel Seminary in Saint Paul, Minnesota, with a master of divinity degree. Some of the dialogue shared in the story is not what one would expect a man of the cloth to use. Those words, however offensive they might be, are not my words, but the words of men who served by my side and made the ultimate sacrifice for their country and the world.

It is to those brave and patriotic men that this book is dedicated.

This story, written from memory, research material, and personal records, is told from the eyes and perspective of a young man.

I was twenty-two years old when the Korean War began.

The Ledge

I was on a promontory at the edge of the world. Before me darkness stretched to infinity. Below, jagged rocks jutted from the sea. Beside me, two men lay severely wounded.

In my imagination, Death waited with me, a shrouded malevolence imperially indifferent, almost bored, and just waiting. My other seven comrades had been killed quickly; I never knew the real identity of those with me, nor those who died. Death seemed to be toying with the last three of us.

There was neither moon nor stars, as if they'd taken shelter from the frigid night, and though sheltered by the cliff from the wind, the chill penetrated to the marrow of my bones. The temperature was near zero.

We had been caught in something much larger than our lives, but in the end we'd been discarded, driven here. Beyond was the void.

Sitting cross-legged between Pearson and Capeman, I tapped the signal light key—dot dot dot—dash dash dash—dot dot dot—SOS—again and again. The signal shot a light beam into the blackness and was swallowed up, insignificant and lasting but a short time, lost.

Our mission lay in ruins thirty miles back. We had come so close, just those thirty miles. Had we reached this ledge yesterday, we'd have been rescued. Now we'd been given up for dead, and we would die with the dawn. There would be no hiding in daylight from our enemy. And we lacked the strength to get off the ledge.

Capeman and I had lowered Pearson, so injured that he could no longer walk, onto this shelf, but we could never lift him up. Capeman had lost so much blood he had no strength left.

Even if we found refuge from the cold and the enemy, we had no food or water. Our only hope was if a ship spotted us and radioed a rescue chopper.

I ran my hand across the top of my flight boot to a hidden pouch. Inside the pouch was a cyanide capsule. I had been told that I could not be captured, yet could I take the deadly potion? Could I cheat enemy capture and torture as Göring had cheated the hangman?

We had joked about the capsule—death before dishonor—but none of us had believed in death, not ours. Others—perhaps the enemy—but not us. Yet what about now?

The clock of survival ticked down. Only hours remained until dawn.

I tapped the key on the signal light again—dot dot dot—dash dash dash—dot dot dot. SOS. I had been doing it for hours, but the flashes kept being swallowed by the darkness.

Scrunching down, I opened my jacket to let the cold revive me. I had done everything to stay awake—talked aloud, sang, stood, stretched, got as uncomfortable as possible, but I was succumbing to exhaustion. As a final resort, I'd pulled frozen clotted blood from my jacket and held it in my palm.

This is the blood from one of the soldiers you killed, I said to myself, a boy really, no more than seventeen. I had held him, my enemy, in my arms as he took his last breath. As he neared death, he forgave me. I fingered the frozen clotted blood and rubbed it between thumb and forefinger. That boy's hopes, dreams, loves crumbled and were blown by the wind over the ledge.

I had killed five enemy soldiers; we had taken their cold-weather quilted jackets saturated with blood and tissue and pushed their bodies into a ravine.

To stay awake I tried to create a past for the boy who was no more, but it was mine I recalled.

I remembered my first day at school and saw a scared little boy at a blackboard, too frightened to draw the cat or bird that the teacher requested. In front of the class, I'd wet my pants, leaving a puddle at my feet. The others jeered. As tears streamed down my cheeks, the teacher gently took my hand and led me away from the howls of laughter.

Where had that little boy gone? Where was the child who played ball and chased dragonflies, the little boy who romped and ran with his dog, Coaly?

He was no more, either. All that remained was a bereft scared soldier soon to die.

I tapped the key again, but now SOS was transformed into Nell Nell Nell, Lanny Lanny Lanny, Nell Nell Nell. I sent a signal of hope into the night. My wife, my son, my wife. Save me. Save me so I can return to you. My loves, my life.

They would never know what had happened to me. That had been part of the devil's bargain we'd made—silence, secrecy, our bodies never returned—in exchange for . . . I struggled to remember. All that bigness we had been caught up in: God, country, honor, duty, glory, peace.

Of course we'd never believed we would die. We were young, warriors, our hearts pure, our cause just. They told us our bodies might not be recovered, but we hadn't believed that, either. Yet seven of us were strewn along a frozen road, riddled by bullets, mutilated, while the last three perched with Death on this slim finger of land, a step to oblivion.

Pulling the jacket tight around me, I sat straighter, revived. Yet maybe we would not die. The ship could still come. It was hours until dawn. There was hope.

Then in my mind's eye I saw Coaly, my wonderful dog who had remained by my side throughout my days as a youth—comforting me, guarding me, protecting me from harm. In his old age Coaly had lost the use of one hind leg, but that wouldn't stop him. He limped along with one leg trailing while we walked the banks of the Trinity River. His affection was above and beyond human compare. In my mind's eye I saw him—he had come to rescue me. As I reached out, he turned and limped away into the cruel darkness. Tears filled my eyes.

Then Death stirred beside me. Pearson whimpered and Capeman groaned; there was nothing I could do for them. I wiped off the frost that had formed on Pearson's and Capeman's beards. They didn't respond to my touch. They were in another world, Pearson's breath so shallow that it seemed his body was shutting down. Capeman twitched intermittently, every stir registering pain.

Nell Nell Nell, Lanny Lanny Lanny, Nell Nell Nell, I signaled. Save us. Let us live. Don't let us die.

My little boy, I cried out into the night. I would never let you go to war, no matter how old you were. Never let you come to this ledge on the end of existence. I will sit here for you. But while I would not send my son to war, I would send another man's, and that man would send Lanny to spare his own son. We would both go to save our sons as our sons would go to save us.

The beam of light disappeared into the night. My spirits sank. There was no ship; there would be no rescue. The abyss was before me, the enemy behind.

Only a short while ago I hadn't known who the enemy was. There was no war; the world was at peace. I was safe, happy with my wife and son. I had not killed anyone. Thousands had already died in this war. Even so, I had believed in this mission; we all had. The president himself had a hand in its planning. Who could doubt the president when he said we might be facing an atomic war? But had we succeeded? The others would never know. Nor might I, for dawn was just beyond the horizon.

I took more deep, painful breaths of air. I looked at Pearson and Capeman. Suddenly I was caught up by the ethic of male valor, by the myths and stories and histories I'd grown up with. Of course I would do it again. I would do anything to save Pearson and Capeman. I would do it all again for Nell and Lanny.

Yet I was afraid. I didn't want to die, to end up like those on the frozen road. I tried to see them in my mind again, resurrect them, but I couldn't. Then I tried to see Nell and Lanny, to conjure all those I loved—my mother, my father, my grandmother, my brothers and sisters, but they wouldn't come, either.

I was alone, cowering on the ledge.

I stabbed the key—dot dot dot—dash dash dash—dot dot dot. SOS.

Chapter One

Texas, the United States, 1950

Very few Americans knew anything about Korea until June 25, 1950—and then everybody knew about it. I was at Fort Bliss, Texas, when I first heard. My wife, Nell, and I were at a party with other Army officers and wives when someone rushed in with the news—North Korea had attacked South Korea. We were going to war.

As a twenty-two-year-old lieutenant, I had mixed feelings. I'd joined the army to fight for my country, but I wasn't even sure I could locate Korea on a map. I knew more about Mars. In my childhood, Flash Gordon and Buck Rogers went there every Saturday at the matinee. Green men lived there, and pointy-headed women with cone-shaped breasts. Mars was a planet, right next to us. But Korea? I didn't have a clue. It was somewhere past the end of the known world.

My friends had mixed feelings, too. We whooped and hollered about the prospect of war, a lot of youthful bravado, but the prospect of getting killed in some far-off place we knew nothing about put a damper on the party.

As Nell and I walked home to our government duplex a few blocks away, a small two-bedroom concrete block with a brown patch of grass out front identical to every other, I knew she was troubled. We'd been married four years and had a young son.

"Does that mean you'll be going?" she asked, huddling close. My arm was around her shoulder. I remember the El Paso night was warm, one of those great nights in Texas where stars blanket an endless sky and the world seems so large, and you so small. It was beautiful and peaceful and I could not believe that the quilt of peace and harmony that comforted the world had been ripped so profoundly, or that so many young men were soon to die.

I had no idea if I'd be going to war, but I didn't want to share my concern with Nell—she was only twenty, and our son Lanny, just three. We couldn't afford a car on my lieutenant's pay, and her folks were six hundred miles away in Forth Worth; caring for a child with a husband at war was more than she had bargained for when I'd asked her to marry me. We were so young, and so was the country—it seemed back then. But everybody was soon to grow up. The world had suddenly turned scary. The war that everyone had called cold was on the verge of turning hot.

Everyone now remembers the fifties as a time of poodle skirts, Elvis, and rock and roll, but that was not the reality.

When World War II ended in 1945, everyone expected a peaceful interlude, a time to catch a breath, but it didn't turn out that way.

I was too young to fight Nazis and Japs, but my brothers weren't—Rhoden Floyd, whom we called R. F., joined the Marines and fought in the Pacific. Donald Junior, who was known as Bill, served in the Army. Even my father, Donald, enlisted in the Army Air Corps while Della, my mom, worked on an assembly line producing B-24 bombers at an air base near Fort Worth. My sister Juanita married and moved away, and my other sister, Emma Lee, went to work at another military installation. I lived at home by myself; I was fourteen and still in high school.

I grew up in rural Texas during the Depression, one of five children in a house without indoor plumbing, arguing with siblings over who would have the first weekly bath because that's when the water was clean. Too poor to include toilet paper in the budget, the family used old newspapers in the outhouse, and I had only one pair of shoes—sneakers to wear to school and on special occasions; the rest of the time I went barefoot.

Alone at home, I became everything the home demanded—caretaker, housekeeper, and cook. After my folks were able to scrape up a down payment, we moved into a new house a mile above the river bottom where we had lived. It was a three-bedroom white frame house perched on an acre of land—with Bermuda grass that took me half a day to cut with a push mower.

My days were full. My mom left early every morning for Tarrant Field, where she joined hundreds of other women building the B-24 Liberator bomber. After doing my chores, I pedaled to school on a bike put together from parts bought in a bike shop. The twenty-mile round-trip was grueling, especially after I landed a paper route that started at 6 A.M., adding another ten miles of bike riding to my day.

This went on for months until I got another job, as a cargo agent with Delta Air Lines at Fort Worth Airport. With a steady salary, I upgraded my transportation, purchasing a very used, dented, modified, high-powered Harley Davidson motorcycle capable of topping a hundred miles per hour. I named my Harley "Lizzy," after the Ford Model T, the "Tin Lizzy."

Being too young to fight didn't keep me from wanting to do my part. I joined the high school ROTC program; I also became an Eagle Scout.

In high school, I studied electronics and took up amateur radio as a hobby. During my senior year I qualified as a high-speed radio operator able to send and receive international Morse code in excess of forty words per minute. Little did I know how important this would turn out to be someday.

After graduating from high school in 1945, I met a girl on a bus; it was the most important day in my life. Nellie Rae Sargent looked just like Judy Garland, and older than her age, which was fifteen; I asked her out, the bravest thing I had done up to then. Our first date was to a wrestling match in Fort Worth. I can't imagine why I took her there, but at the time it seemed natural.

For our second date, we took a picnic lunch to Burger's Lake outside Forth Worth. We brought Nell's mother's favorite kitchen knife; I lost it in the sand, which didn't endear me to Mrs. Sargent.

Six weeks later I proposed to Nell. We lied about our ages, obtained a license, and were married by a Methodist preacher. Though wildly upset and wanting to annul the marriage, our families reconsidered when they learned the marriage had been consummated in a one-night honeymoon at a $5 motel room.

We rented an efficiency apartment and I rode the Harley to work at the Leonard Brothers department store repairing radios, but the job was short-lived because returning servicemen and closing war-industry plants resulted in a surplus of manpower and a nationwide job shortage. One Friday I received a pink slip along with my final wages. My job had been given to a veteran because discharged military personnel returning to civilian life had priority.

Out of work and with no prospects, a billboard caught my eye: "Join the Army. Serve for three years and get a free college education." So I walked into a recruiting station and raised my right hand on January 19, 1946. They sent me that very day to Fort Sam Houston; I didn't even have time to tell Nell. She learned that night when I called to tell her I'd found a job but wouldn't be coming home for dinner, or anytime soon—I was in the Army. Nell, sixteen and suddenly alone, was aghast. I didn't see her again until I finished boot camp and got leave eight weeks later; that's when our first child was conceived.

I was happy; I'd found a home as well as a job in the Army; I had a wife and a family in the making. Sent to radio-repair school at Fort Monmouth, New Jersey, I was halfway through the course when I read a notice on the bulletin board for Officer Candidate School: "Applications are being accepted for special infantry training in September 1946 at Fort Benning, Georgia."

When I went to the first sergeant for an application, he laughed. He was a huge burly man who took his job of kicking trainee ass seriously. I particularly remember his fixation on clean latrines, porcelain that had to be shined with a toothbrush. The idea of a wet-behind-the-ears recruit going to OCS was more than he could bear.

"Not a chance," he shouted. "You're barely eighteen, soldier. They're looking for men, not boys."

"I don't read anything about age," I blurted.

Taking pity on me, and probably to antagonize the first sergeant, the company clerk did everything but sign my application for me, then delivered it by hand to battalion headquarters. A week later I had orders. I think the clerk collected $10 on a bet he had with the first sergeant.

Four months later at Fort Benning, halfway through the course, with the class whittled from 246 to 145, the commanding officer called me to his office. Thinking I was the next casualty, I was surprised when the captain offered me a cigar and handed me a telegram: "Congratulations. You have a son. Both mother and Lanny Allen doing fine."

When I was commissioned at Fort Benning, I was eighteen years old, a father, and the youngest second lieutenant in the United States Army. This definitely had its drawbacks; older noncommissioned officers were appalled at the "ninety-day wonder" now giving them orders.

I returned to Fort Monmouth for the Signal Officer Basic

Course. Included was a course in communication center and cryptographic operation. Six months later, after finishing signal school, I was on my way to Germany; I was nineteen—things were moving really fast.

Stationed with the 7772nd Signal Battalion in Frankfurt, I was assigned duties at European Command (EUCOM) headquarters in the basement of the IG Farben building, a Nazi-style monstrosity that had housed Hitler's munitions supplier and now served as a center for the victorious U.S. Army, and also as European headquarters for the Armed Forces Security Agency (AFSA). As the communication center duty officer, I processed top secret, cryptographic, eyes-only messages and delivered them directly to General Lucius D. Clay, the EUCOM commander in charge of the Berlin airlift, flying in food, clothing, fuel, and everything else to sustain life for the besieged city. I would ride to his residence in a staff car behind a military police jeep and hand him the secret communications. He'd burn them and scribble an answer for me to take back. No one in Europe other than General Clay and I read the extremely sensitive messages. It was heady stuff—a first lieutenant with a four-star general, the man then commanding the largest military operation in the world.

Nell and Lanny joined me several months after I arrived. Nell was pregnant and sick the entire voyage over. She gave birth to our daughter shortly thereafter. We named her LaNell, but she died immediately after birth. Not knowing what to do, I agreed to her body being cremated. I would regret this decision the rest of my life.

When my assignment ended and the Berlin airlift became a success, Nell and I were reassigned to Fort Bliss, Texas, where we moved into those concrete block government quarters just across the highway from the El Paso International Airport; we listened to the hot desert wind blow sand through cracks around windows and doors.

After the party on that fateful day of June 25, 1950, and as a communications officer with access to top secret messages, I read all the army dispatches on Korea. The classified reports were alarming: the North Korean Army was decimating the defenders.

The success of General Douglas MacArthur's brilliant Inchon landing in September 1950 didn't last. On November 28, the chairman of the Joint Chiefs, General Omar Bradley, called President Truman at Blair House with news that General MacArthur had "a terrible message." The Communist Chinese had plunged into North Korea with at least 260,000 men. By Christmas, U.S. forces were reeling in defeat and the Marines were trapped at the Chosin Reservoir.

Americans were dying, lots of them, in a place of which I knew nothing—and they probably didn't, either. How had this suddenly come about? All I knew was the vague outline: communists had attacked free people. The scenario was black and white—bad guys were beating up on good guys. The United Nations forces and the South Koreans were, of course, the good guys—the communists were the bad guys.

We had just fought a war against truly evil men—Hitler's Nazis in Germany and the military dictatorship in Japan. We all understood that war. But who were the North Koreans and why were we suddenly at war with that country?

Chapter Two

Kaufbeuren, Germany, 1951

The world had turned scary in 1951; the atom bomb was on everyone's minds. *Life* and *Look* magazines showed pictures of huge mushroom clouds raining deadly radiation on Enewetak atoll in the Pacific and the Nevada desert. There were tales of mutations and devastation in which nothing could live or grow for generations. Hollywood vampires, werewolves, and mummies gave way to mutant creatures of atomic testing. Mankind would die on a barren planet.

We knew what the future held because we had seen the destruction of the recent past—Hiroshima and Nagasaki. Now our enemy had these weapons. The enemy had infiltrated our government and stolen our atomic secrets. Our cities could be leveled; we—our children—would be victims.

Still, I knew from friends who had TVs that there were funny moments (Nell and I couldn't afford one but we often went to friends' houses to watch the little black-and-white twelve-inch screen). Uncle Miltie Berle pranced and cross-dressed on the *Texaco Star Theater* (the following year he got a $200,000-a-year contract for life, more than double what the president earned), Gorgeous George wrestled in an ermine jockstrap (earning $70,000 a year, nearly the president's salary—and with public appearances, certainly more).

Nell splurged and bought the 1950 big book of the year—*The Betty Crocker Cookbook*—and we saw the Academy Award–winning film *All About Eve* with an unknown actress named Marilyn Monroe. I even heard about a book called *1984* that used such terms as *Big Brother, Thought Police, Newspeak, doublethink,* and *thoughtcrime,* though I didn't know what they meant; I hadn't read the book.

I did, however, know about the term *iron curtain.* Everybody knew that from a speech Winston Churchill gave in Fulton, Missouri, portraying a grim future of slavery under a totalitarian regime that had already swallowed Eastern Europe and was bent on world domination. That's what made Korea so frightening. Korea was the major event on the world stage, and even though Truman labeled it a "police action," the United States knew it was at war and that the world was in more peril than ever before. The Communists were the enemy, the Soviets possessed the bomb, and tensions were at an all-time high.

But I didn't go to Korea; Nell was greatly relieved. Instead, I got orders to join an all-black Signal Battalion preparing for movement to Germany to provide tactical communications for NATO. The downside was that Nell and Lanny couldn't join me right away: families of married personnel had to wait at least eight months because of the critical housing shortage. I had expected this; extended family separations were a way of military life.

I had *not* expected orders to an all-black unit. Integration of the U.S. military was more than a year away when Truman issued an executive order that ended segregation. In 1951, the armed forces were still segregated; blacks and whites could not share the same billets, eat in the same mess hall, or fight alongside each other, even though blacks had fought gallantly throughout World War II and many had died.

Kaufbeuren, at the base of the Alps, was one of the most beautiful military installations in the world, a former Luftwaffe air base with well-kept grounds, shrubbery, trees, and flower gardens. On a clear day you could see the snowcapped Swiss-Bavarian Alps. A lush valley surrounded the post, which was situated on a plateau. Amid trout-filled streams, quaint villages enjoyed peaceful sanctuary spared destruction during World War II. It was like the locale of a Heidi film; people there still wore lederhosen.

I was assigned as a platoon leader of a Signal Construction Battalion whose mission was to train, equip, and retrain so we could deploy within hours to anywhere in Europe our construction capabilities were needed.

The battalion was led mostly by white officers, while every enlisted man was black. My assignment came as a real shock. I had grown up in Texas and been separated from blacks all my life. Blacks were considered inferior; they drank from separate fountains, had separate restrooms, and certainly never ate in the same dining rooms; they rode at the back of the bus and stepped off sidewalks to let whites pass. They had separate seating in theaters, couldn't talk to white women on a social level, went to different high schools—yet suddenly I was thrust in their midst as a platoon leader, responsible for their care and welfare, for their conduct and performance as soldiers.

That's when I learned my previous life had been a lie, that men were all alike and that color has nothing to do with ability, pride, honor, loyalty, and trustworthiness; fear or death either. Indeed, blood spilled from both the white and the black soldiers was a rich red—exactly the same color.

August 25, 1951, was the day my life changed. It was my sixth wedding anniversary and I wondered what Nell and Lanny were doing in Texas; I could hardly wait for them to join me in a few months. After I conducted a Saturday-morning field inspection of my platoon, a jeep screeched up and a company clerk jumped out and rushed over to me. It must be war, I thought.

The clerk snapped a salute and shouted, "Lieutenant, the CO wants to see you immediately. You got a big problem."

"What's it all about?" I asked, but he just shook his head. "Don't ask me, ask him, sir."

The clerk was so shook up I didn't trust him behind the wheel. He just stood there, shaking in his boots. I jumped into the jeep and gunned it away, leaving the corporal to dodge gravel and dust.

My relationship with my company commander had been rocky for weeks. It had started a month earlier when I had applied for transfer to a vacancy within the communications center at U.S. Army Europe headquarters. My mistake had been to apply while my CO was on vacation. He considered this a breach of channels and had been furious when he returned; my application had been immediately disapproved.

Actually I liked my captain; he was fair, straightforward, and an excellent leader whose only bad trait was a hot temper, on the wrong side of which I had put myself. I had applied for the transfer because I'd decided to make a career of the army and knew a big headquarters posting would help. I hadn't intended to slight him. Still, I thought the transfer incident was over, and I hadn't done anything wrong since, so I couldn't imagine why I was in trouble.

I found out immediately, even before I got to his office. The captain's reputation defied his appearance; he was a skinny man on a slight frame. He had a pockmarked face and wore glasses, and his eyes were in a perpetual squint, but he sure could yell.

He started screaming as soon as I entered the building. "Get your ass in here! What do you mean going over my head?"

I was taken aback. "Sir? Going over your head?"

His face was fire-engine red. "I told you that your transfer had been disapproved. That should have been the end of the matter. Going to the top to get what you want is insubordination."

I had no idea what he was talking about. All I could mumble was, "Go to the top, sir?" as I riveted my eyes on one of the standard-issue photos of the chain of command on the wall behind him; it was a photo of Secretary of Defense George C. Marshall.

He was beside himself. "Don't act so damn innocent, Boyd! I just got a call from battalion that you have orders from army headquarters for a special assignment. What the hell are you up to?"

I blurted the truth, "Captain, I have no idea what you're talking about. I gave up on my transfer when you turned it down. Do you mind if I go to battalion to see what this is all about?"

Without waiting for an answer, I saluted and shot out the door. When I got to battalion headquarters, I found an amused adjutant. "I was expecting you. I'll bet your CO is out of his skull."

"Yes, sir, he is, but I don't know why."

"Neither do we. All we know is that EUCOM directed us to cut you orders. You're supposed to be in Heidelberg Monday at 0800. Nobody there seems to know a thing; they're playing dumber than usual. You sure you don't have a clue?"

I shook my head.

"Let me see what I can find out." He picked up the phone and called the adjutant general's office in Heidelberg.

When the connection was made, I heard a series of "yes, sirs," culminating in "I'll get right on it, sir."

The captain set down the phone and cast me a puzzled look. "The AG said the Defense Department reviewed your records and wants you for a highly classified assignment. He said he had no idea what it was, just that it was sensitive and that someone from the Pentagon will interview you Monday."

He left the room but returned directly. "Your orders will be ready in ten minutes. I just called the battalion CO to inform him. He'll call your CO. We know you didn't initiate this; this is coming from the top. We'll tell your captain to loosen his skivvies. Have a good trip, Lieutenant."

I walked back to my billet in the BOQ barracks—a single room of government furniture, with a wooden wall locker, bed, side table, chest of drawers, wall mirror, footlocker, two wooden chairs, desk, and a swivel chair. The only personal touch was pictures of Nell and Lanny on the desk, and wine because officers were allowed to have alcohol in their rooms. I had laid in a good supply of German Riesling.

I now opened a bottle, poured myself a glass, and studied my orders. I was leaving in the morning for Munich. I had to catch a train and be in Heidelberg that night.

But what was this all about? A classified mission? The Defense Department? The Pentagon, an interview? I was a twenty-three-year-old first lieutenant on a remote post in southern Germany. It obviously wasn't a mistake—headquarters hadn't requested me for nothing—but for the life of me, I couldn't figure it out.

It would not have helped to know "the top" referred to by the adjutant was the White House, President Truman himself. Then again, had I known, or known what was to come, I might not have gotten on that train.

I certainly would have finished all the wine.

Chapter Three

Heidelberg, Germany, August 1951

Spared heavy bombing during the war, Heidelberg is a beautiful medieval city on the banks of the Neckar River. Center of German Romanticism and home of the oldest university in Germany, the fourteenth-century city is dominated by the famous castle where folklore has it that the Student Prince leaped from the balcony. But I didn't pay attention to any of that when I got off the train; all I could think about was this mysterious summons.

It grew even more mysterious when I discovered a government sedan waiting, something way beyond what a lieutenant could expect.

I slept fitfully that night at the BOQ, a room just like the one at Kaufbeuren except with no personal pictures or alcohol, wondering about the next morning's meeting with my "Pentagon interviewer."

At precisely 0800, arriving in the sedan sent for me, I reported in a clean, crisp uniform to the adjutant general's office at the massive Army headquarters, a former Nazi garrison with thick concrete-and-stone walls that could have withstood direct weapons fire. I hadn't had breakfast; I was too nervous to eat.

The AG himself, a full colonel, greeted me but had no information about the meeting except that I was to see a visitor from the Pentagon in the conference room. "He wouldn't give me any info," the AG said. "He just wanted to make sure the conference room was secure and had no bugs. You're on your own, Lieutenant. Good luck."

When I was shown into the conference room, a high-vaulted, theatrically impressive chamber with a huge carpet on a gleaming parquet floor, a colonel bent over documents on a massive table looked up with an appraising gaze. He was tall, perhaps forty—young for his rank—fit, and athletic. Taking me off guard, his manner was friendly and cordial, not that of a demanding senior officer, but his eyes remained intent on me, penetrating, belying his offhand manner.

"Let's make this informal, Lieutenant. Don't call me sir; address me as George, George Brown. What do your friends call you?"

"Uh, Art, sir," I stammered. "I mean, Art, George."

"Then Art it is." He directed me to a heavy wooden leather-padded chair. "Sit down. Relax. How about some breakfast? I'm starved." He pointed to coffee, juice, and rolls on the table and helped himself.

I declined and sat, squinting from sunlight pouring through floor-to-ceiling windows, just the two of us in the cavernous room.

Wiping crumbs from his mouth, Brown continued, "What I'm going to tell you is classified. Nothing I say leaves this room. You will not tell anyone—your commander, a friend, even your wife. You will be court-martialed if there's a leak. Got it?"

I nodded, more mystified than ever.

"In fact, none of this will be declassified until 1998. That's on the order of the president of the United States."

"1998?" I repeated. That was nearly fifty years from now. What could he have to say that needed to be secret for so long? And the president? I was a mere lieutenant. What could this possibly have to do with me?

As though reading my thoughts, something he proved very good at, George Brown said, "You're wondering what this has to do with you. All right, here it is: the president has authorized a secret mission. There will be ten team members. The operation code name is Broken Reed. I'm selecting team members. You're being considered."

"Me?" The incredulous "why?" was understood.

"You have everything I'm looking for. I've gone through hundreds of 201 files in all branches of the service. I need someone with top secret-crypto clearance. Believe me, there aren't many of you in the military. Plus, this person must have experience with communication center and cryptographic training. That really narrows it down. Finally, I need someone who can transmit high-speed international Morse code. You have all the qualifications."

He opened his hands. "So there you are." He shrugged as if his next words were an afterthought, which was not the case at all. "Besides knowing cryptology, it also helps that you have infantry training; you graduated in the first all-Army OCS class at Fort Benning."

It turned out the infantry training was not inconsequential. The AFSA, an almost mythically secret organization, had many cryptologists, but they were all civilians. As I was soon to learn, this mission was not for civilians.

Later I learned that George Brown had held back another reason why I'd been selected—he wanted a young officer; younger men were willing to take more risks—they didn't know how fickle the war gods could be. Young men thought they were invulnerable; older men knew better, and civilians certainly did—that's why they remained civilians. But he was right about me; back in those days I *did* think I was invulnerable.

"With me so far?" he asked.

I nodded; this was way too far above me to comment. Besides,

I couldn't think of anything to say. I felt as though I was at the edge of a huge dark ocean not knowing how far it extended, how deep it was, or what lurked below the surface.

Brown came directly to the point. "Art, you have a rare opportunity to serve your country as a member of this team."

I stifled a smile. I wasn't so naive that I didn't know I was being buttered up, or trussed up like a Christmas goose, but I was polite. "I'm honored, sir. George." Though mystified and suspicious, I did feel honored—a first lieutenant talking to a full colonel from the Pentagon about a secret mission. Nevertheless, I knew secret missions had perils—nasty things lurking below the surface.

But a secret mission where? There were trouble spots all over the world. Because I was in Europe and so was Brown, I assumed he meant a secret mission here—perhaps into East Germany, Hungry, Bulgaria, or maybe Greece, or—God forbid—Russia: the last people I wanted to tangle with were the very nasty KGB.

Brown smiled faintly, still avoiding details about the location of this secret operation. "There is, however, a downside to this mission. I want to be honest and up front about it—there's only a 50 percent chance that you'll survive."

I did laugh this time. This *had* to be a joke. "A downside? Getting killed is a little more than a downside, at least to me."

"No guts, no glory, Art. What do you say? Want to hear more?" He had dropped the bomb so casually that it didn't even appear to be a threat, nothing dangerous at all: death was just something you might stub your toe on. Big boys—real men—didn't cry about that.

I must have hesitated too long, thinking he couldn't be serious, because he suddenly got a cold, hard look on his face. "I'm not going to apply pressure; no one is coercing you, but I'll lay it on the line—this mission is vital to the country's security. If you choose not to go, that will be the end of it; it won't reflect on your career. All I want to know right now is, do you want to hear more—given the risks, that downside? If you're not willing to risk your life for your country, you can walk out that door right now. However, if you think you might want to volunteer, I'll give you more details. After that you can still say no, but I have to know first if you'll consider the mission even with the risks involved."

Once again he opened his hands. "Do you want to know more or not?" The bomb was there now, not something to trip over, but real and lethal, yet he had tossed it in such a manner that there was no escaping.

What officer wouldn't be willing to put his life on the line for his country? *That's what service was all about.* My brothers and father had risked their lives in World War II. Of course I would take the risk; it would be cowardly not to, as well as unpatriotic, and despite what he said, a dead end to my career, and Brown knew it. He had cleverly opened with a gambit I couldn't refuse. But it was unnecessary; I really did want to hear more about the mission. After all, he'd told me I could still back out.

I took a deep breath, putting my toe in the water to test it. "All right, tell me more."

A smile creased Brown's face. "Great, Art. I knew I had the right man."

I felt I had no alternative; nevertheless, I wanted to make sure that I had understood what Brown had told me earlier. "But I can still back out, right?"

Brown's eyes glinted in satisfaction. He knew he had his man. "Of course."

That out of the way, he turned all business. "No notes, just pay close attention."

Paying close attention would not be a problem; my thoughts were hardly going to stray.

"Korea is a disaster," Brown began without preliminaries.

So it was Korea! But what did I know about Korea? Nothing, except what I'd read in classified communication center messages while stationed in Fort Bliss, newspaper accounts, and the little history I'd picked up.

"You know Truman fired MacArthur."

Everybody knew that. It was the main subject discussed in the military. It was also on the front page of every newspaper. Just a few months earlier, Truman had summarily dismissed MacArthur. This firing of the country's most celebrated hero had caused an uproar throughout the country, and the debate was still raging. Returning to the United States immediately afterward, MacArthur had addressed both houses of Congress. Papers reported that senators wept openly, and one congressman said of MacArthur that they had just heard "the voice of God." Only years later did I learn that Truman had dismissed the speech as a bunch of hooey.

"Truman thinks MacArthur screwed up in Korea," Brown stated. "He totally missed the Chinese threat. Most of the problem was because he lacked adequate intelligence on enemy strength, capabilities, and intentions. Though MacArthur was upbeat about the war when he met with Truman on Wake Island last October, the president was leery. Despite his 'shoot from the hip' temper, Truman's a cautious man, especially when lives are at stake."

The president's temper *was* legendary, typified by a very public feud with a *Washington Post* music critic who'd given his daughter Margaret an unfavorable concert review. Yet his decisiveness and honesty were legendary, too, as was his "the buck stops here" sense of responsibility.

"MacArthur assured him that China wouldn't enter the war, and could only muster sixty thousand men, but Truman wasn't convinced. After all, Mao had just defeated Chiang Kai-shek and controlled the mainland. It was on Wake Island that Truman started to give serious thought to making an intelligence end run around

MacArthur and his Joint Chiefs. When the Chinese did attack and overwhelmed UN forces, Truman shifted into high gear. He didn't trust anyone any longer. He didn't know who or what to believe. That distrust led to Broken Reed. Truman felt he couldn't rely on questionable information—too much is at stake. That's where we are now—we still don't have good intelligence, but we've got to get it."

Brown held out his index fingers an inch apart. "We're this close to a world war and this one will mean atomic bombs dropped everywhere."

That's what *everyone* worried about. I certainly did. I had a wife and child and knew the Russians had the bomb. We'd all seen pictures of the mushroom cloud and read horrifying stories about atomic annihilation.

"Truman doesn't want a world war, but he's under incredible pressure. There's a real Red Scare in America and many want us to go in with all we've got, arguing that if we don't stop the communists now, we'll be fighting them in our own streets soon. One argument is that since we're stronger than the Russians and Chinese, *now* is the time to go after them."

I knew that was true, and most of my military friends believed it, but I also knew that others urged caution. Secretary of Defense George C. Marshall said we shouldn't get "sewed up" in Korea. Secretary of State Dean Acheson also wanted to limit the war because he didn't think we could defeat China in Korea, but lots of people, including Senator McCarthy, called both of them traitors.

Korea was a mess and I was glad I wasn't there, but I knew the president had a real problem. U.S. troops were already committed; they were under siege, retreating—dying.

Yet even I understood that expanding the war could lead to a bigger war and nuclear holocaust. If I, a *lieutenant,* knew this, I could only imagine what Truman was going through—after all, it was his decision; it was *all* in his hands.

"Intelligence is the key to everything," Brown said. "We didn't know the North Koreans were going to attack, and had no idea 260,000 Chinese troops would jump in after MacArthur counterattacked. Not having that intelligence cost us huge losses."

Suddenly Brown's manner became more personal. "Since you've been involved with intelligence work for years—I've read your file and know what you did during the Berlin airlift—you'll understand the problem."

He added cryptically, "Some of the other team members might not be able to follow this."

I wondered what that meant; I found out later.

"You're trained in cryptographic equipment, codes, and operations. You went to the Signal School run by AFSA at Fort Monmouth. You've worked with agents involved in both communications intelligence (COMINT) and signals intelligence (SIGINT). They're both closely tied into military communications and cryptographic operations. Right?"

I nodded. "I know and understand both COMINT and SIGINT."

"During World War II, we broke the Japanese code and the British broke the German code. We might not have won the war otherwise."

"It would have been a lot harder," I allowed. "It certainly would have taken longer, and many more men would have died."

He leaned toward me. "Do you know the status and quality of our COMINT in Korea?" He didn't wait for an answer. "There isn't any! We used to have intercept stations in China where we could monitor traffic, but that ended when Mao took over in 1949. We have no COMINT on Korea. We're completely in the dark. We haven't picked up anything on troop strengths, movement capabilities, or plans. It's like playing baseball blindfolded."

He sat back in disgust. "HUMINT hasn't given us anything,

either. Our spy effort has been worthless. The CIA hasn't provided any intelligence of value. Not that MacArthur would have listened even if they had come up with something. He didn't trust them. He was *very* territorial—nobody could tell him anything."

Brown shook his head at the futility of the situation. "But it wasn't all MacArthur's fault. He was in Tokyo and the CIA didn't warn him. They completely missed the North Korean threat. Well, *almost* completely missed it. A CIA field agency reported 'extensive troop movements,' but MacArthur's headquarters dismissed the report and forwarded it to Washington, where it got lost in channels. Nevertheless, the key issue on the imminent attack went unreported; as a consequence, U.S. forces were overwhelmed."

That, to me, was the scary part. With all our technology and resources, we were more surprised than we'd been at Pearl Harbor. We'd been caught completely off guard, had no ready military response and no intelligence-gathering capability. Worst of all, the enemy had powerful allies with a million-man army and atomic weapons. No wonder Truman was hysterical.

"There was a total breakdown of intelligence," Brown continued. "We didn't know a damn thing about Korea; it wasn't on our radar. Hell, I had to read up on the place when I first got involved with this mission to find out the basics. I didn't know who Kim Il Sung was, or Syngman Rhee, either, or that their two countries had only existed for two years. I didn't even know the Japs had ruled the country."

He shook his head. "I don't think the CIA knew much, either. How could they? Back in World War II there was the Office of Strategic Services, the old OSS run by Bill Donovan. That was our intelligence agency. Truman dissolved it in 1945 and reassigned its personnel to the State and Defense departments. You can imagine what happened to intelligence gathering then."

Sitting back in his chair comfortably, Brown started a rundown of our intelligence community so detailed that I felt he must have inside knowledge, a suspicion that grew as I spent more time with him. Brown wore an Army uniform, but there was something about him that suggested he wasn't military. Maybe it was his youth—too young to be a full colonel—but it had more to do with his easy and familiar manner, which was out of character for a ranking officer dealing with a junior.

"In 1947, Truman reformed intelligence gathering under the CIA and appointed an old friend from Saint Louis as the first DCI, director of Central Intelligence. This guy's previous experience had been with the Piggly Wiggly food store chain." Brown's disdain was obvious.

"After he lasted only six months, he was replaced by Lieutenant General Hoyt Vandenberg, a nephew of a U.S. senator, but Vandenberg really wanted to be Air Force Chief of Staff, so Truman replaced him with Rear Admiral Roscoe Hillenkoetter. When the CIA missed the North Korean invasion, Truman fired him. Now General Bedell Smith is DCI. It's been a merry-go-round at the CIA from the beginning and there still isn't any good HUMINT coming out of Korea." His voice was dismissive. "So much for the CIA. But COMINT has been worse."

He sat up and pushed his chair from the table, as if trying to distance himself from the disaster that was communications intelligence. "I'll spare you the gruesome details and just give you the highlights. The whole problem can be summed up in one word—*bureaucracy.* During World War II, COMINT worked well: we'd broken Japanese and German codes, knew what the Japanese Navy was doing, knew Rommel's plans for North Africa, and even monitored Hitler's radio traffic to his commanders in Normandy. Then the war ended and the bureaucrats took over. The original agency for COMINT, going back to World War I, was MI-8.

That became the Signal Intelligence Service, then the Signal Security Agency, and then, two years ago, the Armed Forces Security Agency. Running the COMINT show was the ANCIB, then the STANCIB, then the USCIB, and now the AFSAC—the Armed Forces Security Agency Council."

He paused. "Following all this?"

"Should I be? Is there going to be a test?" I smiled. *No one* could follow this.

He didn't smile back; in fact he grew angrier. "Everybody got involved and wanted to run things their way—Army, Navy, Air Force, State Department, Defense Department, and now the CIA, too. It's like fishing by committee. It doesn't work, so it's no surprise COMINT missed the North Korean attack last year."

He brought his chair back to the table and clasped his hands tightly in an effort to control his rising fury. "Here's where we are today with COMINT: last October the AFSAC set up the Intelligence Requirements Committee, a group with representatives from the Army, Navy, and Air Force intelligence offices, to work with the USCIB's Intelligence Committee. Together they're supposed to select the most important targets. Their recommendations go to the Intercept Priorities Board, the IPB. The IPB has about ten Special Intercept Priorities Groups, called SIPGs. Once a month, the SIPGs prepare target recommendations for the IPB, which considers them along with the recommendations for the AFSAC/IRC and USCIB/IC. At this point, the target recommendations go the AFSA."

I was completely lost. All I knew for sure was that it would be a cold day in hell when the final intelligence product got into the right hands.

Sensing my confusion, Brown said tightly, "You can imagine the president's reaction when I explained this to him. It was explosive. He was surprised we hadn't lost the war already."

After hearing the convoluted passage of intelligence, I was surprised, too. However, Brown wasn't finished.

"Worst of all, once the AFSA finally gets the intelligence target recommendations, they go to the Joint Chiefs of Staff because the JCS is in charge of intelligence gathering, *but it's the JCS and the military who are losing the war*—or at least aren't winning it."

Now I could really see Truman's problem; the entire intelligence-gathering system was a failure.

Brown sat back in his chair and let out his breath, as if he'd just finished a long race. "Truman's solution was simple, basically to cut through all this shit. He's done with committees and boards, and he's done with the Joint Chiefs. He wants to know about North Korea, China, and the Soviet Union—now! He can't wait for committees and boards. He's directed a top secret, out-of-channels operation to get the information."

"Which explains Operation Broken Reed," I ventured, though still not seeing exactly what this had to do with me, though my cryptology background gave me some idea.

"Correct. Truman is worried that if he expands the war, the Russians will help the Chinese who are helping the North Koreans, and everything will go up in flames, including Germany here. He doesn't want to make a decision based on faulty intelligence. That's what Broken Reed is about—getting accurate intelligence so he can make an informed decision and have backup for his critics."

"How come Broken Reed? What does it mean?"

"The president picked the mission title. It's an old Indian term. It means something or someone who fails when you need it. That describes the situation in Korea perfectly: no one knows a damn thing about North Korea, China's intentions or its troop strengths, or Russian plans. We *need* that info. Believe me, we've tried everything. The military intelligence guys and CIA have dropped covert operatives out of aircraft, inserted spies through battle lines, even landed them from submarines. *Nothing* has succeeded. Operatives parachuting in were either killed or captured. Enemy and friendly fire killed most inserted through the battle line. Even the few who did get back didn't bring anything substantial. We don't know any more now than before."

But how were we suddenly going to get intelligence if we hadn't been able to get it in the past? And, more to the point—where did I fit into this intelligence-gathering operation?

As usual, Brown was ahead of me. He looked at me coldly—suddenly very definitely superior to subordinate. "Getting that info is where you come in."

At last, I thought. Forget all the national security bullshit and how much your country needs you; here's the part where you're asked to bend over and grab your ankles. I'd been in the Army for four years. I knew how it worked.

But he was smooth and expert, reeling me in slowly. "We've put a long time into this plan, Art. We've studied all the failed missions carefully. We know what went wrong and why. The best minds have worked out every detail and possible glitch. We've put as much thought and work into this as Eisenhower did for D-day. And remember, some of the planners for D-day—General Marshall, Bedell Smith, and Omar Bradley—are advising Truman. They're on his National Security Council. We've had presidential carte blanche on Broken Reed. We know it can work, but I don't want to kid you about the risks. This is a military operation, just like D-day. I wasn't joking about the survival rate. There's a good chance men will die on this mission."

Though now taking this seriously, I tried to keep it light. "Hey, that's what we signed up for, right?"

Brown shook his head. "No, Lieutenant—and that's the last time I'm saying that. This is *not* what you signed up for. This is what you're *volunteering* for now; there's a big difference, and I want to make sure you understand it."

Despite his grave manner, I almost laughed. I knew how the Army worked: nobody volunteers; it's always coercion. They tell you something is going to hurt, and then they ask for volunteers with the clear message that it will hurt more if you *don't* volunteer. So you volunteer. Then they hurt you, but you can't complain—you volunteered. I wasn't complaining—I knew this was the Army way. Hell, I had signed up on my own. I had volunteered.

Brown leaned across the table, his eyes fixing on mine. "I know you're married and have a son. I want you to factor them into the equation before you make a decision. We're not playing games here. This is for real. And maybe for keeps."

Oh my God, I thought, he's bringing out all the big guns—country, family, patriotism. I had played football in high school, had done all the things guys were supposed to do. I was an officer in the U.S. Army—a grown man; I had a wife and child, but Brown was talking about things so far beyond me—the president of the United States, Douglas MacArthur, world war—I couldn't comprehend it. My world had been doing my job as a lieutenant, paying bills, waiting for my wife and son to join me, but now suddenly I was thrust into a world of presidents and generals, wars and death—mine! But what choice did I have? Tell him I was a coward? That when the country needed me, I was busy?

"Okay . . . George," I said, trying to hide my misgivings. "Tell me more, and be real specific about the part that I play in getting killed."

"All right, but let me tell you first who's aboard the mission already: two Navy frogmen; two Army rangers; a B-29 pilot, copilot, and navigator; and two CIA agents. Your billet—the communications specialist—is the last one I need to fill."

Frogmen? Rangers? Pilots, navigators, CIA agents? These

were true secret-mission types, cowboys who would jump at the chance of danger—guys who would volunteer for the craziest thing, and if they balked, a hundred others would take their place—but me, a communications officer? What was I getting involved with? I had nibbled the bait, but hadn't quite bitten yet.

"We need intelligence, accurate information about enemy strength. The only way to get that is with men on the ground—men behind enemy lines. That's the HUMINT. We're going to insert a team into North Korea to determine enemy strength. Relaying the information back is the COMINT, that's you."

I kept my mouth shut and listened, no more nibbling on the bait. I concentrated on trying to suppress my growing incredulity.

"We're going to fake a B-29 going down behind enemy lines. That's easy; we do it with communications traffic that the Chinese and North Koreans monitor. They'll believe we lost a plane because we'll tell them we lost it. Then we'll have the crew captured and conveyed in a Communist convoy across Korea to China."

"What crew?" I asked in confusion. "There's no real plane."

"But there'll be a real crew, men carefully selected for the mission—you and the others. We'll fake a capture by inserting you all into North Korea on a submarine."

My mouth must have dropped open because Brown grinned. "I know it sounds crazy, but hear me out. The B-29 crew consists of eleven men. One will have died in the crash, leaving ten. Three of these men will be Air Force personnel—a real pilot, copilot, and navigator to lend authenticity to the downed-bomber story; they can answer any technical questions if there's an interrogation. Posing as gunners and bomber crew members will be two Navy frogmen and two Army rangers. The frogmen will get the team from submarine to shore, and assist if there is need for a sea rescue. The rangers will get the team to the rescue point, or lead them safely back to our lines if the convoy has to be abandoned.

With me so far?"

I nodded, still waiting for my role.

"Two men from the CIA will pose as crewmen; they'll be in charge of Broken Reed. One is fluent in Chinese, the other in Korean. They'll translate the information collected along the convoy route from twenty-two Chinese and Korean operatives already in there. Your convoy will consist of specially converted vehicles with Chinese troops posing as Communist guards."

"And that leaves me," I said.

"Yes, Sergeant Michael Lavern Baker, U.S. Air Force, B-29 radio operator."

"Michael Baker? Sergeant?"

"Everyone will have a fake name. That's yours. It's for everyone's protection. No one will know anything personal about anyone else—real name, marital status, hometown, religion, background—absolutely nothing. That's so nothing can be extracted if you're captured and, just as important, it's to keep the mission secret—don't want any of you making contact when Broken Reed is over."

I could live with that. "So what does Michael Baker do as a radio operator?"

"You will encrypt the information and transmit it through international Morse code to a communications plane flying over South Korea or the Sea of Japan. Your messages will be relayed to Washington."

Getting no reaction from me except perhaps a dumbfounded stare, Brown said, "All right, one more time, very simply: a B-29 bomber will crash. The surviving crew, ten men including you, will be captured by a fake Communist unit, Nationalist Chinese posing as Chinese Communist troops. They'll have authentic papers and travel across the North Korean peninsula from the Sea of Japan in a convoy of specially designed vehicles toward the Yellow Sea. At predetermined spots, our spies will give you intelligence reports on enemy strength and positions. The reports will be transmitted by radio after they have been encrypted—that's you—to a communications plane over the Sea of Japan. The plane will deliver the reports to Japan for relay to Washington. In the end, before you reach China, the convoy will 'disappear.' A chopper will pick up the team at one of several designated rescue locations along the coast of the Yellow Sea and bring you to safety. The vehicles and com equipment will be destroyed."

Brown looked very pleased with himself; he waited for me to say something but I was speechless. A fake crash, a submarine, Nationalist Chinese troops, a communications plane, a chopper?—I couldn't be hearing this.

Once again, as if anticipating my thoughts, Brown waved dismissively at the problems. "It's all logistics. We can get a sub to the North Korean coast—hell, MacArthur landed an entire invasion force there without anyone knowing. The chopper is simple, too—we'll just tell the pilot where to go and when, and the communications plane will be provided fighter escort."

I finally recovered my voice. "What about the Nationalist Chinese? Where are you going to get them?"

"That's already been worked out by the president and secretary of state. Chiang Kai-shek owes us. Besides, deep in his black little heart, if he has one, he wants to recover the mainland. He fought the Communists for years before Mao defeated him and Chiang fled to Taiwan. Old Vinegar Joe Stilwell, our military advisor, hated him, called him 'The Peanut,' but Chiang has lots of friends in Washington. It's called the China lobby and includes Henry R. Luce, who owns *Time* and *Life* magazines. He and his wife, Congresswoman Clare Boothe Luce, are close friends of the Peanut, and rabid anticommunists. Chiang will help because he needs us to protect him on Taiwan, and someday to get back to the mainland."

Brown grinned, "He'd send Madame Chiang on this mission

if necessary. In any case, there are many Nationalist sympathizers in China who weren't able to get to Taiwan; there are plenty of agents on the ground there. The problem has been contacting them and getting their intelligence out."

I found my voice again. "How many people know about this?"

"*Very* few; only those with a need to know. Except for those on the mission, just a handful of men at the very top: the president; Secretary of State Acheson; Secretary of Defense Marshall; the director of Central Intelligence, Bedell Smith, who used to be Eisenhower's deputy; Omar Bradley, the chairman of the Joint Chiefs; and a couple of others."

I couldn't stifle the obvious question any longer. "What if the team is captured?"

Brown didn't take his eyes from mine. "Each man will be provided with a cyanide capsule. Using it is preferable to being captured."

Before I had a chance to register shock, Brown plunged on. "First off, we're going to ensure you're not captured. Every detail will be worked out carefully. There's a chance something will go wrong—there always is, there are no guarantees in combat—but you can be sure we'll do everything to minimize the risk."

So there it was—a mission behind enemy lines, and my backup was a cyanide capsule. I didn't know whether to laugh or cry, so I just sat there.

"Actually, you're taking this better than the president did when I first briefed him."

"The president isn't going on the mission."

Brown laughed. "No, but he has the responsibility, and he takes it very seriously. Remember, this is the man who ordered bombs dropped on Hiroshima and Nagasaki. He's used to making tough decisions; approving this mission was one of his hardest. That should tell you something right there."

"Okay," I said, "let me see if I've got it right: A B-29 will 'go down' over North Korea; a team will land by submarine behind enemy lines; the team will be 'captured' and conveyed through North Korea by Nationalist soldiers posing as Communist troops; on the way, the team will make contact with spies who will give them intelligence on enemy units; the information will be relayed back to Washington; the team will be 'rescued' and returned to safety."

Brown beamed. "You've got it, Art, or should I say, Sergeant Mike Baker?"

"And one last time, exactly what is Sergeant Baker's mission on the team?"

"You're key to the whole operation. The frogmen will get you from the submarine to shore, the rangers will get you to the waiting convoy, then to the rescue site. The spies will gather the information, the CIA agents will translate it from Chinese and Korean, and you will encrypt it and send it on."

I nodded. "Okay, now let's go over the part about getting killed—the cyanide capsule."

Brown did not try to make a joke of it. "We're taking all precautions, but obviously a mission behind enemy lines is dangerous. That's why you'll have a cyanide capsule. Not only will you use it, you'll *want* to use it."

"Death before dishonor sort of thing?"

"No, death before torture and pain sort of thing. You've heard of their tortures; we don't need to go into the details, but everything you've heard is true."

And that was the end of the briefing. "So now you have it, Art. I'll let you sleep on it. I want your answer in the morning—same time, same place." Brown looked at his watch and nodded perfunctorily, satisfied with the time. He was on a tight schedule; I hadn't set him back. He stood, shook hands, and left the room.

I pulled myself up woodenly and headed back to the BOQ.

But I didn't sleep that night. I pretended to debate my options but I knew I had none—of course I would accept the assignment; rather, I would volunteer. I could never look myself in the mirror if I refused. I could never face Nell and Lanny.

"You look like hell," Brown observed when we met in the conference room in the morning.

"I feel like hell."

"Strange," Brown mused serenely. "I slept like a log."

"You're not going on the mission, either. I am."

Brown smiled. So there it was, a done deal; he had his answer, the one he had expected all along. "Excellent. Any questions?"

"About a thousand, but they wouldn't make a difference. I'm sure you'll tell me the rest when I need to know it. But what will you tell my wife if I don't come back?"

"We'll tell her you were a hero. No specifics, of course, but full military honors. And a great view at Arlington."

"Thanks," I said dryly.

"Actually, I do want you to understand what will happen if you're killed. I've explained this to everyone. Each death will be handled differently so it can't be tied to any other, or to the mission. If disaster occurs, it will be reported that some died in a training mission where their bodies couldn't be recovered. Some will have died far from Korea, others are missing in action. For each there will be an honorable cover story. If something happens to you, if you don't come back, your wife will be informed you died in a plane crash while en route to your home on a military leave status. A cadaver burned beyond recognition will be substituted for your body and shipped to your hometown for funeral arrangements."

I merely nodded; I supposed it didn't really matter what they do with your body when you are dead.

"And along those lines," Brown continued.

"Dear God, now what?" I wondered to myself.

"There won't be any medals or recognition, no matter how this ends. There will be no proof that this mission took place. You will never be recognized for bravery and service to your country—no headlines, no marching bands, no medals, no accolades. Can you live, or die, with that?"

I nodded again. If I lived, that would be reward enough. If I died . . . what would I care?

"Excellent," Brown said. Then he cleared his throat. "Now about your wife and son, there's a bit of a complication."

That's when I almost lost it. "Nell? My God, what's wrong?"

Brown raised his hands to settle me down. "Nothing's wrong, relax. We know she and your son are scheduled to join you in Kaufbeuren shortly, but their port call will be delayed until this mission is over—that's all."

"When will that be?"

"Not for another six months. You're going back to Kaufbeuren this afternoon. You will mention nothing about what we've discussed. You'll tell them you were here for a reassignment interview but you turned it down. You *love* Kaufbeuren and your CO; you wouldn't think of leaving. Assuming everything goes as planned, Broken Reed should be up and running in four months—it'll take that long to arrange everything."

Brown raised a cautionary hand. "There is, of course, a chance the whole mission will be scrubbed, in which case all this dies within you. Understood?"

"Understood. But how will I know it's been scrubbed?"

"I'll call you. I'll simply tell you that the horse we bet on lost. Then you will forget everything we've discussed. However, if everything works out, I'll call you from the States ten days prior to kick off with news of a tragic situation at home. You'll apply for emergency leave. The Red Cross will verify the emergency and

EUCOM will approve orders to send you home. I'll handle everything. You'll go on emergency leave and simply disappear until the mission is over. Then you'll return to Kaufbeuren."

"Or Arlington."

"Or Arlington. It'll be a great show. Sorry you'll miss it."

He stood. "This covers it. I'm delighted you volunteered. I'm going to make sure everything works out. The next time you see me will be at Rhein-Main a few months from now." We shook hands. "Good-bye, Art."

I went back to the BOQ, packed my gear, and rode in the sedan to the train station.

As the train traveled to Munich, I gazed out on peaceful villages, steeples, and domes, a world far removed from the terrifying one we'd been discussing—of submarines, secret missions, cyanide capsules, and atomic warfare. It was too surreal to comprehend. But one thing I fully understood: of course I wouldn't mention this to anyone—who would believe me?

I wasn't sure I believed it myself.

Chapter Four

From Germany to Japan

The headiness of a secret mission, atomic war, presidents, and generals disappeared as soon as I returned to Kaufbeuren. All my company commander wanted to know was what I'd been up to.

When I reported to him in his office the following morning, he was eating a doughnut and drinking coffee. "So what's the scoop? Were you selected for the special assignment or are you back with your platoon?"

"The colonel decided I wasn't qualified." I couldn't believe I was lying to my commanding officer, and I was very uncomfortable doing so.

His eyes narrowed. "So what was this special assignment?"

"I can't tell you, sir. It's classified. I took an oath not to discuss it."

He put down his doughnut and coffee and leaned toward me menacingly. "I have a top secret clearance, Boyd. I could order you to tell me."

Senior officers did not like to be refused; in fact, that simply didn't happen in the military, but there was no way to dig myself out of this. "I would have to refuse that order, sir. I swore not to discuss the assignment. Should you have a problem with that, I was told that you were to call the European Command adjutant general."

That ended the discussion, but not my captain's wrath; he definitely had a problem with it. Though he never mentioned our talk again, he manifested his displeasure for the next four months by sending me and my platoon to remote places throughout Germany, up and down the Rhine, and even to France in support of NATO operations; I lived in barren impersonal BOQs and tents with the few personal belongings I could stuff into a duffel bag.

A part of me really wanted Broken Reed to take place—the part that craved excitement and glory; another part hoped the mission would be scrubbed—the part that wanted to reunite with Nell and Lanny, the part that knew excitement and glory could end in my suffering and death.

During this period, however, I paid ever closer attention to world developments, knowing they might have a direct impact on me and whether I lived or died. I read the *Stars and Stripes* and followed every military and political development closely.

Though General Matthew Ridgway had replaced MacArthur and stabilized the war in Korea, casualties continued to mount, and coffins brought back more American youths.

In Washington and throughout the country, criticism of Truman escalated. While some people wanted the United States to withdraw from Korea, a more vocal contingent urged expansion of the war—still termed a "police action," a misnomer at best. When men died in combat, that was called "war."

Senator McCarthy's Red Scare incited national hysteria. The communist menace had become the focal point of American politics; the Soviet Union and China were viewed as the greatest evils ever to face us: their spies were said to have infiltrated the government, and traitors abounded across the land. Today's fear of terrorism pales next to the anxiety and dread Americans felt about the communist menace. Many believed the nation's survival, indeed the survival of the free world, depended on our resolve to combat this threat. For them, resolve meant all-out war, invading North Korea up to the Chinese border—and, if necessary, a preemptive strike against the Soviet Union itself. Better now, while the United States was stronger than the Soviets, the hawks reasoned.

Whether to expand the war, accept a stalemate, or withdraw was the dilemma Truman faced. His handling of the Korean conflict was criticized by nearly everyone. A few months later, eligible for another term, Truman was considering a run, but he was to be defeated in the New Hampshire primary and announced that he would not seek reelection: Korea was the reason.

What was he to do in the meantime? His presidency had another eighteen months to go and his decisions would have a major impact on the lives of tens of thousands of soldiers, including mine.

Yet it now appeared his decision might be based on a mission for which I had just volunteered, one about which I had dubious feelings, and one completely out of my control. Worst of all, I had no one to share my doubts and feelings with, no one to talk to about them with, not even my wife.

In addition to reading the papers and watching every newsreel at the base theater, I boned up on Korean history. I wanted to know more about the place where my life would be at stake. What I really hoped for was to learn something that could tip the odds of survival in my favor.

But the more I learned, the more nervous and confused I got. I kept running into information I didn't understand. I learned that Koreans were Buddhists and Confucians. But that didn't help, because I had no idea what Buddhists and Confucians believed, except I felt sure it had little to do with Jesus Christ or the Baptist Church back home in Texas.

When I read that Korean culture and art were heavily influenced by Chinese culture and art, I was still mystified. I had no clue about Chinese culture and art. Everything I struggled to absorb pointed toward a society totally foreign to mine—their language, customs, and beliefs.

Korea, in past centuries, had fought off invasions by the Chinese, Mongols, Russians, and Japanese; there had been fierce battles for their land throughout history. The Koreans hated Japanese domination and had gone to the Paris peace talks after World War I to appeal for self-determination, but the Allied powers had not heeded them. They were turned down like Ho Chi Minh and the Vietnamese. Finally, after the Japanese defeat in 1945, Korea was divided in half under American and Soviet spheres of influence.

In 1950, Communist North Korea attacked South Korea. The war could have been viewed as an internal fight for control of one country—a civil war—but it had exploded into a war of ideologies. I understood I was on the side of one of these ideologies, democracy, but I would have been hard-pressed to explain that other ideology—other than that it was communist and therefore evil.

As months passed without any word from Colonel Brown, I thought perhaps Broken Reed had been canceled; it sounded to me, after all, too incredible to be real—submarines, frogmen, and cyanide.

Then, on December 21, 1951, while I was stretched out on my bunk in my BOQ room, a battalion officer poked his head in to say I had a call at headquarters from Texas. My heart jumped. Was this it?

When I got there, only a noncom was on duty; everything had slowed down for the Christmas holiday. Handing me a piece of paper with a number for the overseas operator, the sergeant told me to ask for operator eight. As I dialed, I had an overwhelming urge to run back to my room and jump back into bed, but of course I didn't, and was soon connected. "This is Lieutenant Arthur Boyd in Kaufbeuren, Germany. I was told you have a call for me from Texas."

"No, Lieutenant, I have a call for you from Washington, D.C. I'll place it for you."

The next voice I heard was George Brown's. "Art, is that you?"

My God, this was it. It was happening after all. "Yes, sir."

"I have some very sad news, Art. Fifteen of your father's cattle died mysteriously. Your family needs you. You're going to need emergency orders to return home. Usually that is done only for illness or death, so it may take some time, maybe ten days for your battalion to get the authority; but don't worry, it'll go through. In ten days, call your wife. Tell her you might be out of touch for a while—make up some temporary duty somewhere. In any case, you'll be hearing from me soon."

When I hung up, I told the sergeant there was a family problem. I didn't tell him about sick cows. Cows? Surely Brown could have come up with something better than that. It didn't sound like an auspicious beginning to a top secret mission; nevertheless I went back to my room, knowing the mission was on and the clock ticking.

Ten days later I placed an amateur radio call to Nell that went through a ham station in Blytheville, Arkansas; it was New Year's Eve. Harold Sudsbury, manager of radio station KLCN in Blytheville, patched me through to her. We talked about Lanny, now four and growing like a weed, then I said her port call for Germany had been delayed because of a huge backlog of dependents and a critical shortage of housing.

"On top of that," I continued to lie, "we're going out into the boondocks and you won't hear from me for a month or so." We wished each other Happy New Year, one that would bring us together again, and I hung up reluctantly, not wanting to let go, sever that tie to Nell, profoundly sad that I wouldn't see Nell and Lanny for several months—at best.

I ran to battalion headquarters, manned only by the sergeant major and an assistant adjutant; everyone else had taken leave for New Year's, including the battalion commander, the exec, and my company commander. They had all gone to Munich to celebrate. I told the assistant adjutant that I'd just talked to my wife in Texas who'd told me about a family crisis and I needed emergency leave orders. I gave him the number of the Red Cross representative in Heidelberg.

Expressing sympathy, the young warrant officer placed the call. When he hung up, after scribbling numbers on a pad, he stared at me in bewilderment. "She said they approved your emergency leave and have already been contacted by the EUCOM adjutant general and duty officer. She gave me their numbers to call for verification. What's going on? Why is EUCOM headquarters involved?"

I shrugged. "Maybe it's a slow day and they have nothing better to do."

He called EUCOM, and from then on all I heard was a series of "Yes, sir," "Right away, sir," "No problem, sir," and "I'll get right on it, sir."

I listened with conflicting emotions: fear, elation, excitement, and profound longing for my family. Yes, I wanted to go on the mission, but at the same time, I wanted Nell and Lanny. I wanted to be safe and with them. I wanted to hold them and never let go. The cautious part of me had begun to see the dangers. While the mission was still theoretical, I could allow excitement to reign, but now that it was real, the risks, what I could lose—Nell and Lanny—suddenly became paramount.

When the assistant adjutant finished his call, he just stared at me, completely baffled. "Lieutenant, I'm supposed to cut you emergency leave orders immediately. You'll have them by 0800 tomorrow. You're to take the first available rail transportation to Frankfurt. I'll advise the acting battalion commander. Have a good trip."

That night I hardly slept. It was happening after all. But *what* was happening? Was I really going on a secret mission thousands of miles away behind enemy lines—that submarine and all the rest? I still couldn't grasp it.

At least I didn't have to pack; I'd been ready for a week. Staring at those packed bags, I celebrated a quiet New Year's alone in my BOQ room drinking a bottle of 1946 Rhein Riesling.

At 0800 I picked up my orders and caught the train to Frankfurt. It was an uneventful trip, the train nearly empty. Most people were home recovering from the previous night's celebration.

But it was all business in Frankfurt. I was met by a sedan and brought to Rhein-Main Air Force Base. Brown was waiting for me at the operations center. I spotted him as I entered an area bustling with activity. He was talking with three Air Force senior officers and from time to time glanced at the flight operations board.

Brown had a commanding look, as if he were in charge. One of the officers motioned that I was approaching. He turned and walked briskly toward me.

Though militarily correct, returning my salute crisply, I could tell he was happy and relieved to see me, just as I was glad to see him. Grinning conspiratorially, he patted me on the back and pulled me aside to say our departure was delayed because of inclement weather over the North Atlantic—but it wouldn't interfere with the mission because such delays had been built into the plan. In the meantime, we'd rest and wait at the transient BOQ, prepared to leave at a moment's notice if the weather cleared. He added that the delay would allow him to fill me in on mission details.

Waiting seemed like an eternity. Each hour I grew more restless. Now that Broken Reed was a go, I wanted to get on with the mission; I didn't want to wait any longer. Excitement had overcome my doubts and fears; further waiting might only revive them.

But the weather didn't clear for two days, and Brown had to keep me busy with briefings and entertain me with stories. I learned a great deal more about Brown, Truman, and Broken Reed's origin and planning. I learned it was he, not Truman, who had reservations about Broken Reed, but Brown's concerns had been dismissed.

Once Truman gave the go-ahead, there was no looking back, just like it had been with his decisions to bomb Hiroshima and Nagasaki. When Brown stressed the dangers of sending ten men behind enemy lines where they would face capture and death, he said the president had swept them aside. Mimicking Truman's midwestern twang, Brown gave me a blow-by-blow account of his encounter with the president.

"Damn it, Colonel. You know the track record of the intelligence boys so far. I don't think they know where the toilet paper is. We're facing a full-scale war with China and the Soviet Union. I am *not* going to be the jackass to drop atomic bombs again. Will the loss of ten men be worth preventing a third world war? You bet your butt it will."

Even Brown's fast, choppy body movements mimicked Truman's presence.

"After I met with MacArthur last October," Truman continued, according to Brown, "I had the gut feeling he'd told me only what I wanted to hear and that he had underestimated the North Koreans and Chinese. I need to know the absolute truth, and I don't think our intelligence community is giving it to me. Worse, I don't think they even know how to get it—but I need the truth!"

The "truth" was Operation Broken Reed's objective, an accurate assessment of the enemy's capabilities.

"Make it work" was Truman's edict. "I don't care how it's done."

Making it work was Brown's job, and while he kept the president informed of Broken Reed's progress, he was careful to omit certain details. Indeed, the president didn't want all the details, and for good reason.

In June 1948, the National Security Council, of which Truman was the chairman, passed Directive No. 10/2, which stated that in regard to covert operations, "if uncovered, the U.S. government can plausibly disclaim any responsibility for them."

"Plausible deniability" protected the president from his own actions and directives; he could simply disclaim knowledge of covert actions, especially if he had not been given any details. Very simply, he could deny the presence of the elephant in the corner wearing a party hat if no one had pointed out the festive pachyderm to him.

Now, however, on January 2, 1952, the elephant had moved to the center of the room, preparing to dance. Indeed, Broken Reed was about to kick off; all we were waiting for was a break in the weather. In the meantime, I was given a slide show that laid out the details of the operation. After breakfast, we went into a small conference room.

The first slides showed Yongjin Bay and the deepwater cove where we would land in North Korea. "Note the steep incline you'll have to scale before you reach level ground, where the vehicles will be waiting," Brown pointed out. "It's a long walk, and it'll be cold, probably around twenty degrees. That's the *good* news; the bad news is that temperatures will drop to zero as you move into the interior and I'm afraid the electric heaters in the vehicles won't help much. Other good news is that you will have decent chow, if you like Chinese food; one of the vehicles will have a mobile kitchen."

"How are the vehicles getting there?" I wanted to know. "Who reconfigured them?"

Brown just stared at me. "That is not something you need to know," he said evenly. "I will *tell* you what you need to know."

Chastened, I listened without further interruption.

Other slides showed the terrain we would be traveling through, the vehicles in the convoy, and the kinds of equipment we would be using. I had plenty of questions about the logistics, but I kept them to myself; Brown had made it clear that it was none of my business.

Before he finished the presentation, Brown got a call from the ops center. Our flight, MATS 0409, would be boarding in two hours. Brown told me to go get my bags. We met at the terminal.

On board the 1600th Air Transport Wing four-engine plane, I noticed that the seats in front, behind, and beside us were occupied by mailbags. Acknowledging them, Brown said that was so we could talk without being overheard. And talk we did—or rather, he talked and I listened on the long flight from Germany to Reykjavík, Iceland, then on to Westover Air Force Base in Massachusetts. His voice was soothing, but not what he told me; the more I heard of the mission's details, the more perilous it seemed.

I learned for the first time about my teammates. While I was chosen because of my youth and technical expertise, I discovered that my teammates were all in their thirties, and all had combat experience. It became evident from what Brown told me that they'd been chosen not only for their combat expertise but also because they were seasoned to endure not just the stress of combat, but its boredom, too. "You'll find that fear and danger are no worse than the interminable waiting for something to happen. We're not worried about you, however—cryptology is *damn* boring; we figure you're experienced with boredom. And don't be intimidated by your lack of combat experience—it's like sex and bike riding, after one time, you know what you're doing."

During the flight, Brown told me even more about his relationship with Truman and the germination of Broken Reed. He had great respect for the president, far more than other military men, who thought that if the United States was in a fight, we should charge ahead and kick ass without restraint.

"You only have to be with him a few minutes to see how much he hates war. Probably that's because he was in World War I and saw it firsthand. I think if he could have one wish for anything in the world, he'd ask for peace. He'll rev up the war if he feels he has to, just like he'd use the atomic bomb again, but he doesn't want to. That's why he's so adamant about Broken Reed. He wants as much intelligence as possible before he makes such a decision, but right now he doesn't think he has enough."

"How many times did you meet with him?" I asked.

"Numerous," Brown answered vaguely. "Whenever I needed to, and whenever he wanted. I wore civilian clothes and he never used my last name in the presence of his staff. As far as they knew, I was just George, a family friend."

But what was Brown's real relationship with Truman? I wondered. How did they meet? He obviously was not going to tell me—it was not anything I needed to know—yet I couldn't help but speculate. Was he really a military officer, or CIA? Surely an Army colonel couldn't wander into the White House whenever he wanted. I did know enough, however, to realize that this was classified information to which I would never have access. And I never did learn who Brown really was.

Finally I dared ask him the question foremost on my mind. "Do you really think we're going to make it out alive?"

I was hoping and praying he'd say, "Absolutely"; instead he gave me a long, hard look. "We've lived with this operation for months. Every detail has been planned and executed minutely. There is nothing we have not taken into consideration, but . . ."

"But what?" I pressed.

He started to tick off the possibilities for disaster. "Any change in the battle line could put you at risk. At some points during the mission, you'll be within a few miles of it. If the Communists made a sudden thrust and we counterattacked, it could cause your convoy to be overrun—not a good thing. You see, our commanders will have no knowledge of this operation or your geographical location."

That was disaster enough for me, but he continued. "The convoy could be spotted by our own planes. None of them will know of the op, either. For our pilots, your convoy will be a target of opportunity. They're hungry for kills, and their favorite weapon is napalm. You could be cooked alive."

That was more than enough. I held up my hand.

"Okay," he said. "Then I won't go into the other six thousand things that could go wrong."

I looked at him to see if he was joking. He wasn't, but he didn't say anything further about the operation or its potential dangers.

Only once during the long flight did we touch on personal matters. I asked what he was going to do when Broken Reed was over. "Go back to where I came from. A place you are not privileged to know about. But I will tell you this: you're going to feel my presence for a long time into the future. I'm going to make sure you are taken care of."

We landed at Westover after midnight, where we had only a thirty-minute layover before catching a C-54 to Travis Air Force Base in California. Except for two refueling stops, we slept all the way. At Travis, there was a three-hour layover, time for a hot shower and some food, and then we flew to Hickam Air Force Base in Hawaii. By then I was disoriented from all the time changes and no longer even knew what day it was.

At Hickam we stretched our legs while the plane refueled, then took off for Guam. There we had a three-hour layover before the final leg to Japan. On that flight, Brown went over the entire operation again. Curiously, I found this third briefing reassuring.

I knew Broken Reed cold. I felt confident about my part in the operation.

By the time our plane approached the Japanese mainland, I was more than prepared; I was eager to meet the nine other team members. And ready to meet the enemy. I *wanted* to go to war.

We had flown twelve thousand miles. It was January 7, 1952.

Chapter Five

Camp Drake, Japan

In Tokyo, we were met by one of Brown's assistants, a Naval commander introduced only as Commander Chuck. He was my height, about 5'11", but heavier, probably around 185 pounds with a gut, and older, at least forty.

Chuck said that the other team members had arrived and were already bored with their assignment of having to read about Korea, its terrain, history, and culture. "These guys aren't bookworms," he noted. I could well imagine the frustration of frogmen and rangers made to study books. Later on, I learned that one, a frogman, was indeed a bookworm when it came to history.

A sedan took us to Camp Drake, a U.S. Army installation not far from Tokyo where I was immediately struck by the tight security surrounding our mission. A barracks building had been requisitioned as its staging area; the windows were covered and an MP manned the entrance.

When Brown, Chuck, and I entered the huge dayroom, nine men came to attention. They were in various parts of the room, reading newspapers, separate from one another.

A circle of chairs had been placed in the center of the room. We were told to take a seat and remain at ease; Brown would be back in a few minutes. He and Chuck disappeared into an office.

While waiting, we all sat in silence for about twenty minutes; it was eerie, but it gave me an opportunity to appraise the men with whom I would be working. Sorting out who was who wasn't difficult. I picked out the frogmen and rangers right away—big guys with bulging muscles who looked as if they rarely, if ever, turned the pages of a book. The Air Force guys were just as easy to spot: two men looked exactly like flyboys who would be comfortable in a cockpit or on a bar stool—they even sat with a swagger. The two CIA agents were also obvious; even sitting still, they radiated danger. Only a mild-looking short guy about thirty years old puzzled me.

Then Brown came out of his office and spoke to us for nearly an hour. He began with a pep talk about the mission and its importance, a speech I, and I'm sure the others, had heard ad nauseam: President Truman himself had authorized Broken Reed, the fate of the world hung in the balance, this was going to be a bitch of an op, and we might all die—but it was for a good cause—yet even if we did live, we were never to discuss the mission until 1998, by which time we would probably all be dead anyway. It was not a rousing start.

"You're going to be here for three days, gentlemen. You will prepare as if your lives depend on it, which they do. To start off, I want you to introduce yourselves to one another. Give your real rank, branch of service, and your mission name—which is the *only* name that will be used from now on—and your assignment on Broken Reed."

He pointed to the guy I had already identified as a pilot and said, "Bill, we'll start with you."

A man about thirty, maybe 5'11",180 pounds, with light brown hair and gray eyes, gave us a friendly smile. He looked comfortable and assured. "Major Bill Robbins. My real rank is major. My duty prior to this mission was as a B-29 pilot. My mission assignment is the same—I'm in command of a B-29 brought down by enemy fire over North Korea. Technically, all you guys work for me. I'm the boss." He laughed, which I later learned he did a lot. "Other than that, I want to say that this no-booze restriction we're under sucks."

Everybody laughed, except Brown, who pointed to the man beside Robbins.

"Captain Sam Puller," said a man perhaps thirty, about six feet tall, 175 pounds, with red hair cut in a butch flattop, a very solid, athletic-looking guy with incongruously large thighs. "My true rank is an Air Force captain. My principal duty is a B-29 pilot. My mission assignment will be serving as the copilot of the B-29 that Bill fucked up and got shot down."

Again there was laughter, which did not go down well with Brown—nor did the vulgarity. The colonel frowned and pointed to the shortest man among us, no more than 5'5" and slight—maybe 135 pounds—also about thirty, with curly dark brown hair. His voice, despite his size, was a deep baritone.

"Captain Jim Pearson. That's my true rank and I'm the B-29 navigator, which is what I am in real life."

That succinctness pleased Brown, and he pointed to me.

"Sergeant Mike Baker. I don't know why I've been demoted, but I really am an Army first lieutenant in communications. My mission assignment will be as the B-29 radio operator."

Next up was a blond monster with a crew cut and chiseled jaw, early thirties, around 5'10", weighing some 200 pounds; he looked like a pro wrestler who could toss bulls from a ring.

"Staff Sergeant Tom Capeman. I'm a Navy frogman, a chief petty officer, but on this mission I'm a B-29 crewman, whatever that is." He grinned, but he was serious—he didn't even want to *pretend* he was in the Air Force.

Having got him right, I was proved correct about the next guy, too, a shorter, more slender man, profoundly fit; he looked like a lifeguard, except for a long scar on his chin, probably from a knife fight. He was bronzed from the sun, looked as mean as a drill instructor, and spoke with a raspy Bronx accent.

"Sergeant Reed Lynch. My true rank is chief petty officer. I'm a frogman, except now I'm a B-29 crewman." His disdain for that degradation was unmistakable.

"Gentlemen, be nice," cautioned Brown at the interservice rivalry, moving to the next man, another monster, this one around six feet, 200 pounds, also in his early thirties, tanned, muscular, square jawed, and with short, light-colored hair, a poster candidate for a Charles Atlas ad.

"Sergeant Ted Moody. Master sergeant. Army ranger—now a B-29 crewman."

Eleven words, I counted, and even those seemed a strain for him.

The next guy was just as laconic, just as tall, just as built, a mirror of Moody, except he had a black crew cut.

"Sergeant Dan Kingsley. Sergeant first class. Army ranger." Then, as if he'd forgotten, or wanted to forget, he added, "crewman." Nine words, the record so far. Obviously these guys were chosen for martial, not verbal, skills.

That left, obviously, the spooks. And sure enough, they were CIA. Or rather, they said they were CIA. Even at the time I wondered if it were true. Would real CIA agents admit they were CIA? Once you entered the rabbit hole, reality could get very distorted. Fictions and deceptions were lacquered upon one another until the surface story was impenetrable. The men could have been contract agents serving under the CIA, or former OSS agents working independently, or with the AFSA, or military intelligence, but the surface story was that they were CIA.

The first was a man in his early forties, tall and trim, exuding intelligence and alertness. He had a Roman nose that reminded me of Patton, dark penetrating eyes, and he spoke with a confident authority befitting the man who was really in charge of Broken Reed.

"I'm Captain Jerry Hinsley, the B-29 bombardier on this op. However, I'm not a member of the military. I'm with the Central Intelligence Agency."

"John Tyler," said the last man. Tyler appeared slightly younger, not as tall, with thinning dark hair and a face devoid of expression. There was an aura of seriousness and mystery about him, as well as an unusual reserve; he looked dangerous, and I felt immediately leery, though I didn't know why. "I'll be the flight engineer, a master sergeant." His voice was clipped, as expressionless as his face. "I'm also with the CIA."

That wrapped it up, the ten men on the mission whose lives would be forever linked. Brown gave us a few minutes to shake hands and exchange a few words with each other, and then it was back to business.

"Let's go over the chain of command so there are no doubts in anyone's mind. Jerry is in charge. He speaks Korean and Chinese. If anything happens to him, John will take over. He also speaks Chinese and Korean. After that, military rank in descending order will determine the team leader."

I was sixth in line, just above the frogmen and rangers, four guys that I had *no* business telling what to do or how to do it; together, these guys probably had about fifty years' experience on me, a lot of it in combat, and six hundred pounds of muscle.

Brown then ran down the schedule for our three days, beginning with fittings for our wet suits and flight uniforms that would take up the rest of the afternoon. After that, starting in the morning, we would have "briefings" on a variety of subjects to prepare us for the mission. "You won't find them boring," he said.

I didn't doubt that at all.

First, however, Brown said we would eat; I felt this was more for his benefit than ours. Then, after the fittings, we would eat again, a "get-together banquet," he labeled it.

Or a sacrificial one, I couldn't help but think.

That night we did indeed feast, on a six-course Chinese meal. I had never had Chinese food before and didn't know what to make of it—egg drop soup (and what did that mean? I wondered), sweet-and-sour pork, seasoned vegetables, and meats that lifted the roof off my mouth, rice cakes, finger desserts, all strange and exotic for a guy from small-town Texas. I watched Brown, the CIA guys, the pilots, even the rangers and frogmen shovel food into their mouths with chopsticks, while I had to use a spoon and fork.

The food was brought into the staging area by enlisted personnel and served from thermal containers that kept everything warm. We ate at card tables and sat on folded chairs, but we ate off real plates, and there were even napkins.

There was no alcohol. Still, we spent a lot of time getting familiar with one another. I decided that I liked these men, except for John Tyler, who simply could not bring himself to mingle. The others joked and told stories, though sharing nothing too personal. Nobody mentioned wives or backgrounds, and they made it clear that my youth and inexperience would not be held against me—more in abeyance, I felt; I was worthy until I proved otherwise. I was the baby on the mission, everybody's kid brother.

Before turning in, I went to see Brown in his room.

"What's the problem, Mike?" he asked, using my mission name. "Come in and close the door."

"I'll take only a few minutes, George. You told me that—in the event I was killed in North Korea—an unknown cold-storage burned-beyond-recognition cadaver would be shipped in place of my body to my Texas home and that my wife could choose the burial site. Arlington would be an option."

He nodded.

"I want you to know that I struggled with the idea of my body remaining where it fell, but now I feel okay about it, knowing that dead is dead. Would you do me a favor?"

"What is it, Art?"

"Should that happen, will you make certain that Nell gets all the help she needs in dealing with my death and burial—even if it is not my body?"

"You have my word, Art. Nell will get VIP assistance."

I thanked Brown, closed his door, and went back to my bunk. I heard the slumberous breathing of the others and fell asleep immediately.

Chapter Six

Mission Staging

I felt like I was back at boot camp when Brown moved through the building giving a boisterous reveille call. I grabbed a towel and stumbled off to the communal shower, mumbling a greeting to the others, also groaning at the early hour. While the cold water revived me, I noticed someone doing push-ups on the tiles.

Frogman Tom Capeman glanced up and grinned, then he stood and started calisthenics, something that proved to be a morning ritual. As he did jumping jacks under cold water, he taunted the others, "It wouldn't hurt the Army and Air Force to get in shape."

Well, that did it, of course, for everybody in the showers, causing outrage among the rangers, Kingsley and Moody, and in particular Puller—the Air Force pilot. A friendly, raucous, and ribald exchange of insults ensued. As I passed Hinsley on my way out, I noticed a deep scar on his hip, as if flesh had once been ripped away. He caught my look—I don't think the spooks missed anything—and merely nodded acknowledgment.

The last thing I heard was Puller yelling at Capeman and Moody, something about Army and Navy. It reminded me of high school, showering with a bunch of jocks. I couldn't believe I had devolved so far back in time. My God, I thought, I'm going to war with my old football team. That was not a good omen, I decided; the team I had played on had never had a winning season.

Breakfast was great, however. Only second to the mission itself, what Brown cared most about was food—it was terrific and plentiful: a buffet of sausage, bacon, steak, eggs, pancakes, rolls, and coffee—all served to country-and-western music being played on a portable phonograph that Brown had acquired.

I worried that if I continued to eat like this, they'd have to refit my wet suit, or worse—I'd just sink.

At 0745, we gathered in the briefing room, seated once again in a circle of folding chairs. Colonel Brown took center stage. There was a sense of relief—the staging phase, our final step in preparation for the mission, was under way.

As I looked around the room at the other nine, I recalled a conversation with Colonel Brown just before we landed in Japan. I had asked him a simple question: "What are the other men on the mission like?"

Brown had half-turned in his seat and said, "I can't tell you anything about their personal lives, but I can say that they are great guys, dedicated professionals, and love their country. They are all combat vets. I selected men able to deal with incredible stress and danger, but who have also experienced the hellish boredom of an op like this, so they know the value of patience. They know what fear is, and each has found a way to deal with it. They also know the value of humor when the screws get tight. Some are known to pull some jackass pranks to liven things up. Laughter is a friend, and they know how to use it. When it comes to the superior-subordinate relationship on a dangerous op like this, rank often goes out the window. They see everyone as equal members of the team, trusting one another, each responsible for doing his job. Their language is at times foul and expressive. In short, they're down-to-earth men with one goal in mind—mission success. These men have been together for two days before your arrival. Does this answer your question, Art?"

"Sure does," I answered.

I looked at Colonel Brown entering the room, and then back to the men I would spend the next two weeks with. I was soon to find out what "jackass pranks" were all about.

Just as the colonel was about to make his opening remarks, pilot Bill Robbins waved for recognition. "There's a problem we have to deal with immediately," he announced.

Surprised, Brown acknowledged him.

"As commander of the aircraft, senior man, I have to address a real concern."

We all leaned forward. An Air Force major, the ranking officer—the pilot—already had a problem?

In a somber voice he said, "Someone has been farting."

We broke up, mostly in relief, but he went on in a dead-serious voice, "I mean lethal farting. Mission-compromising farting."

Across from him, Dan Kingsley, the Army ranger, rose up in his seat with a tremendous fart that echoed throughout the staging building.

We convulsed with laughter. Dan obviously had a gastrointestinal problem. All of us had noticed it—he hardly tried to conceal it; in fact, he could pass gas on cue, as he just had.

"It's a secret weapon," he said.

"But we're not the enemy," little navigator Jim Pearson pointed out.

"Gentlemen, gentlemen," Brown said, trying to restore order. "We have serious matters to discuss."

The stern expression on his face signaled that we were to pay attention; this was serious stuff. "Since you are immediately heading for Korea, into the jaws of death so to speak, you need to know something about those jaws."

But Bill Robbins wanted none of this doomsday pessimism; he was already waving his hand. "Jaws of death! C'mon, couldn't we use another analogy here?"

"I got one," Ranger Moody yelled. "How about, heading into . . ."

"Quiet," Brown icily silenced him; this was serious.

What the colonel had told me on that aircraft became real. These guys were human, they enjoyed pranks, laughter was contagious, and what I had witnessed took the edge off what would follow. Nothing was going to turn these guys serious and somber. They were professionals, no doubt had been in the jaws of death a time or two, but they would not be intimidated.

"We're going to give you some background information on Korea." Brown motioned to Commander Chuck, who had been standing silently beside him all this time.

Chuck delivered a "briefing" on Korea that consisted of little more than recent headlines—a free country (South Korea) had been invaded by Communist oppressors (North Korea) backed by Red China and Russia; America had jumped in to save the free country. Lives were being lost and a stalemate was in progress. The situation was extremely dangerous and World War III was right around the corner.

I couldn't imagine what the CIA agents must have thought of this oversimplified summation of history, but the rest of us were not overly impressed, though Moody, Kingsley, and the pilots seemed relieved at the brevity. They had no interest in sitting through a historical or political lecture. They had heard and read it before.

Everybody seemed eager to move on to the nuts and bolts of the mission, except for one of the frogmen. Tom Capeman had a question.

He raised his hand as though he were in a classroom. "What's the long-term solution?"

Chuck was perplexed. "I don't understand your question."

"I mean, what's this all about? Where are we going with this?" He leaned forward in his chair, an extraordinarily big man, with muscles powerful enough for the circus, incongruously caught up with his next question, "What's the goal?"

Chuck glared at him. He was a senior officer and an enlisted man was asking him a geopolitical question about which he had neither clue nor interest. "The goal," he responded slowly, as to an obtuse child, "is to stop the Communists."

Capeman shook his head impatiently. "So we stop the Communists from pushing across the thirty-eighth parallel, then what? Have we got some plan?"

This was too much for Moody. "The plan is to kill Commie bastards," he exploded. "What's the matter with you?"

But Capeman was not to bc deterred. "Korea has been known for centuries as the Hermit Kingdom. They've been fighting off foreigners for four hundred years. Aren't we just another bunch of foreigners? Even if we stop the Communists this time, eventually aren't the Koreans going to get together and reunite? So what's our role in this?"

We all just stared at Capeman.

"And I thought you were just another pretty face," Robbins said.

"What the hell is wrong with you?" Moody repeated.

Capeman appeared embarrassed. "I like history. I read up on Korea. Just 'cause I didn't go to college doesn't mean I'm stupid. I wanted to know about their country, and China, too. The Manchus defeated the Ming Dynasty in China in the sixteenth century. They had already taken over Korea. But the Koreans finally got out from under them. The only people to have beaten them were the Japs, but now they're free of them, too. I'm saying that this is a real mess we've gotten ourselves into and I'm curious how you guys with the brass are planning to get us out of it."

The frogman read history? It was like hearing Attila the Hun recite poetry. Nobody said a word until Brown stepped in; he was not happy. "It isn't our place to question policy decisions. Perhaps later you can share your knowledge with the others. Right now we need to move on."

Moody cast Capeman a suspicious look. He obviously had no interest in history or political intricacies; he was the ultimate warrior—he did what his leaders told him. If they said, "Go to Korea," his only question was, "How many grenades do I get?"This, after I had thought about it, was pretty much my question, too.

But instead of going to the number of grenades we would carry, Brown had something else in mind. He went directly to the heart of the matter: how we were to deal with one another on a mission in which our lives depended on the very core of combat—trust.

"Let's talk about what counts most to you: life and death—yours."

Now he had our riveted attention. "This is a team. You must function as one, yet we, the directors of the mission, are making it very difficult—in fact, almost impossible. We are asking you to trust one another with your lives, but telling you that you can't know anything about the guy next to you, who may have control of your life. How can you trust someone if you don't know anything about him? You see the problem. Well, let's see if we can overcome it."

He pointed to Jim Pearson (Tom Thumb) and Ranger Ted Moody (Mr. Charles Atlas), the two oddest ones. "You guys are a team. Your lives depend on each other. You must trust one another. It's life or death. I want you to tell one another something that will inspire each of you with confidence—something that counts, something personal and profound, but nothing that will reveal anything that could identify you. This is a real test. Jim, you're first."

Pearson didn't hesitate. "I went to Harvard."

Moody stared at him in disbelief, and then he doubled over in laughter. Here was a muscular man who could have hurled Pearson through the staging building wall, going to put his life in the hands of someone whose main attribute was that he had gone to Harvard. Moody raised his hands in mock surrender. "That's it; I give up. I'm killing myself."

Even Pearson laughed, but Brown pressed on, not overly impressed with Jim's answer, which left me wondering, too. "Okay, Ted, tell Jim why he should trust you."

Moody thought a moment, then another. You could almost feel him grinding thoughts into words. He seemed to be searching deep within himself, maybe for the first time. Then at last, eyeing Mr. Harvard, he said, "All right. My wife was screwing another guy. I divorced her but I didn't kill her. Or him."

The silence was stunning. Finally it was broken by Reed Lynch, the other frogman. He nodded to Pearson. "I get it. He wins. Trust him. The rest of us would have killed the bitch. If he spared her adulterous ass, he'd sure as hell save your Harvard one."

So it went through the rest of the morning, paired together, working until we had a feel for one another, even though we didn't know anything factually specific about each other. It was a great exercise in which we tried to bond and be accepted without revealing anything personal. We eventually found ourselves communicating on a primal level: trust me, believe in me, but no, you can't know anything about me.

What it seemed to boil down to in the end was instinct—we "instinctively" trusted one another, something no more definable than "gut feeling." But that should not have been surprising, because Brown had chosen us carefully; we were not randomly selected. He had selected us with cohesiveness in mind.

The result of the exercise was an affirmation of Brown's

selection process—I *did* begin to form trust for these men. Like myself, they had been chosen because they were willing to sacrifice their lives for our country, to give up everything for a belief we all shared. Being aware of this dedication and commitment about one another made it easier to trust one another.

Whether we realized it or not, we had each questioned the fundamentals of our existence by asking ourselves: what counts? Is it country, freedom, our children? And we had all come to the same answer—that there existed something beyond self, more important than life, and we were willing to die for it. We could not be bought, and we would not sell one another out.

We were soon given a break for lunch, another feast of too much food intended to knit us more tightly together. The meal did not have the desired effect: the rangers and frogmen bonded in muscular fraternity at one table; the pilots teamed up at another; the CIA agents remained aloof at theirs; and that left Jim Pearson and me, the smallest and the youngest, at our own table.

Brown studied us from his vantage point at the front of the room, obviously disturbed—the bonding needed more work, so how do you bring a frogman and a pilot together, a ranger and a CIA agent? He knew he had to try again, and try harder.

After lunch, he went at us with a different strategy: fear.

Gathered again in a circle like kindergarteners, we listened to Brown introduce our first guest speaker, a young Army captain wearing medical insignia and a no-nonsense look.

"Gentlemen, we're going to get a few unpleasant issues out of the way so we can move on to the mission itself. This is Captain Medic. He is a doctor who served with a Mobile Army Surgical Hospital unit, MASH, in Korea. He will tell you about combat injuries and how to treat them. He'll demonstrate with a slide show."

Oh, great, I thought: blood and gore, and right after lunch.

Without preamble, the doctor, a not particularly military-looking man in his early thirties, hit the highlights. "I believe I've seen more shattered bodies and lives within the past several months than I'll witness for the rest of my life; I certainly hope so. I have brought some slides of these injuries that will show you what artillery, mortars, hand grenades, bullets, burns, combat accidents, and subzero weather can do to the human body."

What followed was sickening, a graphic depiction of the horrors of war; more than a few of us almost lost our lunches.

The first slides showed shrapnel damage—blood; guts; bones; and torn, mutilated, and burned bodies—a kaleidoscope of punctured organs, ripped flesh, muscle, tendons, severed arteries, and broken bones.

"But this isn't the worst," he said, readying another slide.

I wanted to look away, but I was riveted to the gore on the screen.

"Filth is the worst."

So we saw gangrene, flesh rotted and turned black, withered stumps, and bone eaten by bacteria.

But all this was just the warm-up. Bullet wounds and burns came next. Most graphic were slides on the effect of dum-dum rounds, outlawed by the Hague Convention but a favorite of the enemy. Dum-dum rounds are soft-nosed lead that enter the body at 2,700 feet per second, expand, and explode, ripping out chunks of whatever gets in their way. One slide showed the entrance point, the size of a normal bullet, but the exit wound was the size of a baseball. If the round strikes a bone, it shatters the bone, sending pieces in all directions like miniature bullets. Captain Medic stated that no one he'd treated had survived a dum-dum impact to the head.

After the burn presentation, a particularly gruesome series of slides, we were given an account of concussions, broken backs, fractures, sprains, and lacerations.

The finale was the worst of all—frostbite.

"With windchill, temperatures in Korea drop to thirty degrees below zero. Here's an example of what can happen."

Up popped a slide of two human feet frozen solid.

During the entire presentation, no one spoke, joked, or made flippant remarks; everyone concentrated on keeping their composure. I certainly did; I struggled hard not to get sick or show squeamishness.

Shutting off the projector, the doctor looked at us serenely. "Now you know what can happen to you. But here's the bad news: there won't be a doctor with you, no MASH unit to treat any of these wounds. You will have to rely on one another. Your lives, literally, are in each other's hands. So let's go to work on saving one another."

For the next two hours, we took a first-aid course on how to use the emergency medical kits that would be on each vehicle. No one's attention strayed, no one joked, and the result was exactly what Brown desired—we were brought closer together. We were all vulnerable men of weak and mortal flesh indeed, and we needed one another to survive.

At the end of his presentation and training session, the doctor wished us well. "Perhaps our paths will cross again, gentlemen, but I hope not in my professional capacity."

When he left there was silence.

Finally Bill Robbins, the pilot, broke the somber spell. He stood up. "I think I forgot something in my locker; I need to go get it."

"What locker?" Brown asked.

"My locker back at Travis Air Force Base."

Brown smiled but immediately jumped ahead to the next atrocity show. "You've met Commander Chuck, now let me introduce my other assistant—Colonel Andy. Andy is with Air Force intelligence. He specializes in aerial surveillance but today he is going to tell you why you do not want to be captured."

A trim man of medium height in his mid-thirties, with dark-rimmed glasses and professorial, humorless manner, stood before us.

Robbins, despite his cocky manner, had been profoundly affected by the doctor's presentation. I noticed how frequently he had averted his eyes during the slide show, but now his swagger and bravado returned. "Do we really need this?" he asked. "They're going to cut off our nuts and jam needles down our dicks. We get the picture."

"Perhaps we could see a demonstration," joked frogman Capeman. "On you."

The room filled with laughter, including Robbins. Andy waved for silence. "I'll be very brief, since you already have an idea of what can happen; however, beyond damage to the testicles and penis, there are a few other tortures the North Koreans and Chinese favor."

I definitely did not want to hear this, but once again was riveted, as were the others, several of whom I noticed had unconsciously brought their legs together and cupped their crotches.

"Spying is considered the greatest crime by our enemy, and there is no limit to the degree of cruelty that interrogators will use to get information. You do *not* want to be interrogated. They will pull out your teeth one by one without the use of anesthetics. They will extract your fingernails and toenails. They will puncture your eardrums, gouge out your eyes, burn you with cigarettes. They will shove a hot poker up your rectum. You *will* talk. There is no question about that; no one can withstand the torture. Whether you have been able to provide them with information or not, they will execute you with a single bullet to the back of your skull."

He opened his hands. "That's it. Any questions?"

No one wanted more details; we indeed had the picture.

"Then, moving right along," Andy said, "let's discuss ways for you not to get captured. Assuming everything goes as planned on the mission, the issue will not arise. However, we must consider that everything may not go according to plan. If, for any reason, you are not able to reach the rescue point and face capture, you have one, I repeat, *one* option."

He held up a flight boot that had been on the floor beside him. "This is a right boot. You will be fitted with an identical one. Note that there is a nylon cord knotted on the end protruding a half inch from the inside top fold of your boot."

Andy walked around the circle and showed each of us the knotted cord.

"When you pull the cord, the leather fold will open. Inside the fold is a small, smoke-colored waterproof glass tube with a rubber-sealed screw-on lid."

He pulled the cord, removed the tube, held it up, and passed it around. "Note that it reads, 'Potassium Cyanide—DANGER—POISON.' There's even a skull and crossbones."

The glass tube was returned to him. He then unscrewed the lid and emptied a small capsule containing a white powder into his palm. He handed it to Robbins and told him to pass it around.

Robbins did so, gingerly, and each man in turn handled it like a hot coal, except for the CIA agents, who barely glanced at it, as if they had seen one a hundred times before. Perhaps they had.

Retrieving the capsule, Andy continued. "The last step is to place the capsule between your back teeth, bite hard, crush it, and swallow."

He put the capsule in his mouth, bit down, and swallowed.

I almost fell off my chair.

"After you swallow, you will die. Very soon. Painfully. Your vital organs will shut down; this will be followed by convulsions, coma, then death."

I think we were all waiting for him to convulse. We stared at him, transfixed. My mouth hung open.

"Any questions?" he deadpanned.

"Thank you, Colonel," Brown said. Then he grinned. "You don't think we'd let you guys handle a *real* cyanide capsule, do you? The temptation might be too great. We don't want any of you taking the easy way out of this op. We want you to suffer a *lot* more."

He clapped his hands sharply. "Okay, class dismissed. It's 1740. Chow is at 1900. You have a little better than an hour of free time."

We felt an incredible release of tension. We all jumped up, freed from hours of gore and death. There was laughter, backslapping, and horseplay, exactly what Brown had been aiming for, except for Tyler and Hinsley. The CIA agents seemed unfazed by what we had just been through.

"I'm going to do my daily-dozen exercises," Moody said, which of course goaded Kingsley and the two frogmen to join him. The rangers wanted to run the length of Japan, but we were virtual prisoners within the staging area. Brown wasn't taking any chances with Broken Reed's tight security.

I could just picture their workout—Hercules and his buddies running through fifty repetitions of military exercises. Though I could have used some exercise, especially after all the food, I wasn't about to join those guys. I knew I could never keep up; it'd be humiliating.

The meeting room was converted into a gym.

"Officers are welcome, sirs," Moody said pointedly to the Air Force pilots.

"No way," barked Bill Robbins, not stepping into that trap, either. "I'm going to go take a bubble bath."

Actually a bath was what *I* wanted, or at least another shower to wash off the past hours' horrors. Or better yet, a stiff drink. No wonder they had forbidden us booze during this period; we would all have gotten wasted after these briefings. Except maybe Hinsley and Tyler. I watched them calmly walk off together. Too calmly, I thought. There was something about Tyler that bothered me, but I couldn't put my finger on it.

Back in my room, on my bunk trying *not* to think of what I'd just been told, I considered the men on the mission in whose hands my life would be. Did I trust them? The frogmen and rangers, absolutely. Bill Robbins and Sam Puller? No question; these guys had flown many combat missions; I had no doubts about their composure or bravery. The same with Jim Pearson; he might be short and slight, but I saw steely determination in him. Besides, I thought, nobody stupid or lazy got into Harvard, even if the frogmen weren't impressed; if nothing else, he could brilliantly bullshit his way through this op.

That left the spooks, Hinsley and Tyler. Deception and subterfuge were their lives. So how could you trust them? They lied for a living. Yet there was no question about their dedication, professionalism, and willingness to sacrifice their lives for the mission—but for one another? There was the rub, of course. I could picture Dan Kingsley or Ted Moody, certainly Tom Capeman and Reed Lynch, even Robbins and Puller carrying a wounded Jim Pearson or myself on their shoulders to the rescue point. But Tyler or Hinsley? Would John Tyler risk his life to carry me to safety?

Hinsley was in charge; he was also the oldest among us. It was his job to ensure the mission was carried out. From what I'd observed, he appeared calm and competent. More than likely, he'd do a quick mental analysis of the situation, weigh risks, balance lives against the goal, and make a dispassionate, ruthless decision. That was fine with me; I understood the mission was more important than any of our lives, and I trusted Hinsley to do the right thing.

But what about Tyler? He hadn't done anything to incur anyone's dislike, but even so, I didn't like him; I could not picture him risking his life for me. He was going out of his way to remain aloof. He didn't want any part of us. Why?

Then it occurred to me; he might have another assignment altogether.

We could not be captured. Killed, that was okay—regrettable, of course, but all in the line of duty. Capture would destroy the mission and create an international crisis; it would damage Truman's credibility not just with foreign governments, but with his own military. That's why we'd been given a cyanide capsule and a graphic demonstration on how to use it.

But what if someone hesitated? Or couldn't bring himself to take it? Or *couldn't* take it—if he was wounded or unconscious? There had to be a backup plan. The cyanide was the backup plan for capture. Was John Tyler the backup plan in case the cyanide failed?

I saw Tyler in my mind, removed, cold, calculating, observant, and felt his cold eyes on me. Oh, yeah, he could do it, I decided. How much easier would it be for him if he never bonded with any of us?

Then I realized, no question, I was getting paranoid. But here we were, talking world war, atomic bombs, presidents, and a mission behind enemy lines—maybe paranoia was in order. In any case, an operation this important, this elaborately planned, would surely have a contingency plan for disaster. The more I thought about it, the more convinced I became that John Tyler was that contingency plan.

Terrific! Now, not only did I have to worry about the six thousand things that could go wrong—equipment breakdowns, mutilations and dismemberments, *cyanide*—there was John Tyler lurking behind it all, watching for any mistake or weakness.

I was pondering this when we were called to dinner, this time Deep South home cooking: fried chicken, barbecue ribs, potato salad, baked beans, coleslaw, hot biscuits, pecan pie, and ice cream. The rangers and frogmen ate with gusto, but then they had probably just established a world record for push-ups, sit-ups, and squat thrusts, expending as much energy as it would have taken to climb Mount Fuji. I, however, didn't have much appetite. I wanted to talk about Tyler with Jim Pearson, but that wasn't allowed. Still, we all joked and laughed throughout the meal, and there was a great deal of interservice teasing and put-downs, but I kept my eyes on Tyler, ever quiet, ever removed, just watching us, and watching me watch him.

Chapter Seven

Rehearsal

The next day, which was again miserably overcast, cold, and wet, we got down to the nuts and bolts of Broken Reed. We had our wet suits and flight uniforms; now it was time for a dress rehearsal. First was the submarine run-through in wet suits, prepped with a slide show about the terrain where we would land. I had never worn a wet suit before; it was like an immense girdle, extremely uncomfortable. It looked great on the rangers and frogmen, accentuating their muscular physiques, but poor Jim Pearson and I looked like carrots dressed in rubber gloves.

The frogmen, Tom Capeman and Reed Lynch, were in charge of this initial phase. All the rest of us had to do was don our wet suits and row the rubber rafts to shore. Brown emphasized that the passage from the submarine to the coast was particularly dangerous. Any mistake or misstep could cause us to be swept out to sea, where we'd freeze to death or end up at the bottom of the ocean. We were to do exactly *and only* what Capeman and Lynch ordered. Brown seemed to direct that point primarily at Robbins, who had already demonstrated his independence and reluctance to take orders from men junior to him.

After we reached the coast, the two rangers would take over. Dan Kingsley and Ted Moody would lead us from our landing point on Yongjin Bay to our rendezvous point with the armored convoy. This was where they earned their pay, it was their area of expertise. Then, at the end of the mission, they would lead us from where we would abandon the convoy to one of several designated rescue points along North Korea's west coast. While we were on foot, they were in charge. Brown's order was to do exactly what they told us.

So far, so good, I thought; I felt I was in competent hands, and if all I had to do was row and walk, I could manage my part.

"Now I'm going to tell you about the convoy," Brown said. "Again, you are going to be in expert hands. So let me tell you about your 'captors.'"

For the first time we learned that Lieutenant Lee and his unit, sixty-six Nationalist Chinese soldiers who had infiltrated North Korea, had forged North Korean and Communist Chinese military directives ordering Lee's platoon to transport captured American airmen across the Korean peninsula to a port on the Yellow Sea. A covert operative serving within the Chinese high command headquarters had been successful in preparing authentic-looking forged documents in such a way that there would be little chance of their being questioned.

"You will do what they tell you. They are your captors, but their lives are at stake as much as yours—maybe more so because if captured, they would be considered traitors and suffer far worse than you. You are all unsung heroes, but these men are going above and beyond."

"Will they speak English?" Bill Robbins wanted to know.

"Lieutenant Lee is fluent and the guards who'll be with you inside the vehicles speak English. I'm not certain about the others."

"Forget the English," Moody said. "Can they play poker? It sounds like it's going to be a cold lonely week inside those refrigerators."

Brown ignored him to go into the details of the eleven-vehicle convoy. The lead vehicle would be a Chinese reconnaissance truck manned by Lieutenant Lee and three men.

Lee's vehicle would be followed by a Soviet T-34 tank, two reconfigured and modified American half-tracks, a second Chinese recon vehicle, four wheeled vehicles, a second Soviet T-34 tank, and, bringing up the rear, a third Chinese recon vehicle. Plans called for a fifth wheeled vehicle to be added, if needed.

We laughed when Brown told us that Lee's men had stolen two Soviet T-34 tanks from under the noses of a Communist Chinese armored unit.

The modified U.S. Army WWII half-track, supposedly captured by the Chinese, would be identified with the Communist Chinese Army insignia.

I noted that Brown did not explain how the two half-tracks got into North Korea, and where the balance of the vehicles came from, but remembering how he'd slapped me down when I'd asked about such details earlier, I kept silent. I surmised that the half-tracks must have been modified at an ordnance shop outside of North Korea and landed by ship earlier; after all, MacArthur had landed an entire invasion force without detection a year ago. The rest of the vehicles must have been captured or swiped from enemy units.

Next we learned how the team would be divided. Brown told us that Pearson, Capeman, Moody, Kingsley, and I would be in the lead half-track.

I felt happy with my assignment; these were the guys I would have picked if it had been left to me. I liked Pearson, and felt comfortable and protected with the one frogman and two rangers. I was relieved not to have to share tight quarters with the CIA agents, and I thought the pilots would also have been too much, like being in a raucous fraternity house. These men, plus Reed Lynch, the second frogman, were to be in the half-track behind us. The only change I might have made was to swap Lynch for Kingsley. I liked Dan, but the ranger's gas attacks had been growing even worse, surpassing what any one of us would have thought possible. I realized that close confinement with him in the half-track could become intolerable.

We would travel only at night. Before dawn, we would pull off the road and camouflage the vehicles for protection against being bombed or strafed by our own planes searching for targets of opportunity. Lee's men had been trained as masters of camouflage, able to hide even the T-34 tanks from aerial sight during daylight hours. Bivouac sites were chosen for maximum protection from aerial detection.

We were then told about the twenty-two operatives who had been inserted the previous June and July to infiltrate enemy units and gather intelligence about enemy positions, commanders, strength, supplies, combat readiness, intentions, battle plans, and resolve. They were the ones most at risk.

Each operative was issued map coordinates along a convoy route and given a window of time to make contact, when they would turn over their intelligence reports. Not only did they have to avoid capture under darkness in order to make contact with us, they had to slip away afterward without detection—then exit North Korea following a complicated escape plan.

Of the twenty-two operatives, fourteen were Chinese from the Nationalist Army on Formosa. Eight were from the South Korean Army. All twenty-two had been handpicked and trained by the CIA and the U.S. military, and could speak English. They had undergone HUMINT training, harsh physical training, escape and evasion training, language indoctrination, communications training, and cold-weather and mountain survival. All were ranger-qualified. Eight had parachuted or been dropped by helicopter. Six were inserted by boat at selected landing sites along the shore of the Sea of Japan, and the final eight had slipped through the battle lines from South Korea. All had been in country collecting information for six months.

Every operative carried identification and orders enabling him to infiltrate North Korean and Chinese military units.

Each had been assigned a specific mission or geographical sector within North Korea, extending from the battle lines northward into Manchuria.

All carried a radio so they could establish limited contact with other operatives on preassigned frequencies. Because of distance and terrain, they would not always be able to contact the convoy, but they would be able to receive strong signals that would provide the convoy's precise location at all times.

The original intelligence reports would be in Chinese or Korean, which Hinsley and Tyler would translate into English for my encryption and transmission. After the CIA agents verified that their reports were acceptable, the operatives would be released to make their escape out of North Korea.

As far as we knew from their most recent covert transmissions, the operatives were ready.

In addition, Brown had received word that the convoy was in place. "They're waiting for you guys. The cover story is that your plane was shot down north of Kumsong; the crew survived and was captured, and now you're being brought by a recon patrol to the east coast, where your captors will transport you across the peninsula to the Yellow Sea. From there you will be taken to mainland China. Everything is a go. All that's left is to finish preparations here, get your submarine to the coast, and load you onto your vehicles."

It sounded so easy. I knew better; we all did.

We spent the rest of that day and the next exploring ways to minimize what could go wrong and familiarizing ourselves with the equipment. For me, that meant rehearsing with the transmitting and cryptology gear. Jim Pearson was my backup and worked with me. A complete inventory proved that every item was present and in operational condition. Every spare part was included. The signal operating instructions (SOI) and special signal instructions (SSI) were complete. Everything was ready to go.

Capeman and Lynch practiced mock rubber-craft landing with the team and went over charts and currents while Moody and Kingsley digested maps of the terrain from the coast to the rendezvous point, and alternative routes to the rescue point. Hinsley and Tyler, off by themselves, did whatever CIA agents do, and that left Robbins and Puller with the brief task of telling us what they thought we should know about the B-29, which wasn't much because there was no B-29, and in any case we were not supposed to let ourselves get captured and interrogated.

Finally, Brown had the flyboys check the contents of the four emergency kits, which took only a few minutes.

"Now what?" Robbins complained. "Isn't there anything else Sam and I can do?"

"You already did it," Capeman retorted. "You crashed the fucking plane."

"And a good job they did," Brown said with a laugh. "You're all alive. Lesser pilots would have gotten you killed."

"Better pilots wouldn't have been shot down, sir," Lynch commented. The frogmen had *no* sympathy for the Air Force officers.

I spent hours working with the SOI, the communications bible I would use. The SOI contained all the classified codes, frequencies, and procedures. Having to encrypt all messages made everything more difficult and time-consuming. It would be easier to transmit everything in the clear, but that would provide the enemy with a clear text of everything our operatives had collected. Another slowdown in transmission would be caused by radio frequencies that had to be changed often to prevent the enemy from plotting a fix on our location. Practice and more practice was required to cut down the time for encryption and frequency changes.

Making contact with the operatives would be critical, but transmitting their reports to the airborne operator would be even more critical and require the tightest security. There was no room for error.

Two phases would be involved. The first was to convert the reports with a sophisticated encryption machine into gibberish five-letter code groups. The second phase was to use a high-speed code key, known as a vibroflex, or bug, to transmit the five-letter code groups using international Morse code through the use of a series of keyed pulses, representing dots and dashes.

For example, a simple message, "Ten artillery weapons are dug in twenty-one kilometers south of Kumchon," would be encoded as "HFNMF IPDSG LDJDV HVUYW HDCBJ AYASN DKVDO PBDKL SLSCH GSTYT DSIAZ FDVJH TWHQQ KKSCS."

This message, if intercepted, could make no sense. To break it required an identical cryptographic machine with identical components and settings. The more confusing and complex the system, the more secure it was, and of course, the more difficult to break. Basically, it could be likened to speaking a foreign language using an obscure or invented third and fourth language, all transmitted as fast as possible in a code only one other person has.

Once this complexity is grasped, one can appreciate the marvel of anyone breaking such a code, as the British in World War II cracked the German code with the Enigma machine, and the Americans cracked the Japanese code. It also explains why American code transmitted by Navajo Indians in the Pacific theater was never broken—there was no reference point for the Japanese monitoring the transmission; nothing made sense because no one on their end understood Navajo, which was the basis of the code.

For two days I worked with the SOI, with Jim backing me up.

We worked behind screens and used the actual equipment we'd have on the mission and practiced removing and replacing it from a mock-up of the secret storage compartment in the half-track because speed was critical, and detection fatal.

After that, we rehearsed destroying the equipment and SOI, which under no circumstances were to fall into enemy hands. At the end of the mission, or if discovery by the enemy was threatened, we were to strap six Thermit bombs over the SOI, SSI, radio, and crypto equipment, attach an electronic timer and detonator, and let it blow, transforming the classified material and gear to ash and molten metal. The timer was preset for six minutes, theoretically enough time for us all to bail out of the half-track before the Thermit bombs ignited. This timing couldn't be altered.

When we finished practicing, we placed the equipment in watertight containers and packed it for transport. Color coding was added to the containers to identify the contents.

By the end of our preparations, I was stunned by the mission's intricacy. Everything had been designed to fit like a masterpiece watch, hundreds of details, maybe thousands I didn't even know about, perfectly synchronized—the Nationalist Chinese troops and mechanized convoy ready when we arrived, operatives at their designated assembly points, the encoding and transmission—and this on top of the overwhelming challenge of outwitting the enemy and getting to the rescue point for extraction.

The odds for success seemed remote; too many things could go wrong—maybe more than the six thousand Brown had alluded to. Adding to my worry was the anxiety and foreboding on the faces of the others. It bothered me that the rangers and frogmen seemed worried; these were guys for whom fear was supposed to be alien. Nor did I like it that Robbins and Puller were subdued. When pilots got quiet, it was definitely time for concern. I didn't want these men, all combat veterans, to be nervous; their fears heightened my own. That Hinsley and Tyler appeared nonplussed did not help; these men's profession demanded stony expressions. If anything, their stoicism aggravated me even more.

I felt overwhelmed. Even if the landing and the convoy went right, should I fail to get the transmissions off, the mission would fail. If everything else went without a hitch, if everybody—frogmen, rangers, CIA agents, Nationalist Chinese, operatives—performed perfectly, the mission's success or failure still fell on me—and I had never been in combat, never been tried under stress, let alone proved myself. The responsibility was so awful I felt sick to my stomach. I felt like a man waiting for the hangman's noose. But there was nothing more to be done. We had to rely now on our skills, and an immense amount of luck.

That night we had a celebratory meal, or, as it seemed to me, a Last Supper. It was a sumptuous feast, but I wasn't hungry. I noticed the others didn't eat much, either.

I slept fitfully that final night in Japan; blood and horror saturated my dreams. I wished I hadn't come; I wished I could change my mind and go home; I wanted to see Nell and Lanny, and for the first time, I wondered about death—what was it like? Would I meet it bravely? Death had suddenly become real. The youthful bravado and game playing were over. I was experiencing what every soldier faced on the eve of battle—mortality.

I was stepping onto the fields of Mars, a puny man like uncountable millions before me who had been slaughtered by the war gods, scythed unmercifully by Death.

Then I felt shame—I was an American officer. Of course I would be brave. Besides, it was too late to back out; John Tyler would see to that.

Chapter Eight

From Japan to North Korea

Maybe I slept that night, but if I did, my sleep was intermittent and not restful. I didn't eat much breakfast, either, though the combat vets chowed down hungrily. Perhaps for them, the hardest part had been prepping for the operation; now that the battle was joined, so to speak, they were ready—and hungry. The frogmen and rangers cleared everything on their plates and went back for more, fueling themselves for the fight ahead. I could barely keep down two slices of toast.

Despite their gung ho manner, I remained subdued, not a little due to the weather—it was another cold, grim, overcast day like all the others I had experienced in Japan. Moreover, this would be my first combat insert, and I acted like the novice I was—a rookie in his first game, not a seasoned jock playing for the championship. The others were pumped up and ready to hit the field, while I found myself wanting to cling to the bench.

We loaded our gear on trucks for the haul to Tachikawa Air Base, and while I took minor comfort in the boisterous, almost eager behavior of the others, I didn't say a word. Capeman and Moody tried to engage me, even gave me reassuring pats, but I sat like a damp dark mushroom in a rain forest.

Arriving at Tachikawa didn't improve my spirits. Three

choppers were waiting to fly us to the coast, where we would meet the submarine. But the lead pilot told Brown the mission might have to be delayed because of strong winds en route.

Brown shook his head emphatically; he would not put off the mission. "Whether we crash or make it to the Sea of Japan isn't your problem, Captain. I'll take responsibility. Get us on our way."

Crashing clearly was a problem for the pilot. He muttered an obscenity as he walked away, adding further worry to the fearsome burden I was already carrying.

The burden became crushing when we barely cleared Tachikawa's perimeter; strong winds felt as if they were tearing the choppers apart. I looked to the others for cues on how to react. They were no help; their faces were intense and worried, too, all horseplay and bravado gone. I could tell each was fighting fear in his own way. That's when I realized no one ever got used to facing death. Each new encounter was terrifying; death didn't distinguish between the brave and the cowardly, or favor the experienced over the novice. This encounter and all to come would each be a roll of the dice for all or nothing. Capeman, Moody, and the others had no advantage over me. Experience and stoicism carried no weight or respect with death. The war gods mocked us all.

We were *all* afraid, and for the first time I saw those sitting beside me as men who could really die. I saw them now as men with wives and children, mothers and fathers, hopes and dreams. I didn't want to die not knowing anything about these men with me. I didn't want to die without them knowing anything about me. I had a wife and a son and I wanted to tell everybody about them. For the first time I felt the incredible bond men form in combat and the tremendous need to reach out to a comrade.

But we were forbidden to do this. We were each on our own.

The flight became so turbulent that we feared our equipment would be destroyed; we had lashed it down, but no one had expected such violent buffeting. I saw the others trying to hold down their breakfasts and was glad I'd skipped the meal except for the toast.

Just when I thought I couldn't take much more, the choppers throttled back and started a bouncing, stomach-tossing descent.

When we landed harshly, there was a mad rush to exit; we couldn't get off fast enough. In a moment we were all standing on a long wooden wharf, blown by winds that threatened to knock us into the sea. A motor launch bounced wildly on the waves below us.

I saw the submarine way offshore, moored to a buoy in Tsuruga Bay. I was ready to say to hell with it, and we hadn't even left Japan yet, but the frogmen seemed suddenly to be in their element. They grinned lovingly at the sight of the sea. Though Japanese longshoremen were supposed to load our equipment onto the launch, Capeman and Lynch took over and secured everything to their satisfaction.

Brown watched us board. His face was grim and determined, but when we were ready to shove off, he smiled encouragingly. "Good luck, gentlemen. God bless. I'll see you next week at Kempo Airfield in South Korea." He saluted us and we cast off.

In minutes I went from airsick to seasick, and I stayed queasy the entire hour it took to reach the sub. It took another thirty minutes to transfer the equipment into the sub, then we went aboard. Except for the frogmen, this was the first time on a submarine for the rest of us. I didn't know what to expect, but the reality was worse than I could have imagined. Picture hell underwater and you have a starting point. Cramped, claustrophobic, sardines in a can—that doesn't begin to capture the interior of a World War II submarine. I couldn't fathom why anyone would choose such a duty station, and this was before the damn thing submerged or began to vibrate.

We were led down a corridor so narrow the rangers and frogmen had to inch through sideways because their shoulders were too broad. We were brought to a galley, a relatively large room, and welcomed curtly by the skipper, a Navy commander who shook our hands and immediately left us; he did not appear happy.

I had a moment of panic wondering if he might be jumping ship, but we soon heard his voice from the bridge giving orders for getting under way.

Immediately vibrations thrummed through the vessel, and we began a series of not-so-gentle corkscrew rolls in choppy water. As though it was an attempt to distract us, coffee and doughnuts were brought out. I couldn't touch a thing. Neither could anyone else, except the frogmen. I had the distinct feeling they were showing off.

Minutes later the skipper returned. He was in his late thirties, lean and mean, and I had been right—he was *not* happy. "On behalf of the Pacific Naval Command, welcome to the United States submarine ferrying service," he began without warmth.

His eyes narrowed and his voice growled. "I have no idea what this is all about. All I was told on short notice was to pick up some seamen with their equipment and deliver you to specified map coordinates off the east coast of North Korea, which, I do not need to tell you, is behind enemy lines. This is a combat mission, except we don't have any weapons."

Then, looking at Pearson and myself, he said accusingly, albeit accurately, "You are *not* seamen. This is *my* ship, and before we go any further, we have to get something straight. For those of you who might not know, let me inform you of the first law of the sea—on a ship, the captain is supreme. I am the *only* authority."

He let that settle in, and then he started in earnest.

"I have been instructed to enter in the captain's log that this is a routine patrol. My ass! Going unarmed to North Korea is not routine. I can't even enter that I picked you up, where we left from, or where we're going. Manning this boat is a skeleton crew pulled off liberty, including myself. We have been ordered to cover our nametags, and my men have been told not to talk with you.

Bullshit! I can't run a ship this way. I want to know who you are and what you're doing here."

He gazed out upon us with a ferocious look. No one said a word.

The commander's jaw set. What's next? I wondered. Is he going to make us walk the plank? Did a submarine have a plank? I was definitely intimidated; I knew I didn't belong on this man's vessel, and he certainly knew it, too.

When the room reached maximum tension, Hinsley stood up. The CIA agent appeared calm, not in the least intimidated, and his voice resonated with authority. "Commander, I am in charge of these men. My name is Captain Jerry Hinsley."

The commander balked. Obviously, as Hinsley intended, he mistook Jerry for a Navy captain, not an Air Force captain, a rank higher than his own.

"You'll note," Hinsley continued, "that none of us is wearing name tag or rank insignia, either. In addition to your orders not to enter anything about us in your log, our anonymity should give you some idea of how sensitive and classified this mission is."

Having established his authority, Hinsley went on more diplomatically. "I appreciate your frustration about your orders, but we are operating under puzzling orders as well. All I can tell you is that we are on a classified mission of great importance and are not at liberty to discuss any aspect of it. You have your orders—to deliver us to the coast of North Korea. You must obey them and not ask any questions. We have our orders, to land on the coast of North Korea and tell no one, including you, about this. We must obey those orders; therefore, we will answer no questions. Do we understand one another?"

The two men stared at each other for a long minute. Finally the commander relaxed. "We understand each other perfectly, Captain." He smiled for the first time. "Welcome aboard, gentlemen. The sea is running a bit rough; it will take thirty-two hours to reach our destination. After you've settled into your quarters, we'll give you a tour of the sub. You're welcome on the bridge and can get a good view from the conning tower. We'll travel most of the way on the surface. About fifty miles off the coast, we'll dive and proceed underwater at periscope depth until we reach the designated coordinates off the coast of North Korea. We'll surface after dark a few miles offshore. Then you're on your own. Now I'm going to turn you over to my executive officer."

He nodded crisply and left.

"Serves the prick right," Moody whispered, referring to the commander's reprimand from Hinsley.

"No," said Capeman, coming to the naval officer's defense. "It's his ship. That's how the Navy works."

"Air Force, too," Bill Robbins concurred. "On my plane, what I say goes. All things considered, he was pretty gracious."

We were shown to our bunks, then given a tour of the sub; it didn't take long—there wasn't much to see, and none of it was interesting.

We gathered in the galley afterward to compare notes. Robbins and Puller said that when they were on the bridge, they had overheard crewmen bitching about this assignment, saying they were dragged into temporary duty from another sub. Another sailor said he'd been pulled from shore leave. Tom Capeman noticed the torpedo racks were empty and there were no crew members in the torpedo room.

"Hey, that explains all the empty bunks," said Moody.

Lynch nodded. "A sub this size should have about sixty men. I haven't seen but half that number."

"All the sub's identification markings have been whitewashed over, even on the life jackets. Some of the stuff is still wet," Pearson pointed out. "Look at the ship's plaque on the galley bulkhead. That heavy cardboard covering it has been taped over so we can't see the sub's identity. Hell, they don't even want us to know the name of this ship. Just like ourselves, we don't have the foggiest idea of the names of the crew. Somebody's gone to a lot of trouble to cover up this op."

"And it will remain covered," Hinsley barked. His message was clear: mind your own business! We then knew that Hinsley knew all about the sub and her crew, and was enforcing the cover-up.

Stripped down though it was, the sub nevertheless had plenty of chow. Now I understood why submarine crewmen had a tendency to put on weight: no room to exercise, and not much else to do except eat. But I still had no appetite.

I spent a lot of time on the conning tower, mesmerized by my first encounter with the sea. Watching the sub slice effortlessly through swells was breathtaking. Snow-white foaming water seemed to boil as the bow dipped below the surface, then rose to meet the next crest, sending tons of water cascading over her deck. I watched the ongoing romance between the sub and the sea, each caressing, penetrating, then conquering the other.

The rangers, however, were unimpressed by the aquatic wonders. Kingsley and Moody spent their time poring over maps, for after Capeman and Reed got us in our small boats to shore, their job was to link us to the waiting convoy—or get us to our rescue point, if anything went wrong. They had to know every terrain feature, every road, trail, river, stream, lake, bridge, and village, every yard from the coast to our destination, so they could lead us in the dark from any given spot to safety. Our lives depended on them, and they took their job seriously.

Everyone else tried to catch up on their sleep. Surprisingly, the hours passed quickly; funny how time flies as danger approaches.

When we were summoned to the galley for our final briefing, the commander greeted us far differently than upon arrival. He was friendly, almost jovial, which made me wonder if he wasn't just happy to be getting rid of us so he could return to Japan, hot baths, and massages.

"In about fifteen minutes, we're going to periscope depth, then we'll travel submerged to within a few miles of the coast. We'll hold the position until dark. Once we make contact with the unit on shore, we'll surface. Then you shove off. I'm turning everything over to Captain Hinsley from here. I'll be on the bridge. Good luck, gentlemen."

Hinsley took over, but only to call up Capeman and Lynch. "No gung ho speech, no pep talk. This is it. We know what we have to do. We know how important it is and we know how dangerous it is. From this minute on, Tom and Reed are in charge. As soon as we reach shore, Dan and Ted take over. Does anyone have a last question—except for Bill, and the answer to yours is no, you can't go home."

There were no questions, just laughter, even from Robbins.

The frogmen ran down the procedure. They were not polished public speakers, but Capeman had our full attention.

"As soon as we dive, put on your wet suits. When we surface, remain down here until Reed and I finish loading and securing the gear in rubber boats. When that's done, we'll bring you up. The deck will be slippery so *don't* remove the lifeline attached to your body harness until you're in the boat." He turned to Reed. "Did I forget anything?"

"Yeah. Keep quiet. Sound travels well over water, so don't bang the oars." He looked at Kingsley. "And don't fart. They could hear you in Beijing."

"Or he'd blow a hole in the rubber boat," piped up Robbins, unable to contain himself.

"I said quiet. From here on, only four words will be used. 'Port' means only those on the left side of the boats will pull on their oars; 'starboard' means those on the right will pull; 'ahead' means everybody strokes; and 'stop' means, for those rangers among us—stop rowing."

"That's it," Capeman said. As soon as he finished, Kingsley farted.

Everybody threw something at Kingsley, and we were about to jump him when the intercom exploded with a blast—OOOH-GHA, OOOH-GHA. DIVE. DIVE.

There was a horrendous racket of valves opening and closing, metal on metal, then a terrifying rush of water filling the ballast tanks.

I thought the damn thing was sinking. Well, of course it *was,* as it was supposed to, but the rattling and vibrations were so powerful that it seemed the ship was coming apart. We all looked so frightened that Capeman and Lynch laughed. Jim Pearson later told me that he almost crapped in his dungarees.

After recovering from the shock of diving, we put on our wet suits and sat quietly. No one said a word. We were all intent, waiting for water to burst through the bulkheads. I was a wreck; going behind enemy lines definitely seemed preferable to being trapped underwater in a submarine.

We applied a dark, gooey substance to our faces and hands, designed to reduce the reflection of light and prevent exposed skin from freezing.

Capeman and Lynch got up to leave.

"Where are you going?" Bill Robbins demanded, not wanting to be left without them.

"To supervise loading the gear onto the boats. We'll see you topside." Capeman looked at Moody. "That means, for ground-pounders, on deck." He pointed up.

None of us was happy to see them go; we wanted the comfort of their presence, if only to keep reassuring us that all was well, especially when the submarine surfaced, another shattering cacophony—ballast being blown and clanking valves. God almighty, I thought; there was nothing stealthy about a submarine.

Who needed radar and sonic soundings? A deaf drunk could hear one coming.

Indeed, and unknown to us at the time, a diversion was created onshore by the Nationalist Chinese to cover the sound of the surfacing sub. Lieutenant Lee's unit, we later learned, was in place near the beach; when they got a signal from the submarine, the eleven vehicles started their engines and his men began to talk loudly and laugh to distract any attention from the sea.

When called topside, released from thirty-two hours of confinement belowdecks, we were slapped by bitterly cold wind. Five rubber boats were in the water, tied together so they would not drift apart, and already loaded. As we exited the hatch single file, a crewman attached a D ring to the lifeline harness we wore over our wet suits. The lifeline was fixed to a stanchion on the sub's deck.

The crew guided each of us down the slippery deck to the boats and helped us aboard. Moody and Kingsley looked as out of place as the rest of us and held on to the lifeline for dear life. So did I.

Tom Capeman was in the lead boat, Reed Lynch in the last. When Tom gave the command, the crew cast off the line from the sub and we were released, inside Yongjin Bay, heading toward the coast of North Korea, over a mile from shore in water so choppy we had to hold on to keep from being thrown out of the boat by foot-high swells.

Within minutes, the sub backed away. It made a gentle turn to port, bringing the bow about toward the open sea, and slowly slipped under the water.

We were alone. I kept staring at where the sub had disappeared. As the darkness engulfed me, I had never felt so exposed and vulnerable in my life.

"Ahead," Capeman said firmly, and we all began to row. Though it was below freezing, it was not long before I was sweating.

Although we were over a mile out, we could see a small blinking light from shore; it was all we could see. It flashed three times, then four, paused, then repeated the sequence. This was the prearranged signal guiding us to our landing.

Capeman had been right about sound traveling over water, for we could hear vehicle engines and Lieutenant Lee's men shouting and laughing. They were creating a great distraction, so much so I found it hard to concentrate on my rowing.

We rowed steadily toward the signal until a strong bright searchlight suddenly cut a swath along the shoreline. Lee's signal light immediately went black, and Capeman ordered "Stop," which was unnecessary. We were all paralyzed with fear.

Had the enemy heard us? How long before the searchlight would start to sweep out into the bay?

Almost immediately we began to drift back out to sea, pushed along by strong currents and a stiff breeze blowing from land.

Instinctively we ducked low in the boats.

I looked fearfully toward Capeman's boat. He faced a terrible decision—continue to drift or push on in. If we drifted, we could be carried out to sea where we would freeze. There was no hope of contacting the sub. Yet if we rowed toward shore, we risked detection, capture, torture, and death. Despite my terror, I almost laughed at the irony; we were indeed caught between the devil and the deep blue sea.

Then a single rifle shot rang out and the searchlight shattered and went dead, followed by even louder noise, cheering, and cursing from the unit on shore. They must have been playing drunk, with Lee ordering a marksman to knock out the light.

"Ahead," Capeman ordered, and we put our backs into rowing toward the once-again blinking signal.

Nothing else disturbed us as we moved steadily landward, rowing against the cold, rolling, punishing sea.

As we approached shore, we saw several men waiting for us in the dim night light. When the boats finally scraped bottom, they jumped into the water and pulled us closer. God, what a welcome sight they were.

Ice had formed at the water's edge. We stumbled out of the boats and into the arms of our Nationalist Chinese "captors."

We lifted our equipment out of the boats and passed it to Lee's men. In minutes, our gear had been safely off-loaded. Capeman and Lynch assisted in loading rocks onto the rubber boats, slashed them with bayonets, and shoved them out to sea to sink. Then, in a detail that stunned me, they tossed the metal oars far out into the bay. I realized then that had the oars been made of wood, they would have floated, giving away our presence; every single detail about the operation had been considered.

Bill Robbins sank onto the sand and kissed the ground, but Kingsley, now in charge, pulled him up and directed us to fall in with Lee's soldiers, who had picked up the equipment; then he and Moody led us off, eager to prove they were as expert as the frogmen.

We stumbled single file along a narrow steep trail behind Kingsley, who was being guided up the trail by one of Lee's non-coms. Moody assumed the rear position, herding the others to keep ahead of him. Despite waterproof, insulated footwear, we kept slipping and losing our footing on the icy slope.

Finally we reached the area where the vehicles were waiting. A man about 5'8", perhaps thirty years old, wearing a Communist Chinese officer's uniform, stepped forward. He greeted us in perfect formal British English. "I am Lieutenant Lee. I am pleased you have arrived safely." He pointed to a large group of men behind him. "This is my unit. There are sixty-six of us. We will talk later, but first you must change and load your equipment on the vehicles."

In below-freezing weather, in front of curious Chinese soldiers, we stripped off our wet suits down to thermal underwear and put on our Air Force flight suits. The flight jackets and pants didn't appear to be newly issued and just removed from a supply shelf. To keep up the ruse, all had been splattered by oil and showed parachute harness stain marks brought about by bailing out of a disabled bomber. Lee then directed his men to burn the wet suits in a fifty-five-gallon drum.

After we changed and loaded the equipment, we crowded together inside one of the half-tracks; at least it was warm. Lee studied the name tags sewn into our flight suits, then addressed Robbins. "I am sorry your plane went down, Major. I regret that we must transport you and your men to China. You are our prisoners, but we will treat you with every courtesy."

He turned to Hinsley, clearly familiar with the facts about each of us and our assignments. He knew of course that Jerry was in charge. "Before we go, I want to tell you how matters stand."

His speech was so formal and precise that I had to suppress an urge to laugh. "We almost did not make it here. When we arrived in the area, we were challenged by North Korean sentries."

Every time he said the word "Korean," his mouth turned down in disdain. "Communist" always evoked a disgusted grimace.

"I was brought to a North Korean lieutenant colonel in charge of this sector. He disputed my orders and wanted to know why he had not been informed that our convoy would be arriving in his area. It was very disagreeable. However, I convinced him that our orders must remain secret. I also offered to have my men relieve his men on guard duty until we got word that the recon patrol which had captured you had arrived. I told him an armored platoon was more than sufficient to guard this deserted stretch along the bay. It helped that I was able to offer him numerous bottles of rice wine."

He smiled. "I am sure he and his men have been celebrating ever since. That's probably why the disturbances tonight went unnoticed."

"You mean shooting out the searchlight," Hinsley said.

"Yes."

"But now we're ready to go?"

Lee turned to me. "As soon as Sergeant Baker installs and checks his equipment."

"We know our vehicle assignments," Hinsley said. "We'll be ready whenever you give the word."

Lee raised a hand in caution. "I must first brief you on what to expect. We will travel only at night. Before each dawn, we will pull off the road to camouflage the vehicles from airplanes. Your Marine, Navy, and Air Force pilots are very good."

Robbins gave a thumbs-up.

"Some are," Moody said snidely.

Lee, not understanding, looked perplexed. "However, I must warn you that we will probably be stopped many times while we are on the road at Communist and North Korean checkpoints. Each stop will be dangerous. I will have to show our orders. They will undoubtedly be challenged. The vehicles will be searched. Therefore, before we are stopped, you will be handcuffed. My guards may have to . . ." He searched for the proper words. "Be uncourteous with you to impress the enemy soldiers. I regret that, but it is necessary. Of course, when we are stopped and before you open the hatch on your half-track, you must hide any equipment. I will give you a few minutes."

He looked at us. "Do you have any questions?"

"Do you play poker?" Robbins asked.

He thought a moment, then said, apropos of absolutely nothing, "I am a married man."

When no one else spoke, he gave a slight bow. "I wish you well on your mission."

After he was gone, we stared at one another. "So, does he play poker or not?" Robbins asked.

"I wouldn't play against him," Kingsley said.

And that was it. We had arrived safely. Now it began for real.

Chapter Nine

Behind Enemy Lines

Capeman, Moody, Kingsley, Pearson, and I stowed our gear in the half-track and met our "captors." There was no awkwardness, as we were as happy to see them as they were us. Knowing we would be sharing cramped quarters for the next five days, we wanted to get along as well as we could.

Sergeant Chou was a well-built man in his late twenties, shorter than me and in superb physical condition. He told us proudly that he had been a bodyguard for Chiang Kai-shek. Corporal Liu was younger, lithe, and very fit looking; he, too, had been a bodyguard for Chiang. While neither appeared a match for Capeman, Moody, and Kingsley, I felt sure both possessed martial arts skills that made up for our guys' bulk.

They were friendly, and their English, though not perfect, was understandable; they told us their Korean was better—not that we would have known—and that they would alternate in twelve-hour shifts; one would be with us at all times. Both were armed with holster-mounted .45-caliber automatic pistols and would have a U.S. Army Browning automatic rifle in the compartment. These weapons reinforced the impression that they were our guards, but in fact they were armed to protect us.

For the next thirty minutes, I installed the communications and crypto gear in their brackets, then did a test run. Field strength meters indicated the emission of a strong radio-frequency signal from the transmitter, and a check for cryptographic operation proved that everything was ready to go. A quick run-through on all frequency bands of the receiver was positive. There was no damage to the components or spare parts. I gave the thumbs-up to Sergeant Chou and he went off to tell Lieutenant Lee. Chou returned shortly and said we would be leaving immediately.

Kingsley claimed a corner of the half-track and settled in, wrapping himself in his bedroll and blankets. I threw my bedroll and blankets by the fold-up seat where the com gear was hidden. Jim Pearson tossed his stuff next to mine. The others chose the other corners, with Chou or Liu closest to the rear hatch. With six of us inside, the vehicle was cramped, yet that worked to our advantage—at least initially, because the closeness seemed comfy and took the edge off the cold. Later, of course, the closeness became oppressive and the air stuffy and fetid.

It seemed strange to be suddenly separated from the other five men who were riding in the second half-track; we would see little of them from here on.

Before the convoy pulled out, we familiarized ourselves with what was to be our home. The half-track had been heavily modified. All its standard gear, including weapons, had been stripped from the vehicle's carriage platform, which now was completely enclosed with armor plate. With the exception of adjustable side air vents installed near the top, plus an armor-plated rear hatch, the compartment resembled a 10-by-16-foot maximum-security prison cell. The ceiling height was about six feet, tall enough for Jim and me to stand; the others had to stoop.

Moody pounded on the compartment wall and told us it would withstand small-arms fire and artillery shrapnel, but not a direct hit from a larger armor-piercing round or a tank main gun.

Along the right side was a long, hinged metal seat—welded to the wall and designed to fold up. When the seat was in the down position, the hinges were hidden from view, giving the seats the appearance of being permanently installed. The radio transmitter, receiver, crypto machine and components, the SOI, and six Thermit bombs were secured under this seat.

Across the front bulkhead, separating our compartment from the cab, was a hidden storage box that contained six heavy-duty batteries for all our electrical needs—including two electric heaters, electric lights, the radio, and crypto gear. A heavy-duty generator in the engine compartment would keep the batteries charged. Also along the front bulkhead was another hidden box containing five .30 caliber carbine rifles, ammunition, rations, and two survival kits containing signal rescue equipment and medical equipment.

A one-hundred-gallon water tank with hand-operated pump was mounted under the bench on the left side of the compartment, along with a small porta-john.

Two electric heaters mounted on the ceiling fore and aft provided faint warmth, merely taking the bite out of the frigid air we were breathing. The cigar-box-size heaters barely radiated enough warmth to keep the equipment operational.

Knowing the importance of quickly hiding the com and crypto equipment if we were suddenly stopped at an enemy checkpoint, the five of us practiced breaking down the gear and stowing it. We got the process down to less than two minutes, plenty of time; if we needed more, Chou and Liu could stall the enemy by fumbling with the hatch.

"If we stop, don't talk," Chou told us. He pointed to himself and Liu. "We say everything. Don't answer questions."

Then, taking us by surprise, he unholstered his .45, chambered a round, and handed the pistol to Kingsley. "Shoot me if you do not trust me."

Dan grinned. "I'd rather shoot Robbins, but he's not here." He handed the pistol to Capeman.

"Tell you what, Ranger Man, keep farting and I'll shoot you."

"What is 'farting'?" Liu asked, apparently unfamiliar with American slang.

"You'll find out," Moody said, and in demonstration, Kingsley farted.

Chou nodded. "I see. Maybe I shoot you, too."

We laughed, comforted to know our "guards" had a sense of humor and trusted us. We took turns handling the weapon ceremoniously, and then handed it back to Chou. I had the feeling that the surprise passing-around of the pistol had been carefully planned by Chou and Liu to break the ice and make us comfortable, an overture of friendliness and trust that, despite our cultural differences, as soldiers we would all understand.

Chou and Liu spoke together a moment, and then Liu opened the hatch. "Sergeant Chou will take first watch with you. I will sleep."

Within minutes, the six overhead lights in the compartment dimmed as the half-track engine cranked alive; then the vehicle lurched. We all pitched forward, then rolled backward, as the half-track traversed a wide ditch. This rocking was followed by a hard turn to the right that almost dumped everyone off their seats. Eventually the ride smoothed out, and we began picking up speed.

"We on the coastal road now," Chou explained. "We go to Wonsan, maybe eight hours."

At last we were on our way, yet it seemed so sudden—and final. All the preparations were over, the talk done, the anticipation finished. We were in the midst of war. Our separation from those we loved was complete, our alienation total. We settled back. No one spoke. Everyone seemed to be absorbed in their private thoughts. Our lives were out of our hands now. We were behind enemy lines on this improbable mission.

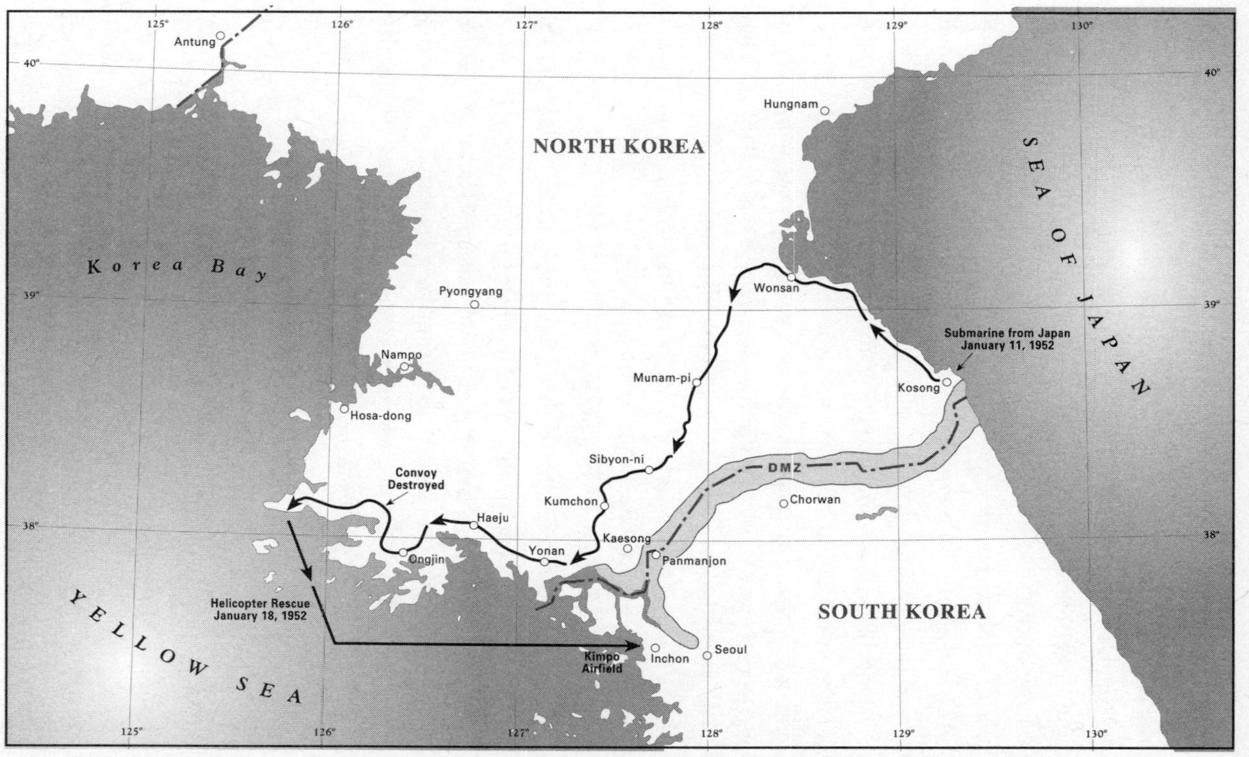
SEA OF JAPAN
NORTH KOREA
SOUTH KOREA
Korea Bay
YELLOW SEA
Antung
Hungnam
Pyongyang
Wonsan
Nampo
Hosa-dong
Munam-pi
Kosong
Submarine from Japan
January 11, 1952
Sibyon-ni
DMZ
Kumchon
Chorwan
Convoy
Destroyed
Haeju
Kaesong
Yonan
Panmanjon
Ongjin
Helicopter Rescue
January 18, 1952
Kimpo
Airfield
Inchon
Seoul
125°
126°
127°
128°
129°
130°
40°
39°
38°

I hadn't thought about the odds for survival in a while. Everything had happened so fast, yet here I was, five thousand miles from my wife and son. Nell didn't even know where I was, and Lanny—he might never know his father. In my mind I could see him jumping into our bed on weekend mornings, wanting to sleep with Mama and Papa. There we'd be, the three of us snuggled down under a comforter, feeling warm love flowing over our little family. We'd wake early on Saturdays to go to the zoo, where Lanny would point at every animal, try to imitate their sound, and laugh.

Now here I was, crouched inside this steel box just like an animal.

I gazed about at the men with me. Sitting forlorn and preoccupied, they didn't look like heroes, certainly not men all those important words rested upon—war, peace, annihilation. They looked like an average bunch of guys lost and out of place. I'm sure I looked the same. We were ordinary men caught up in something too far beyond us to comprehend.

Overwhelmed, we sat silently.

Cold fresh air blew through the air vents, and I could hear the roar of the tank's engine in front of us as we bumped along the road. It seemed impossible that we were here, but now that it was real—I could imagine the enemy up ahead lying in wait for me, I felt every swerve and jolt of the road—it suddenly seemed likely that we might never get back home. Go back to what? I wondered. Would anything ever be the same again after this?

Perhaps sensing our loneliness and fears, Chou said quietly, "You are a long way from your homes. So am I."

We all turned to him, grateful for any respite from our thoughts. "I was born in China," he began, as though telling us a story. This too had been planned, I thought, an attempt to put us at ease and divert our fears. I had read that the Chinese were polite and courteous people and felt Chou's story was another gracious overture for trust and friendliness.

We all listened raptly; we wanted a diversion.

"This was before Mao Tse-tung. Even before the Japanese came and took our country. It was during the time of Sun Yat-sen, after the Ching Dynasty, but before Chiang Kai-shek. There were no emperors and empresses. The old dowager empress, with fingernails as long and sharp as knives, died in 1908. She was the most powerful woman in the history of my country, a concubine who became empress. On her deathbed, she ordered the new emperor murdered, her own son."

It seemed so long ago, though Chou was the same age as Capeman, Moody, and Kingsley; like a fable, foreign and mysterious.

Capeman was as bewitched as a child hearing a bedtime story.

"My father was educated as a mandarin," Chou continued. "He arranged my marriage, and those of my sisters. Then the wars came. First the Japanese, then against Mao. My family was not communist. I fought with the Kuomintang. Chiang Kai-shek is a very great man. But he was betrayed. In 1949 we had to leave China. My family lost everything. When I got to Formosa, I became a bodyguard for Chiang. I was chosen for this mission because I hope America will free my country someday and my family can go back to China. I thank you for helping." He lowered his head in a bow.

I was stunned. I wasn't here to free China; that thought had never occurred to me, nor to the other guys, I was sure. It was an odd sensation to realize that you think you know something, or have a grasp of what is happening, but it's not at all what others think or believe. Your reality is completely different from theirs. I was here because I believed in my country, because of Nell and Lanny, but Chou was here for a completely different reason. And yet, we were on the same side. But I didn't pursue that because I knew where it would lead—to how our enemies thought they were right, and believed in what they were doing;

it would explain how communist China and North Korea were on the same side; I didn't want to go there. I wanted to avoid the quagmire of thought, the bog of gray. It was easier to keep things simple, black and white.

Moody, however, couldn't resist a dig at Capeman; he still hadn't forgiven him for his knowledge of history, something Ted considered worthless, maybe even treasonous. He nodded at Chou and pointed to Capeman. "You and the sailor can have great talks about China. He knows everything."

"Better than knowing nothing," Capeman rejoined.

"Okay smart-ass, tell us something."

But Capeman was still captivated by Chou's story; he wanted to hear more. "I never knew the old empress killed her own son."

Moody was dismissive. "I'm sure there's a lot you don't know, but tell us something you do know."

Chou deferred to Capeman politely. "Yes. You tell us."

Capeman's knowledge of Chinese history was phenomenal, like that of a professor of Far East culture. He spoke of an old empress who was the last ruler in the Manchu Dynasty. He went on to tell of the rulers, the Mings, whose dynasty lasted three hundred years, until around 1650. They were the ones who got China involved with Korea. Then "our professor" explained how the Manchus ascended to power.

When Capeman mentioned "Manchus," Moody butted in by asking, "Like Fu Manchu?" When Moody said he'd seen the movie with Boris Karloff in it, we all broke up.

Capeman rolled his eyes and said, "Something like that," before explaining that the Manchus were from Manchuria.

Listening to Capeman recite Chinese history did more than help pass the time; it took our minds off of where we were, surrounded by a North Korean and Communist Chinese Army.

Before listening to Capeman, I had no idea that the Mings

and Manchus and the Japs had started fighting over Korea and that they had slaughtered each other for years.

Moody was interested, and so was I, though I wasn't sure how accurate all this was. Even Pearson, Mr. Harvard, seemed to be listening. We had five days ahead of us, 120 hours to fill. This was a good start, telling stories; it would keep our minds occupied.

I learned that war had been fought for centuries over the Korean peninsula. The Manchus, with the help of the Koreans, beat the Mings and started the Ching Dynasty in China, also known as the Manchu Dynasty.

Every so often, Capeman would glance toward Chou for verification.

Chou would nod approvingly and look impressed, telling Capeman that he was "very smart."

That, of course, only aggravated Moody. Like a college history major eager to learn, he pushed Capeman to "get on with it."

Capeman continued by telling of the lack of peace between the Manchus and Korea. Korea pretty much did what China said, until the Japanese got more powerful.

Chou couldn't contain himself. "They are awful people," he said. "They destroyed my country."

"And Korea," Capeman said.

Then Moody and Capeman got into a conversation about Chinese concubines. Moody was on the edge of his seat as Capeman related that one of the members of a concubine became a princess, guarded by eunuchs.

It was then that Moody got a glint in his eye. "Eunuchs? They must have been sailors from their navy."

That did it. Capeman dove on Moody and the two started pummeling one another. Kingsley tried to separate them, and in a moment the three were tumbling about on the cold steel floor, laughing.

Chou, at first horrified at the fight, not understanding any of it, in the end was perplexed.

Finally Capeman sat up and said to Chou, "Anyway, you're welcome for us helping you. We're here to help you kick Communist ass."

"Yeah," added Moody. "And thanks for helping us do it."

Chou bowed in gratitude, though still confused, and now a bit wary of the foreign devils.

Amazing, I thought. The mammoths had managed to say exactly the right thing to Chou while Mr. Harvard Jim Pearson and I sat mute.

Our somber mood disappeared; Chou had lifted our spirits. Capeman, Kingsley, and Moody were not introspective men; they were physical types who liked to joke and horse around. For a time, sitting in the half-track alone with their thoughts, they had been brought to a place where they didn't want to be—deep inside themselves, and they resisted, because perhaps they knew instinctively it was a forlorn, barren patch of existence. Why go there? What was the point?

Now, with the mood broken by Chou, they'd happily latched onto a diversion.

Moody wanted to talk. "I don't think this is breaking any rules, compromising the mission or anything. I was born in northwest Texas, on the panhandle," he announced, starting his own story.

"Texas," murmured Chou. I suppose to him it was as fabled as empresses were to us.

"So far it's not communist," Moody continued. "Calvin Coolidge was president. My family was poor as piss."

"Piss?" asked Sergeant Chou. More slang he didn't understand.

Kingsley pointed to his crotch and made a whizzing sound.

Chou nodded in comprehension.

"Nobody arranged my marriage," Moody continued. "In fact, my brother unarranged it. He married the bitch."

"Bitch?" asked Chou, confused again.

"Bad woman," Pearson explained, his first comment of the night.

"Ahh," Chou said knowingly, making a disapproving noise, clicking his tongue with the roof of his mouth, eager to hear more from Moody.

"I had a girlfriend in high school, Louise. She was wild. As soon as I got some money, I was going to marry her." Moody got an almost soft expression on his face, what I suppose passed for tenderness, but it immediately disappeared.

"Then my brother came home from the war. He was in the Marines, a lifer, but he got wounded on Iwo Jima. When he was discharged and came back, everybody felt sorry for him because he walked with a cane. So he started hanging out with us. We'd go on double dates."

Suddenly the half-track started to brake, ending Moody's story. We felt the tracks clawing to a stop, and in a moment we halted.

"Is this a checkpoint?" Pearson asked Chou worriedly.

Chou didn't answer. He grabbed the Browning automatic rifle and motioned us silent.

In a few moments, Lieutenant Lee banged on the rear hatch and ordered it opened. Since all the gear was stowed, Chou unfastened the latch.

Lieutenant Lee stood in the middle of the road with a single North Korean soldier, obviously drunk. He had trouble with his balance and almost fell backward. Lee steadied him.

Upon closer look, I saw the soldier was not just drunk, but filthy and unshaven. He tried to climb into the compartment, banging his Russian burp gun on the metal floor. We all instinctively moved away, except for Chou, who blocked his entrance.

The two started to yell, and the soldier waved the burp gun at us threateningly. Chou pressed his Browning to the soldier's left temple. The man's bloodshot eyes widened in fear. Behind them, Lee took out his pistol and aimed it at the soldier also, but at the same time spoke soothingly to Chou. Now it was our turn to be horrified.

The standoff ended when the soldier lowered his burp gun and backed out of the hatch. Grinning, he said something to Chou. Chou nodded, smiled, and responded in a pleasant voice.

The soldier turned to Lee and said something else, and Lee closed the hatch behind him.

"What was that all about?" Moody demanded.

Chou shrugged as if nothing had happened. "North Korean roadblock. The guard wanted to see inside. He wanted wine. He thought we had some. I told him that you American dogs had drunk everything long ago. I said that if any had been left, I would have drunk it. That's when he laughed and left."

"Jesus," said Kingsley. "I've never had a drunk wave a burp gun at me."

"I wasn't worried," Moody boasted. "Didn't you notice he still had the safety on?"

I certainly hadn't noticed, but I was grateful for Chou's quick thinking. I didn't mind being an American dog, as long as I was a living one.

Chou was full of disdain. "North Korean soldiers drink too much. Sometimes they drink antifreeze."

"You got any?" Moody asked, not altogether in jest. "I'll drink it."

Chou shook his head. "It is very dangerous, but these soldiers don't care. They are so cold. And bored. But drunk soldiers are not a problem for us. Communist soldiers are much better soldiers. When they stop us, it will be worse."

Pearson patted his boot as if to make sure the cyanide capsule was still there. He made his first joke of the trip, beginning to feel more comfortable with the enlisted beasts. "I hope one of these is enough."

"Want mine, Captain?" Capeman offered pleasantly.

"Maybe."

Now the beasts were happy. It appeared that the officers had a sense of humor.

The engines revved up again, and we continued past the checkpoint, where we could hear other North Korean soldiers shouting and laughing; they all sounded drunk. No one thought of going back to Moody's story; we were drained and unsettled from the confrontation with the drunk soldier. Besides, we knew we'd have lots of time later. The pace picked up and the ride was smooth for about an hour, then we ground to a halt.

"Another roadblock?" Moody asked.

Chou shook his head. "I think we are at the first contact point."

He was right. We had stopped for the first intelligence report. We'd come to the heart of the mission. Before this, everything had been mere preparation. The essence of the mission was the intelligence these operatives had obtained. Even the frogmen and rangers acknowledged these men as the real heroes.

Kingsley couldn't imagine what they must have gone through. "We've been behind enemy lines only a few hours and were almost killed by that asshole with a burp gun; these guys have been here six months. We're in a half-track; they've been on foot, sleeping in caves and Christ knows where when they weren't tangled up with some Commie soldiers. Ted and I know what it's like to wade through mud and snow up to your ass with somebody after you, but not for six months living on the edge like these guys."

Moody agreed. "Besides, these guys have been completely on their own, having to fake being Communist Chinese soldiers. Plus, they're navigating in unfamiliar surroundings and humping a radio on top of everything. No question about it, they're going through the worst. Nothing can compare to ground-pounding like that."

That sparked yet another skirmish, this one about who had it worst in war. Pearson wouldn't concede anything to the Army. "Try putting yourself in a bomber. Sit thousands of feet in the air while the sky explodes all around you. Watch your buddies take flak and see their planes ripped apart, and then go down in a trail of smoke. Or sweat blood as your crippled bomber limps back to base, worrying about MiGs chasing after you. It ain't easy up there. You're just a target with everybody shooting at you."

Tom Capeman jumped in. "Try swimming in heavy seas so cold your asshole turns blue. Frogmen are dropped into the ocean from a craft going fifteen knots. We're always the first in, long before the landing crafts, to blow traps and clear obstacles. We take out fortifications. Being underwater is scary; you can't see anything, and a thousand things could go wrong—you could get tangled and not get out, your breathing apparatus could fail, your wet suit could tear and you'd freeze. Forget the ground and air, water is the worst."

Chou listened to all this with great seriousness and growing concern. He thought we were angry at each other.

Finally the others turned to me, but what could I offer? I hadn't been in combat. So I put on an inscrutable look and said, "Like Lieutenant Lee, I am a married man."

That broke them up and ended the biggest-dick contest as we strained to hear what was going on outside the half-track, but we couldn't pick out a thing. In minutes, we were on the move again.

"Did we make contact?" Moody asked.

There was no way to be certain; we just hoped the operative had made it to the rendezvous and delivered his intelligence report, and that Hinsley and Tyler could translate it.

Less than thirty minutes later, we stopped for the second contact. Again we tried to glean what was going on but learned nothing, and in a couple of minutes, the convoy rumbled on.

This time we didn't advance more than a few miles down the road before we halted. This, we realized, was not a scheduled stop. Chou grabbed his rifle and motioned us to a corner away from the hatch.

Lee banged on the door. The communications and radio gear were still hidden. Chou opened the hatch and we were confronted by a North Korean soldier, very different from our first checkpoint guard. This one was all business. His uniform and greatcoat were sharp, his face clean shaven and his manner professional; he had not been drinking. He looked well fed, alert, intelligent, and dangerous. Gazing about the interior, he nodded to Chou, ignored us, then backed away, apparently satisfied.

When he was gone, Moody said begrudgingly, "That's how soldiers should look."

Kingsley agreed. "Not the kind of guy you want to meet on the battlefield."

But probably a lot more representative of the enemy than the first, I thought.

The convoy resumed its journey. We traveled for another thirty minutes and stopped for what we imagined was the third operative, but this stop turned out to be different. Lee banged on the hatch and we could hear Hinsley beside him. "Time to go to work," he said.

Hinsley handed me a sheaf of papers. He was exuberant. The report in English was richer with intelligence than he'd expected. He told me the operative was already on his way out of the country and that he and Tyler were working on the second report.

"So far everything is going without a hitch. You're going to be busy the rest of the night. Get on with it."

As soon as the hatch closed, we broke out the crypto gear. Jim Pearson and I worked as a team. As I entered intelligence information from the report, the crypto machine spat out a paper tape with adhesive backing containing five-letter encoded word groups, identical to a stock market ticker tape. While I operated the crypto machine, Jim pasted the encoded tape on lined sheets of paper, carefully numbering each sheet. Together it took us a little over an hour to encode the first report.

While we worked, the convoy stopped for the fourth intelligence report, and Hinsley handed me the second one that he and Tyler had translated.

We were stopped only one more time that night. Again, a North Korean soldier looked into the compartment, chatted briefly with Chou, ignored us, and walked away. It took us only a couple of minutes to hide the crypto machine, and less than that to bring it back out when the soldier left.

Around four in the morning, Corporal Liu relieved Chou.

Jim and I worked throughout the balance of the night encoding the reports. The detail was stunning, and very disturbing. The first two reports provided information on enemy troop strengths and their locations extending from the Pukhan River eastward along the battle line to Kosong on the Sea of Japan, then northward past Wonsan, Hungnam, Sinchang, and Tanchon to Najin, just south of the border with China.

They detailed a massive North Korean Army buildup, from the Sea of Japan stretching west along the battle line to where they joined with People's Liberation Army divisions near the Pukhan River. North Korean infantry and artillery were dug in for up to twenty-five miles north of the battle line, so deep they prevented any UN flanking movement.

Both Jim and I were exhausted by the time the convoy pulled into its first bivouac site south of Wonsan, just before dawn.

We took a break to watch the camouflaging of vehicles. We had made it safely past several North Korean checkpoints, but now an even greater danger threatened the convoy during the day; our own American planes patrolling overhead, seeking targets of opportunity.

Camouflage netting was pulled over the vehicles, and broken limbs and brush were added to conceal them from discovery. Moody, Kingsley, and Capeman pitched in to assist the crew on our half-track as Jim and I tried to revive ourselves by stretching our legs in the cold air. We still had a couple of hours of encoding to complete before contacting the airborne operator and transmitting the reports, which was scheduled for noon.

Though exhausted, Jim and I went back to our task while the others tried to sleep; we had to break every thirty minutes or so to clear our heads.

It took us another four hours to finish, mostly because we were so tired. The snores of the others were a constant distraction. Outrage and shifting positions on the floor occurred when someone took a foot in the face from a sleeping comrade—another event impossible to ignore.

The third and fourth reports provided even more disturbing news. These dealt with the elaborate defense measures taken to prevent UN landings from the Sea of Japan, with emphasis on fortifications around the coastal areas adjoining Wonsan, Hungnam, Sinchang, and Tanchon. Enemy commanders, both North Korean and Chinese, were determined to prevent another landing such as MacArthur's at Inchon. Key to their defenses were dozens of heavy- and medium-artillery batteries.

In addition to identifying defensive positions, the reports provided details about unit identities, their commanders and key staff officers, and combat readiness, all crucial factors in intelligence analysis. The North Korean Second, Third, and Fifth Corps, with over 100,000 troops, were prepared to meet any UN offensive. The reports stressed that these units were composed of battle-tested, well-equipped troops with high morale. Ordnance consisted of thousands of small-arms automatic weapons and tons of ammunition, along with hundreds of light to heavy artillery pieces, all functional and preregistered on key targets. The units had armor support and extensive communications.

When we finished at 1100, Jim and I broke out the com gear by ourselves so the others could sleep, but they jumped up when we began burning the clear text copies of the reports Hinsley had given us.

"I thought we were on fire," Capeman said when he saw the paper burning in a metal container. He immediately rushed to the box to warm his hands over the flames; the others quickly gathered around.

"Next time, let us know before you do that," Moody said. "It's the only heat in North Korea."

"What day is it?" Kingsley demanded, working off his boots to try to defrost his toes over the fire, but the flames had already died down.

"January 12," Pearson provided. "Got any plans for the day?"

"Yes. To stay alive."

"I gotta piss," Moody announced, heading for the hatch. We all followed him outside and a couple of guys headed into the brush while our "guards" watched.

"Let's light another fire," Capeman said when he returned. "My ass is frozen."

Pearson, more comfortable with these guys than before, shook his head, probably because he had a classified assignment that they could never handle, and said, "I do not want to see your ass thaw, Sergeant."

Back in the vehicle, we broke out rations and waited for the time to send the reports. Most of our meals consisted of soups, rice, and highly seasoned vegetables provided by the convoy's Chinese cooks. Chunks of unknown meat were often included in the soups. For snacks we had rice cakes and sweet cookies. However, to vary our diet, we had standard-issue C rations—ham and beans, beans and franks, canned bread, stew, and crackers—all of which appealed more to Capeman, Moody, and Kingsley.

At 1145, I switched on the transmitter and receiver to the radio transmission frequency indicated in the SOI. At exactly 1200, I received a strong signal from the airborne operator. The plane was in position, and the operator ready to receive the reports.

During the next four hours, I changed frequencies several times to avoid anyone getting a fix on our position, but managed to get all the reports off by 1600. When I got a "Roger" and message reception receipt, I let out a whoop. "Done!" I cried out. "They got it all. The first reports are on the way to the president. Help me put the gear away."

Everybody congratulated me.

"You mean all that gibberish made sense?" Moody asked.

"Yep," I said, sinking down on the floor in exhaustion. "It's being flown to Japan and will be transmitted to Washington within a few hours. Now I'm gonna crash; I haven't slept in thirty-six hours. Wake me up when I have to go back to work."

Everybody else jumped out of the half-track to stretch as I settled into a corner to sleep. But before I dropped off, the others scrambled back in, almost pushed inside by a very agitated Sergeant Chou. He slammed the hatch shut and tossed us handcuffs. "Put them on. A Chinese general and six soldiers are approaching. Lieutenant Lee is very worried."

Seeing him upset, and knowing that Lee was concerned, threw us into a panic. For the first time I saw real fear in the eyes of the rangers and frogmen; that was more frightening than anything.

We slapped the handcuffs on and huddled together, away from the hatch.

We didn't know what to expect, but it turned out to be worse than we imagined.

Chapter Ten

A Brush with Death

Lieutenant Lee banged on the rear hatch. His voice was severe and demanding. Taking the cue, Sergeant Chou opened the hatch, his rifle trained on us. Our cowering in the front of the compartment was genuine.

"Get out, dogs!" Lee yelled.

We scrambled on our hands and knees to comply. Chou roughly booted us out of the half-track and we tumbled onto the frozen ground.

"Get up!" Lee demanded. We struggled to stand, but not quickly enough. Chou pulled us upright by our hair.

I don't know if the Chinese Communists in front of us were convinced of his authenticity, but I was, even before Chou jabbed Capeman in the gut with the butt of his rifle, doubling him over. I was shaking violently, and not from cold.

The Chinese general was short, powerfully built, and very angry. He walked the line in front of us, stopping before each to stare into our eyes. When he got to me, I tried to maintain his steel-gray look, but had to avert my gaze at the incredible contempt and hatred emanating from him.

When he reached the end of the line, he reversed direction and once more moved in front of the five of us, taking time in front of each man to spit in his face.

Capeman, Kingsley, and Moody stood immobile, expressionless, letting the sputum slide down their faces. Both Pearson and I flinched. Maybe it was my obvious fear that brought the general to a standstill in front of me.

He started to yell in Chinese. I felt his hot breath and tried to hold myself steady and upright. Then his right hand dropped to his pistol, a .38 caliber chrome-plated revolver, and unholstered it.

Lieutenant Lee's men immediately took a position at the end of the line with their rifles at the ready.

The general raised the pistol directly into my face, only inches from my forehead. My eyes were level with his trigger finger. I watched his finger take up the slack. His hand began to shake as he yelled at me even louder.

I had never been so afraid in my life. I knew I was going to die. My entire body began to convulse. I closed my eyes tight, waiting for the explosion that would blow my brains out.

Suddenly I heard Lieutenant Lee's voice, his mouth inches away from the general's ear. He spoke sharply, interrupting the general's tirade.

Anger erupted in a loud verbal exchange from the two men. With my eyes closed I waited for the end to come. Suddenly there was a loud explosion. The general had raised his pistol, aiming within inches over my head, and fired a round.

The report was deafening. I was certain I was dead. My knees folded and I dropped to the ground. Finally realizing that I was still alive, I opened my eyes and looked up.

The general stood motionless, smoke still curling from the barrel of his revolver. He looked down at me, jammed his pistol into his holster, turned on Lee, shouted a few words, then signaled his men to follow and stormed away.

As his vehicle disappeared from sight I started to puke; I doubled over and heaved my guts onto the ground.

Chou unlocked everyone's handcuffs. Kingsley and Moody helped me to my feet and guided me into the half-track. I crawled into a corner and tried to disappear.

Capeman immediately went to the ration box and pulled out a can. "Damn! That kind of excitement works up an appetite."

Pearson crouched beside me. He didn't say anything, just reached out a hand and stroked my head.

"So what was that all about?" Kingsley asked Chou, "besides the fact that he obviously didn't like the looks of Baker."

"I think it was his hair," Moody joked, trying to rouse me. "It's a dopey haircut. I think you should go for whitewalls."

Then I totally disgraced myself. I began to cry.

Moody smiled, but it was a compassionate smile. "Hey. Forget what I said. Keep your hair the way it is." He went to the box of rations and sorted through them until one met his approval and he grunted happily, death forgotten.

"You asshole," Capeman said to him, moving beside me. He lifted my face so that I was looking into his eyes. "It's okay," he said. "We all would have shit in our pants."

"I did, anyway," Kingsley said, now also attacking a can of C rations.

"How could you tell, Fart Master?" Moody said, breaking everybody up. Even I smiled. I wiped my eyes and saw everyone look away to spare me further embarrassment.

Relieved that we were all right and that I had recovered, Chou told us what had happened. "The general said he'd gotten a report from one of his roadblocks that there was a strange convoy moving down the road with American prisoners. He came to check it out because he hadn't heard anything from his headquarters about it. Lee showed him our orders. He didn't challenge them, but he wanted to see the prisoners. That's when Lee told you to get out."

Chou got an apologetic look on his face and bowed toward Capeman. "I am sorry I hit you."

Capeman looked surprised. "You hit me? When? I didn't feel a thing."

"Yeah, right," muttered Moody. "I thought you were going to cry."

"Next time hit him," Capeman said. "Anyway, go on. Then what happened?"

Chou continued. "The general was very angry."

"We could tell," Pearson said dryly.

"He said American bombers had killed his best friend. He wanted revenge. That's when he pointed the gun at Sergeant Baker. But he was going to kill you all next."

"Whoa," said Moody, while spooning rations. "The rest of us, too? Now that's serious."

Chou added, "Also the men in the other half-track. So Lieutenant Lee told the general to look to his right, where his men had taken aim at him. He said he had orders to bring the prisoners to the Yellow Sea, where a gunboat would take you to mainland China. He said he was sorry about the general's friend but that we were at war. He told the general that if he killed his prisoner, he would be dead before the smoke cleared from his pistol. So the general raised his pistol above Baker's head and fired."

Chou thought a moment. "Maybe the general's friend was Mao's son. American bombers killed Mao's favorite son."

Capeman was incredulous. "We killed Mao Tse-tung's son? When?"

Chou nodded. "In November 1950. American planes bombed Pyongyang. Mao's son was there."

"Too bad Mao wasn't there," Moody said. "And Joe Stalin. And my ex-wife."

"Two days later, Mao's armies attacked Marines at the Chosin Reservoir," Chou said.

"Mao's son was killed? I never heard that," Capeman repeated. "No wonder he attacked."

Chou shrugged, unconcerned about the fate of Mao's son or whether he had been the general's friend. "Anyway, here we are, everybody fine."

Not quite, I thought, but I was feeling better, though still embarrassed. I had seen the other guys stand up before the general; they wouldn't have cried. In fact, I think Chou might have worried they were going to spit back at him, setting off a massacre. I didn't think Chou would have flinched in my place, either.

Everyone but Chou and I dismounted to stretch their legs and relieve themselves. When we were alone, Chou knelt beside me. "Lieutenant Lee saved your life, but you were very brave. All you did in the face of death was throw up. That's not dishonor."

He gestured to the others outside. "They won't tell you, but they think you were brave, too. I know." Then, looking toward the open hatch, he shook his head. "Americans are very strange. I don't understand you." He shook his head. "Always fighting. But then they are not fighting and everybody is laughing."

I smiled, in gratitude for his thoughtfulness, and because I understood those guys.

Chou looked at me for verification. "True? They are not angry at one another? Even though Moody is from Texas? A cowboy? I saw cowboy movies in Taipei. They are always fighting and shooting."

I laughed; we were characters out of a fable for him. "No. They are just joking with one another."

Chou nodded. "I must tell Corporal Liu. He does not understand. He is afraid your big men are going to fight. They are always yelling at one another. He asked me about Americans but I did not know for sure."

"Tell Corporal Liu we are all friends and he should not worry."

Suddenly Chou looked up anxiously. He cocked his head, then grabbed me. That's when I heard the roar of approaching aircraft through the open hatch. American planes were our greatest fear during daylight hours; they had almost total control of the skies, and our Communist Chinese vehicles were targets of opportunity.

Outside Pearson yelled, "Navy fighter-bombers, two of them coming in from the Sea of Japan."

From the urgency in his voice I knew that the fighter-bombers were making a pass.

The pilots had plainly spotted something suspicious and were coming in low for a closer look. The planes roared overhead, flying within feet over our half-track, then started a tight banking movement; they were coming back for a second run.

I heard Pearson scream as he dived behind the half-track. "Get out of the half-track. Take cover! They're attacking."

Before Chou and I had a chance to jump clear of the vehicle, the first fighter-bomber, a Navy F4U, screamed past, just above us; the sound was deafening.

Chou pulled me down inside the hatch and dove on top of me. When the second made its run, we heard a loud swoosh, followed by an explosion that rocked us, and a flash Chou and I could see inside the metal compartment through the open hatch. Then all was silent.

Chou pulled me up, and together we leaped from the compartment. I saw the others scrambling for cover and dove into the brush beside them.

We waited anxiously for another bomb run but heard the fighters fade into the distance, heading inland toward the mountains. In a moment, Lieutenant Lee gathered us all together; this was thc first we'd seen of the rest of the team in the other half-track.

Lee was angry and explained that one of his men on the T-34 tank—only ten meters in front of our half-track—had started removing the camouflaging nets too soon. "The American planes must have spotted this and come back. We were very lucky not to be killed."

His soldier was probably not going to be so lucky, I thought.

"What happened to the first plane? Why didn't he fire?" Moody wanted to know.

"Probably he had trouble aiming; it's almost dark and they were unable to see their target clearly," Bill Robbins said, obviously shook up; this was his first time on the other end of a bomb run. "He must have pulled up because he couldn't fix the target. The second pilot hit the bomb release a second too late."

He pointed to a burning knoll a hundred meters beyond us. "Napalm. If he'd hit his target, the tank would have exploded and set the rest of us on fire." He shook his head. "We'd be charcoal now."

"Why didn't they make another run?"

"Too dangerous. They'd already been spotted, and maybe they were on another mission."

Puller added, "Or maybe the first plane malfunctioned and the second was out of bombs. There's no way to tell. Just that we were lucky."

As usual, Dan Kingsley took it best. He didn't seem perturbed; he was already assisting the half-track crew in removing the camouflage netting so we would be ready to move out. "Stupid flyboys. They can't do anything right—even hit a tank bigger than my mother-in-law. How we gonna win a war when pilots can't hit a tank?"

Robbins had recovered. "Those were Navy pilots. Air Force pilots would have hit us. If it'd been me up there, you'd be barbecue right now."

Kingsley laughed. "No, you'd have crashed the plane. We'd have more prisoners with us."

Not understanding any of this American interservice rivalry,

Lee oversaw the removal of the netting and directed us back to our vehicles. "We're behind schedule. We must go."

Though we tried to be nonchalant about this second brush with death, we were all shook up—even Kingsley, despite his bravado.

"How bad would that be—killed by our own men," Capeman said when we were settled into the half-track. "You think there'd be some way to get word to our pilots that we're out here. It's bad enough facing the Chinese and the North Koreans. Now everybody is out to get us."

Moody looked puzzled. "I keep forgetting: why is it our people don't know about this mission?"

For once I had an answer. "Brown told me that Truman didn't want anybody to know about this op, even those in the top chain of command, because he was going over their heads. If he couldn't tell them, he sure as hell couldn't let his field commanders know. The same reason the sub commander wasn't told anything about us."

Moody was not appeased, and voiced the first challenge to the mission. "There's got to be a better way to get intelligence than this. Too many things can go wrong. There are twenty-two operatives out there. Any one of them could get caught and give us up. I don't like it."

I was stunned. Ted Moody was the most gung ho of us all, the last person one would expect to voice a concern or question the mission. The rest of us might have toyed with such doubts, even Capeman with his knowledge of history, but not Moody; he would execute his orders exactly as told.

All I could think was, good thing John Tyler wasn't in our vehicle to overhear this. He would be on the lookout for such doubts or signs of weakness.

I tried to allay Moody's fears. "They've tried everything else; nothing worked to get this intelligence. The CIA and MacArthur were caught completely off guard by the Chinese and North Koreans. Other operatives have been working behind enemy lines for a long time, but Brown told me their radios couldn't transmit long distances, and even when they were successful, by the time they contacted our personnel, the intelligence was out of date, inadequate, or incomplete. Some operatives had been killed in their attempt to infiltrate or get out. When others made it to safety with intelligence information, local commanders didn't pass it on. So, as complicated as all this is, Broken Reed is the only workable plan."

Seemingly mollified, Moody shrugged. "I was just bitching; I'm entitled. It's kinda late for second thoughts, anyway."

True, but I'd sure keep them to myself; maybe I should warn him, I thought. But I didn't want to voice my suspicions about Tyler. The last thing we needed was more worry, or dissension among ourselves.

Just before we got under way, we were brought food. Besides the C rations that Capeman, Moody, and Kingsley had already seriously depleted, we got hot chow three times a day. Tonight we had meat, rice broth, and bread.

Capeman speared the meat and held it up. "What is this?"

"Woof woof," said Moody.

Capeman chewed it slowly. "I've had worse."

Probably he had, I thought, but I still wasn't interested. Food was the last thing on my mind; I needed sleep. Since the submarine, I hadn't slept more than a couple of hours; I was exhausted. My only chance to sleep was during the day, but there had been those disruptions today—the Chinese general pointing a pistol in my face, then Navy fighter-bombers trying to roast us. I drank the broth and lay down, trying to get a little shut-eye.

We were on the coast road from Wonsan, already past Munchon, when we turned westward on a narrow road that wound through a mountain pass. We were two thousand feet up, and were going to descend into the Imjin River basin to near Munamni, where we would bivouac and spend the second day, but I didn't last more than a few minutes on the road before the clacking of tracks and gentle roll of the vehicle eased me into a deep sleep.

I don't know how long I slept—not nearly enough—when Pearson shook me awake. He had let me sleep through the first contact; now we were at the second. "Jerry has the first report translated. He wants to talk to you."

I crawled out of the half-track; cold air immediately slapped me awake.

John Tyler stood beside Hinsley, appraising me carefully. Jerry clasped my shoulder and stared into my eyes. "We know what happened with that Chinese general. We think you did great. Don't worry about being scared. None of us could have handled it any better. Anyway, you're part of the club now; you're not a cherry anymore."

Tyler just stood there, eyes boring into me.

Hinsley handed me the first report to encode, then warned, "It's going to get worse tonight. We're passing through a Communist Chinese–controlled area. They'll have roadblocks, and their guards could be much tougher than the North Koreans. I'll get you the second report when we finish with it."

Back in the vehicle, I told the others what to expect tonight, then Jim and I tackled the report.

The first part covered Chinese forces north of the Yalu River, which separated North Korea from Manchuria.

As we read through it, Jim and I glanced at each other in disbelief. We could barely keep the information to ourselves. The Soviet Air Force had a heavy bomber group at Mukden in Manchuria, fully loaded with atomic weapons in their bomb bays, and ready for takeoff on minutes' notice. Joint battle plans by the Soviet Union, Communist Chinese government, and the North

Korean government were in place, approving the use of atomic weapons in the event of a preemptive atomic strike by the United States, such as General MacArthur had proposed, or a failure to stop any new all-out military offensive launched by United Nations forces.

In addition to the Mukden group, there were heavy Soviet bombers located near Changchun, China, deep within Manchuria, and strong Soviet Air Force fighter contingents near Port Arthur and Darien on the northernmost shores of the Yellow Sea. The distance from the main Korean battle line paralleling the thirty-eighth latitude to the Soviet airfields in China ranged from two hundred to four hundred miles. This meant that if Soviet bombers were directed at targets in South Korea and Japan, an overwhelming number of Soviet fighters could provide air cover for bombers manned by Soviet crews.

The information was chilling. If the United Nations launched a ground campaign to drive the Communist Chinese back across the Yalu, the Soviets were prepared to jump in, possibly with atomic weapons.

Colonel Brown had been right when he'd told me a hair-trigger scenario was being played out in Washington and in Moscow. The world indeed teetered on the brink of atomic war.

I felt that if this report reached Truman, it alone would justify Broken Reed. He would not escalate the war if he knew Soviet bombers were standing by with atomic weapons in their bomb bays and fighters on the flight line. MacArthur, we'd heard, had wanted to use atomic weapons along the Yalu River in China, but the president had not authorized their use; he certainly wouldn't now that he knew the Soviets would retaliate with their own.

The rest of the report contained disturbing information concerning supply lines, combat-ready reserve troops, and ordnance storage dumps that would permit rapid resupply for Communist units along the battle line. It was apparent the enemy was not just entrenched a few miles beyond the thirty-eighth parallel, but dug in well beyond the Yalu, deep into China.

Realizing the significance of this report, Jim and I rushed to encode it.

I looked behind me to the others; they were oblivious to the threats and danger, and I didn't feel I could inform them; they didn't need to know. Besides, they were having too good a time.

Kingsley had brought out a deck of cards, and they were playing poker. The stakes were high. They had made play money from scraps of paper and drawn pictures on some of the pieces to represent yachts and cars.

Their betting became hilarious. The bigger they bet on riches beyond belief, the louder they got. It was as entertaining as watching the Three Stooges in a vaudeville act.

Watching from beside the hatch, Sergeant Chou asked if they would teach him how to play. The three looked to one another and said, "Sure." You could almost feel their hands rubbing together in anticipation and glee.

I watched them patiently instruct Chou in the rules of poker, then turned back to my job.

Even with the electric heaters going full blast, frost formed on the inside hull of the compartment. My fingers were so numb that it took me much longer to encode these messages. I was glad that one heater had been mounted on a swivel base and extension arm so that heat could be directed toward my hands, the crypto machine, and the radio transmission key. Even so, Jim and I had to stop again and again to place our hands close to the heater.

I didn't realize how cold it was until we were stopped at a Chinese checkpoint. There was plenty of time to stow the crypto equipment and for Moody to hide his deck of cards.

The Chinese guards forced us outside while they searched the vehicle. They plainly took their time to torment us in the below-freezing temperatures. We were made to stand outside for at least fifteen minutes. When finally let back in, we found our bedrolls and blankets tossed into a corner, but nothing else disturbed. They had not discovered the secret compartments or the communications and crypto gear. Had they done so, Lee's men would have killed them.

The only tense moment occurred, according to Sergeant Chou, when the guards asked about the bedrolls; they wanted to know where they'd come from. Lee told them they had been taken from a U.S. truck abandoned by the Seventh Marines near Hagaru in the Chosin Reservoir. When the Marines retreated from the Frozen Chosin—or, as Chesty Puller famously put it, were "attacking in a different direction"—they left on foot. The guards accepted the explanation.

Shortly after this stop, we made contact with the third operative for that night, and Hinsley gave me the second report to encode.

The others were back to their poker game, but things had soured. Sergeant Chou had proved a fast learner and was now winning most of the pots with a surprising number of full houses and flushes.

"You sure you haven't played before?" Capeman demanded.

"It must be beginner's luck," Chou answered with a straight face.

Jim and I finished encoding the second report, which focused primarily on supply routes and the incredible amount of matériel pouring south, not just in vehicles but carried by civilian "porters" loaded with food, ammunition, and spare parts on A-frames. Each of the porters carried up to a hundred pounds, and they didn't stick to the roads, but snaked along mountain trails like a long line of ants.

Just as troubling as the tonnage pouring into North Korea were the reports on enemy fortifications and supporting artillery.

Enemy units were entrenched along every major valley and highway approach extending from the northern highlands south to the battle line.

Before we could rendezvous with our next contacts, the convoy screeched to a halt. We rushed to hide the crypto gear and waited.

The delay lasted a long time. Finally Lee had us open the hatch and explained what was going on. American bombers with high-explosive bombs had hit a Communist Chinese ammunition convoy earlier in the day. One bomb had scored a direct hit, and the secondary blast from over two tons of artillery ammunition had blown a huge crater in the road, rendering it impassable.

Many Communist personnel had been killed, and medics were still working on the wounded. Lee did not want us out of the vehicles for fear the Chinese would take out their anger on us.

Lee had come for an emergency medical kit because the Chinese had exhausted their supplies and one of their medical officers had asked if we had anything to spare. Since we had two kits, Lee gave one to the medical officer.

Outside we could hear the wounded scream while a road crew tried to repair the damage. Normally, repair crews could fix a road in a few hours, but this air strike had been particularly severe; the crater caused by the exploded truck was very deep. Adding to the crew's problems were the extreme cold and early darkness.

The crew eventually came up with a temporary solution by making a gradual slope into and out of the crater. The first tank and then the half-tracks managed to make it through without stalling, but at one point we were tipped forward at a steep angle, then at another dangerous angle as our half-track climbed out. We were tossed about like dolls. The wheeled vehicles got through only when a cable strung from the tank reeled them out. The operation took more than an hour and put us way behind schedule.

As we rolled away, leaving behind the wounded enemy, I

looked to Capeman, Moody, and Kingsley to see how they were reacting. Did they take pleasure in the enemy's misery? Their faces were set impassively as they heard the cries and moans of the enemy soldiers; they showed no joy or satisfaction. They seemed to realize we were all caught in something beyond ourselves, that those men were serving a cause just as we were, that our fates could be the same. Warriors, I saw, did not rejoice in the suffering of other warriors. There was indeed a brotherhood of arms, and that brotherhood embraced foes.

Only when the sounds of this suffering passed did they again take out their cards.

During the night we stopped two more times for operatives' reports, making a total of five. The last three reports focused on six Communist Chinese units entrenched along the battle line, responsible for occupying a defense posture adjacent to the Sea of Japan. Each army had established a rearguard unit along attack and defense corridors that extended from their bunkers northward to deep within difficult mountain terrain. These rearguard soldiers numbered close to a quarter million. If Truman needed further proof of the enemy's strength and the peril of escalation, these reports would provide it.

Because of the delays along the route that night, Jim and I were unable to encode everything before we pulled into our bivouac site just south of Munam-ni. We had made lousy time, but at least we had made it.

I wanted desperately to crash for a couple hours' sleep, but I had to finish encoding the reports. I was exhausted, my nerves shot, my hands numb.

The other guys were beginning to feel guilty. Having lost all their paper money and make-believe yachts to Sergeant Chou, they watched Jim and me work feverishly.

"Isn't there anything we can do?" Capeman asked. "I could at least paste that tape to the pages. And if Moody and Kingsley worked together *real* hard, they might even be able to get the numbers right."

I shook my head. "You got us here, and you're going to get us out; that's more than enough. Jim and I can do this part. Thanks anyway."

Breakfast was hot cereal, dried bananas, and hot coffee, but even all the caffeine wasn't keeping me awake.

When the others got out to assist in camouflaging the half-track, I jumped out to relieve myself and let the cold air slap me alert.

Standing alone off the road as dawn broke over the mountains, I was awestruck by the beauty, and the desolation, too.

Majestic snowcapped mountains towering in the distance were slowly unveiled as the darkness receded, but all around lay waste and destruction. Barren skeletal trees listed as charred sentinels over the scorched, cratered, bombed earth. Wrecked vehicles and abandoned weapons were scattered about on the frozen ground. If you looked up, the scene was beauty, God's art, something you might see painted on an old Chinese screen; but when you looked to the ground, it was hell on earth, man's art—a tableau of annihilation and misery.

How many had died fighting over this lonely, desolate place? I wondered. I had heard the agonized cries of wounded and dying men only a few miles back. The battleground here, I knew, must be soaked with blood.

War was far worse than I had imagined, nothing at all like what my friends and I had talked about at Fort Bliss; then it was a game, boasts, and glory. That seemed a lifetime ago now—when I was young. Yet I knew the gruesome waste before me was just a shadow of what could follow in an atomic war.

That was what we were here to prevent.

I looked about to the men stringing camouflage netting, using even more care than before; they didn't want to risk another air strike. I'd been with them a week but didn't know much about them. Now I wanted to know everything about them—where they were from, what their childhoods had been like, whom they loved, what they dreamed, what their hopes and fears were.

Capeman glanced over, catching me staring at them. "You could get your ass over here to help us, Baker," he joked.

"I'll finish that for you if you finish encoding the rest of the reports." I still had hours of work. Then I'd have to contact the airborne operator and send them off; it would be afternoon before I got a chance to sleep.

"You win," he said, dropping to the ground to do push-ups. "You finish your work and we'll get your ass back safely."

I watched him do calisthenics. They weren't for my benefit; he did them at every stop, just as he had done in the showers at Drake, not just to keep in shape, but to work off pent-up energy. "Wouldn't hurt to work out, Army boy; no pain, no gain," he called.

I shook my head. I was in enough pain, and if I dropped to the ground, I was afraid I wouldn't be able to get back up.

I took a last look at the majestic mountains and climbed back into the half-track.

Chapter Eleven
Danger Intensifies

Jim and I, somewhat to our surprise, finished the encoding with two hours to spare before the time to contact the airborne operator.

"Wake me at 1130," I called to the others, falling onto my bedroll in the corner, asleep before I heard any response.

The next thing I felt was Moody shaking me awake. "You gonna sleep through the whole damn war, Baker?"

"Yeah, princess," said Kingsley beside him, kneeling over me, "it's been almost two hours."

Capeman called from his corner, "Funny, even with all that beauty sleep, he doesn't look any better. But do me a favor, will you? Talk a little louder in your sleep next time. It sounded like you were having a great dream. And give us more details."

I looked at him in embarrassment. "Was I talking in my sleep?"

"Oh, yeah, sir," Moody said. "Some really hot stuff. I never expected that from you. You always seemed a straight-arrow guy. An officer and a gentleman."

Kingsley nodded. "It was good stuff all right, but I'm not sure it was your wife you were talking about."

I was mortified, but I laughed. They'd been kidding and I'd fallen for it. I struggled up to get out the communications gear, but they had already set it up for me.

I turned on the transmitter and at precisely noon, the airborne operator acknowledged my signal. I transmitted in Morse code for three and a half hours. When I finished, I had sent off a cumulative ten intelligence reports documenting enemy troop strengths and unit locations.

The reports revealed a staggering enemy buildup—hundreds of thousands of troops we had not known about, numerous artillery and armored units, and tons of supplies and munitions. Commando units and reserves ensured rapid replacement for casualties, while artillery was registered on major targets. Elaborate field-wire communications networks, as opposed to tactical radio transmissions, were established to prevent monitoring by UN intelligence intercept units. Well-maintained supply routes extended from North Korea into Manchuria.

I was shocked at the enemy's strength and preparedness. MacArthur's counterattack in 1950 had been foolhardy, but an offensive now, after fourteen more months of enemy buildups, would be even more disastrous.

This ominous intelligence aside, I had a personal issue to deal with; I was still smarting from the "dream" joke the guys had played on me that morning and I had been thinking about payback ever since; it helped take my mind off the Chinese and North Koreans. There wasn't anything I could do about the enemy, but I could at least get back at Capeman, Moody, and Kingsley.

After they all had helped me break down the com gear and put it away, I told them the reports had been bad. "It's a lot worse than anyone expected."

"How bad?" Kingsley wanted to know.

"You know I can't go into any details, but Soviets, Chinese, North Koreans are all waiting to pounce. Nearly a half a million of them."

"You can't tell us *anything?*" Moody asked.

I shook my head. "It's for your own protection. Besides, you don't want to know. You don't want them to torture you for info."

"They'd torture us anyway," Capeman noted. "That's why we have the cyanide."

"You'll want to use it, too," I said. "There's some crazy stuff out there."

"Like what?" he demanded.

I pretended to think, then gave in. "All right, I guess it won't hurt to tell. There's a half-million Chinese out there and we're right in the middle of them." I held up one of the encrypted reports. "This gives the details of all units operating in this area. One of them is the Chinese 324th Division. They moved down from Manchuria. They're all queer. An entire division."

"What!" Moody shouted.

"Queer?" Sergeant Chou asked, puzzled.

Capeman blew him a kiss. Chou looked startled, then understood. "Ahh," he said.

"You're putting us on," Kingsley said.

This was 1952, and these were macho military men. I knew I could get them riled up with this little ruse.

Kingsley grabbed the report out of my hands, but of course it was in code and totally meaningless to him. "You're lying," he said.

"Yeah, it's just bullshit," Moody concurred, though he didn't sound completely convinced.

I shrugged. "Suit yourself, but I'd be careful dismounting the vehicle around here. They see you guys and . . ." I left it to their imaginations.

They all grew silent, their imaginations in overdrive.

"Well, there's a torture they didn't tell us about," Capeman said, patting his boot to make sure the cyanide capsule was still there. "But you know, lots of armies had queer soldiers."

"I don't want to hear it," Moody said. "Keep your damn history to yourself."

Capeman persisted. Riling Moody even more, he said that the Greeks all had boyfriends; so had the Romans. He went on to say that "the Amazons were lesbians and they kicked everybody's ass." Moody's mouth fell open when Capeman said that Japanese samurai soldiers made it with each other—Alexander the Great was queer, and so was Julius Caesar.

Moody looked at him levelly. "Capeman, if you don't shut up, I'm gonna deck you."

Realizing that Chou was growing nervous because of the tension, Pearson turned to Capeman and tried to defuse the situation. Jim was the ranking officer, and he had combat experience. He didn't have the best social skills with the enlisted men, but he was very smart. "You're right about Alexander and Ceasar, but don't scare Moody about that. Tell us some more history. You left off with the Japanese after they took over from the Manchu Dynasty."

Capeman brightened, flattered that the Harvard guy was interested and had been paying attention. "You really want me to go on?"

"Oh, shit," Moody muttered, but Capeman happily resumed his lecture by saying that the Japs wrecked Korea in 1910. We all paid attention as our "professor" stated that they got rid of the king and made slaves of everybody. They did everything they could to destroy Korean culture. They didn't allow Korean history to be taught and made kids learn Japanese in school. They wanted to make Korea a colony, and nobody did a thing about it.

"That's because nobody gave a damn," Moody said. "Why would they?"

A new dialogue had started up between Capeman and Moody. Capeman answered that if the United States had cared back then, we wouldn't be fighting in a Korean war.

Capeman continued by telling everyone that by the time the United States did care, it was too late. The Soviet Union had already come in and backed some of the people who had been fighting the Japs.

Capeman went further by saying that Kim Il Sung turned communist because no one else helped him; that's why a civil war started.

History proved that the same thing happened in Vietnam. Japan took it from the French, but the people there didn't want the French *or* the Japanese. The civil war that went on there was for the same reason—the communists were backing those fighting for freedom against the French.

Chou, who had been listening intently, finally had a comment. "Communists are very bad. They destroyed my country."

That brought the conversation to a halt. China *had* been destroyed. Mao's triumph had humiliated both Chiang's government on Taiwan, and his American ally—us. Out of politeness and embarrassment, we didn't pursue Chou's comment.

"I need some fresh air," I said, jumping out of the half-track.

Jim joined me, but the others remained inside. "That was evil about the queer division," he said.

"Payback for that talking-in-my-sleep stuff."

He laughed. "Remind me not to screw around with you."

I smiled. "There's a reason we're officers. Still, I don't think I'll let on that I was joking."

Jim agreed. "Not to Moody, anyway. He's tough. I definitely don't want to be on his bad side."

He was right. There was a raw edge to Ted Moody. While Capeman and Kingsley were hardly lambs, there wasn't a volcano festering beneath their surfaces; Moody seemed as if he could erupt at any moment over anything. I'm sure he had. Once he had alluded to previous service in the Marines, two hitches in a prior enlistment that had not ended well. The separation apparently had been mutually agreed upon. None of us had questioned him about it; I'm not sure that I wanted the details—it might be just one more thing to worry about.

Back in the half-track, I slept until we got ready for the night move. We were going to travel southward from Munam-ni to Kumchon, eighteen miles north of Kaesong. During the night, we would follow the valley road that skirted the forbidding mountainous terrain of the north. Beyond those mountains we would enter the open expanse of the Imjin River basin and travel west toward Pyongsan, cross the Yesong River, and head south to our third daytime bivouac location. It was going to be another long night.

After we ate, we settled into our bedrolls and tried to get some sleep, but there was none to be had; the convoy ground to a halt after only thirty minutes on the road.

Outside we heard angry, loud voices and straining engines; then Lee opened the hatch and told us what was going on.

"Many Chinese Communist vehicles are blocking the road. We can't get by them until they're removed. It's a supply convoy. Their fuel tanks are contaminated and froze up. They want us to help them."

Lee looked to Chou, who spoke rapidly in Chinese. Lee gazed at me, then snorted in little-concealed amusement. "I'll tell them to hurry or our tanks will push them off the road."

We overheard an angry verbal exchange, but in a short while we were on our way again. Not long afterward, we stopped for our first operative contact of the night.

Kingsley got out his cards. Tonight they decided to play for beautiful women, but they wouldn't let Chou join the game.

"You can keep the money," Moody said, "but you can't have all the women."

Soon, after they had drawn pictures of women on paper, they began a raucous game, betting beauty queens, raising one another with cheerleaders, nurses, and entire harems.

In the meantime, the "adults"—the officers, Jim, and myself—removed the crypto equipment that was stowed in brackets under the seat. I was worried that the cold weather as well as the constant jostling might have damaged it, but to my surprise and elation everything worked perfectly.

When we stopped for the second operative and Hinsley handed me the first report, we were ready to go to work, but hadn't gotten much done before the convoy again halted.

Lee came and told us to put everything away because we were passing through a dangerous area and could be pulled over at any time. He said we were just beyond Sibyon-ni, where there were massive Communist troop night movements.

When we resumed, our pace was excruciatingly slow. Outside we could hear enemy troops marching in double columns along the road. Our own guard soldiers were yelling at them to get out of the way. As we passed through their columns, we heard Chinese soldiers slamming the butts of their rifles against the sides of our half-track and shouting what must have been obscenities. Apparently *all* armies are alike: those pounding the ground resent those riding in vehicles.

The road we were traveling was now within twenty to twenty-five miles of the main battle line. I remembered Brown's warning that any change in that line could threaten us. If these troops were on their way to attack, and UN forces counterattacked, we could be caught in the middle.

As we came ever closer to the battlefield, we heard artillery from both sides. What had before been faint rumblings in the distance had turned to earthshaking roars. We were now within range of our own long-range artillery.

I grew very tense, though the others didn't seem disturbed. Their coolness in the face of danger was comforting, but also embarrassing to me. I wished I could be as brave as they were. Even Jim took the artillery calmly, but then he had been in an airplane while flak burst all around him.

Finally we got beyond the enemy troops and Lee gave us the all clear to get out the crypto gear. Pearson and I were still encoding the first report when we stopped for the third operative.

Because we were so close to the battlefront, the reports this third night were concentrated on enemy forward units, those already dug in on the battle line, and those moving toward the front—everything from army group headquarters to battalion-size commands.

The number of enemy troops reported to be battle-ready was stunning. The depth of combat units along the battle line was immense, up to miles in some places, backed by heavy artillery and armored vehicles. The network of fortifications facing our troops ensured a bloodbath for any units that tried to advance. Moreover, in the rear, the training of combat troops had been intensified, with what appeared to be an effective plan in place for rotation between line and reserve units.

The second report detailed an enormous stockpile of supplies and ammunition, evidence of the efficiency and integrity of well-established supply lines. There could be no doubt that tons of military supplies that had originated in Communist China and in the Soviet Union were smoothly flowing southward into the hands of the Chinese and North Korean armies. Our Air Force interdiction efforts had only minimally stemmed the stockpiling of this matériel.

As we worked feverishly to encode the second report, Hinsley brought us the third. This one spelled out the command and control system linking units from battalion strength down to company size. Enemy commanders and staff officers were, for the most part, combat veterans who had served in World War II fighting against the Japanese, then with Mao against Chiang Kai-shek.

The report even identified the preregistered targets on UN positions, including major terrain features and road junctures.

When I finished encoding the third report and before tackling the fourth, which we had picked up earlier, the last one for the night, I took a break. I figured I had plenty of time to complete it before the scheduled transmission time later in the day.

I dropped down in a corner and watched the others. Corporal Liu had relieved Sergeant Chou and was watching the card game, too, nestled in his corner, wrapped in a blanket, his rifle across his legs.

Kingsley looked over at me. "Want to join the game?"

I shook my head. "Just taking a break."

"So what's out there tonight?" Moody asked. "A division of lesbians?" He looked over at Capeman. "Chinese *Amazons?*"

"That I could deal with," Capeman said.

At that they threw in their cards; they wanted to talk. And I wanted to listen. I craved some human contact, even just words. I wanted to know anything about these men. By this time I had concluded that I was the only married man, that the others were single, some divorced, while others had never married.

"Surely we can talk about ourselves without getting too personal," I said. "We can't say much, but there's gotta be something. We know Ted was in the Marines before he became a ranger, and we know Jim went to Harvard. That's not giving away anything."

"Okay," Moody said. "Tell us something about yourself, I mean something we don't already know from your talking in your sleep. We don't know anything about you except you look like you just got out of puberty and started to shave last week. And you have dirty dreams."

I thought a moment. What could I say, some piece of me that I wanted them to know but wouldn't violate Brown's orders? I looked directly at Moody. "You're right. When I pinned on my gold bars at Fort Benning I was eighteen, the youngest second lieutenant in the Army. Let me tell you, it wasn't easy giving orders to jokers your age. More than once I overheard remarks like, 'Our ninety-day wonder is still wet behind the ears. Where's his mommy?' I learned quickly to let that stuff go in one ear and out the other. I started trusting my noncommissioned officers, letting them run the show. I didn't go to college. I learned how to lead the hard way—by making mistakes, and learning from them."

"But you're an officer," Kingsley said. "I thought all officers had to go to college." He looked to the others and winked evilly. "I mean, that's why officers are so much smarter than the rest of us, right?"

I shook my head. "I went to OCS because of my com skills." I pointed to the crypto gear. "You don't have to go to college to work that."

"What else can you tell us?" Moody asked. "Something *interesting* this time."

"My folks were real poor during the Depression," I continued. "We had an outhouse and used newspapers for toilet paper."

Kingsley pointed to the bucket latrine and laughed. "You ought to feel right at home here. Except we haven't even got newspaper."

"Poor?" Capeman piped up. "You don't know what poor is."

Moody rolled his eyes. "Oh, God, here we go."

Apparently my story time was up, they'd lost interest in me.

"Seriously," Capeman said. "We were *poor*. I grew up on the Gulf of Mexico."

"I knew it!" Moody shouted. "You wetback. That's where you learned to swim—crossing the Rio Grande. Becoming a frogman was a natural career move."

"Wetback?" Corporal Liu asked, but I doubt he understood the explanation, "Mexican," or its significance.

"Shut up," Capeman said, "this is my story. Tell your own next. We lived in a shack and my dad sold scrap iron, but there wasn't much iron down there and nobody had any money to buy it anyway. Some days we didn't eat. Then a hurricane blew down the shack and we couldn't fix it up. We found another run-down shack. The only thing that got us through was my mother. She slaved for us at home, cooking, washing, and keeping us all together. She stood by my dad and wouldn't ever eat until he and the rest of us kids finished all we wanted."

He didn't say anything for a moment, but we knew he wasn't finished. We waited respectfully; you could not interrupt when a man talked about his mother. That was sacred.

"Her love made me a better man. Every time I start to feel sorry for myself, at boot camp, or even here, I think of her." He took a deep breath. "That's what I want to say—I really loved my mother. She died during the war. I couldn't even go to her funeral."

Nobody said anything. We were all thinking of our mothers, but Moody of course broke the spell. Actually, I would have liked to have heard a story about *his* mother. But that's not what I got.

"I'll tell you a family story, the one I started the other night. It's about my brother, the Marine, a sergeant, a couple years older than me. I had a draft deferment because I was working in a defense plant, but my brother got shot up on Iwo Jima and came home using a cane. Big hero! I'd been going with Louise since high school. We were going to get married as soon as I made enough money."

Corporal Liu, fascinated by all this, struggled to keep up.

"When my brother came back, he and Louise started seeing each other behind my back. They ended up getting married. That's when *I* joined the Marines, to get out of there. I caught the tail end of the Pacific fighting, then re-upped. When I got back to the States I got married. Bad mistake; it was a rebound thing. We'd only known each other a couple weeks. A few months later, I caught her in the sack with my first sergeant. That was the end of us and the end of me in the Marines."

"Sounds to me like you have trouble keeping your women," Capeman said. "I need to give you some pointers." He was getting Moody back for the "wetback" remark.

A very tense moment followed as the two men stared at each other. I *never* would have said anything like that to Moody, but Tom got away with it. It struck me as a small-scale demonstration of superpower détente—two guys facing off, each capable of doing serious damage to the other, with the result being a draw.

Corporal Liu hovered on edge, glancing from one to another, until he realized nothing bad was going to happen, relieved, I'm sure, that the cowboys were not going to kill each other after all.

"So *you* tell us something," Moody said to Kingsley, defusing the moment. "Other than the fact you got some monster gas problem that is destroying us."

"It's a gift," Dan tried to joke, but it was evident that Moody's comment had cut deep.

There was a long period of silence, then Kingsley spoke up. "Times like this, I realize I don't belong. I've always felt that, even when I was a kid. I grew up in Arizona. My dad was a rancher and there weren't many people around us. Even when I joined the Army, I didn't feel like I fit in." He shrugged, almost in embarrassment. "Most of the time, I don't understand people. I didn't go to college. I don't know much. I knew about the Japs and Nazis but until Capeman told me, I didn't know about Korea. I still don't understand it. I don't know why people have to fight, especially over things like Korea. I love my country and I'm ready to die for it, but I don't get what it's all about. People are pretty evil, that's what I learned. So when I finish up my twenty years, I'm heading back to Arizona. I'm gonna have a couple hundred acres and live out there with nobody else around."

We all felt awful. No one wanted to hurt Dan, but Moody was not about to give in to squishy feelings. “Living by yourself is a good idea. You can have fart contests with cows. And win.”

I recoiled at the cruel remark, but to my surprise Kingsley laughed; he was not one to wallow in self-pity. He could take a joke.

Dan’s tale of alienation, however, put a damper on our storytelling. Moody shuffled the cards and dealt while Jim and I went back to the fourth report.

To my surprise, the operative delivering the fourth report had obtained enemy offensive and defensive battle plans that revealed detailed orders for attack and withdrawal, commitment of reserve units, and designated secondary lines of defense. It was evident that UN units would face a determined enemy with a well-designed and rehearsed battle plan.

There was no question that the enemy was well equipped, well trained, and fully combat ready to meet any UN offensive. In fact, they were just waiting, a trap ready to be sprung.

The final report hardly cheered us; it detailed the Twentieth and Fortieth People’s Liberation armies operating in this sector closest to the battle line. Besides listing troop strengths—tens of thousands more soldiers than had previously been reported, all dug in and connected with interlocking tunnels and trenches along every hillside within their zone—the information centered on morale and tactics, and these were frightening.

Enemy morale was extraordinarily high; unit commanders had whipped their troops into a frenzy of hate.

We had all heard reports of enemy troops, arms linked, prepared to advance in hordes to their deaths, “the Yellow Peril,” it was called, but now it was in writing. Battle plans ordered them to attack with no regard for their lives, and they were reportedly willing to do so in massive frontal assaults. They would attack at night on a signal of bugles, screaming across the thirty-eighth parallel, backed by punishing artillery to overrun UN positions.

Here was the nightmare in black and white.

What had we gotten ourselves into? I wondered. The only way we could stop their onslaught would be with atomic weapons, but the Soviets were standing by with their own. The chessboard was so lethal that any move would be disastrous; thousands, maybe millions would die. Where would it end?

I thought of my brother, Rhoden Floyd, who had fought with the Marines in the Pacific in World War II, and of our troops in Europe after D-day. Much of that fighting was small-unit actions involving tactics and strategy based on casualties. But here was an enemy with men, perhaps millions of them, willing to throw themselves against us without any regard for their own lives. This would be an entirely different war, one in which human life meant nothing, with tactics and strategy of overwhelming mass and unlimited casualties. We were not mentally equipped to fight it.

Capeman, Moody, and Kingsley were incredibly brave men, but what chance would they and others have against an enemy that cared nothing about casualties, an enemy with limitless men, twenty times more than the Germans and Japanese combined?

One of the great tenets of war is that an enemy's strength is not based on how many men are willing to fight, but on how many are willing to die. Here we faced an enemy like no other: an enemy with millions ready to sacrifice their lives.

By the time we reached our fourth daytime bivouac position near Kumchon, just before dawn, I was profoundly depressed.

And I wondered about what Capeman had said. Was Korea a civil war? How could we, or anybody, settle a civil war? Tom had asked a question in Japan that still bothered me. He wanted to know what our plan was, what we were going to do if we stopped the Communists? No one had answered him. These people, the

North Koreans, were serious—they had a million men ready to fight and die. They seemed not about to give up if we stopped them at the thirty-eighth parallel. We could bomb them, but that wouldn't solve the long-term problem. They would keep coming.

What had started out for me as a straightforward issue—kicking Communist ass—had turned complex. Korea was not like World War II. That had been a clear case of right and wrong, good and evil, but this was different. We were fighting a dedicated enemy of whom we knew little, one that believed in a cause that transcended a single leader. Nazism ended with Hitler's death, and Japanese imperialism with Emperor Hirohito's surrender. A civil war, like a religious war, survived the death or surrender of a leader.

Even more disturbing to me than this realization was that there seemed to be no plan beyond stopping the enemy at the thirty-eighth parallel, no long-term goal, no strategic thinking—no solution to further conflict. The strategy was all defensive, and anyone who had ever been on an athletic field knew defense alone didn't win.

When we got to the bivouac position, we all dismounted to stretch our legs and relieve our bladders.

After watching Lee's men string camouflage netting to conceal the vehicles, I was overcome with the cold gray grimness that was the dawn. I climbed aboard the half-track and fell into a troubled sleep.

Chapter Twelve
A Botched Rescue Attempt

For once I got several hours of uninterrupted sleep. Though hardly rested, I felt somewhat restored when I got out the com gear to call the airborne operator; today's transmission was scheduled for 1230.

I turned on the radio transmitter and receiver at 1215. There was no response when I tried to contact the airborne operator on schedule. When by 1245 I didn't get a response, I checked and double-checked the SOI for time and frequency, but I had them right. I began to fight panic. What if something had happened to the plane? We *had* to send out the reports. There was no other way.

The others picked up on my anxiety, and together we waited for a response. By 1300 hours I was frightened; the plane had never been late before.

Kingsley had another worry—that we might be too close to the main battle line; he was afraid a UN offensive would put us in the middle of a fight between our troops and the Chinese.

I worried about that, too, but for a different reason. Many of the agents providing reports were using low-power radios to contact Lee as the convoy moved across the peninsula. This close to the battle line, the Chinese could pick up their signals. I recalled Brown saying that every previous effort to insert spies into North

Korea had failed. Intercepted radio signals probably had a lot to do with it. One of our agents was missing and had not shown up. Had the Chinese detected his signals and captured him? If so, the Chinese would be monitoring other signals—maybe mine.

Could the Chinese intelligence triangulate my signals and zero in on the convoy? Each transmission was a possible compromise of our position, and should someone be monitoring the signals, they could detect and plot our route down these westward roads. That, coupled with reports about a strange convoy transporting American fliers, could give us away.

The longer I spent transmitting the reports, the greater the chances of being detected.

Then, at 1310, I finally picked up a strong radio signal from the airborne operator. He signaled that his crew had had trouble with their port engine and takeoff had been delayed. He promised that from now on, they would arrive early for the scheduled transmissions.

Relieved, and knowing the importance of last night's reports, I took particular care transmitting them. After the final report had been acknowledged, I knew that no matter what happened from here on, our mission was a success; we had provided Truman with more than enough intelligence to make an informed decision on how to conduct the war. He could not possibly expand the war now that he knew what was lying in wait for our troops.

Relieved that the transmission was a success, we all settled back to rest prior to the fourth night's move.

After sleeping most of the afternoon, we ate a hot meal and dismounted for a break. I watched as the netting was removed for the night move. Unlike the first day, we waited until it was completely dark—we had learned from our mistake; we wouldn't risk another air attack.

Before we left, Lieutenant Lee told us that tonight's travel toward Ongjin near the coast would be the most perilous segment;

this was where the Chinese had launched their counteroffensive against MacArthur—a heavily built-up Communist area where we'd likely be stopped often at checkpoints.

Knowing that we had hours of boredom ahead (I *hoped* for boredom, not excitement), I glanced expectantly to Capeman. I wanted a story. The last storytelling among ourselves had not ended well; Kingsley had been wounded by Moody's snide remark about his gas problem. I felt we would be on safer ground with another history lesson from Capeman.

"Tell us more about Korea," I said. "How did we get involved in the first place?"

Tom brightened; he needed little encouragement to discourse on history.

Moody motioned to Chou. "Gimme your rifle."

Chou responded with a smile.

"I'll tell you the story of why you're here," Capeman said.

"I know why I'm here," Moody snapped. "To kill Commies."

Capeman ignored him and settled back comfortably against the bulkhead. "It happened about a hundred years ago," he began, as though telling a bedtime story to children. I quickly became absorbed. Out of the corner of my eye I saw Kingsley and Moody listening grudgingly; even Pearson, though pretending to be busy opening a can of rations, was paying close attention.

Capeman spoke about the time European countries went to the Orient looking for trade and colonies, sending Catholic missionaries to save the heathens. The English went to China, the French to Vietnam, and even the United States sent Commodore Perry to Japan.

Actually I remembered some of this from high school history lessons, though I had no idea it would some day involve me.

The English who settled in China, Capeman pointed out, caused lots of trouble by doping people with opium.

"If I lived there, I'd want opium, too," Moody said, caught up in the story despite himself. It did not take much to weave a story that captured Moody.

Capeman didn't care for Moody's interruptions. He told Moody to keep his trap shut and then went on to tell us that the Koreans saw what was happening, and saw missionaries pouring into China, Vietnam, and Korea, too. The Korean king didn't like the foreigners coming and he killed thousands of missionaries and Christians. He didn't like the Americans coming, either.

"When did we come?" Pearson seemed as surprised at his question as we were, given that he was spooning beans and franks into his mouth and pretending not to listen.

Capeman responded by telling us that the United States first came in 1866, right after the civil war, twelve years after Perry went to Japan. We sent a trading ship. The Koreans burned it and killed twenty-four sailors.

Moody looked at Capeman. "Sailors?" He shrugged, "That's not so bad."

Capeman shot back at Moody by saying that if he didn't want to have a fat lip, he would keep quiet and listen.

Our "professor" went on by saying that five years later we sent more ships. The king's men fired on those, too, and we withdrew to China, where we had bases. But it ended well. In 1882, we signed the first treaty between Korea and a Western country, and we started to trade with one another. But then everything turned sour.

He lay back on his bedroll, the story done.

"What do you mean? What happened?" Moody wanted more. "You can't leave it like that. I mean, I know it's all bullshit and you're making this all up, but go ahead and finish."

I didn't think he was making it up and wanted Tom to keep going, too, but I also knew he would tell us the rest later; there was plenty of time.

Kingsley had been quiet throughout the story, but he was curious. "How come you know all this?"

"I told you, I like history. In school I couldn't do science and math to save my life. I mean it—if my life depended on passing algebra, I'd take the cyanide capsule. But I liked history, the dates and people; it was like a great story. So I read it whenever I could, and remembering that stuff wasn't a problem."

He grew serious. "Reed Lynch will tell you this, too—in between saving the world and getting laid, we have plenty of time on our hands." He nodded to Moody and Kingsley. "You guys know that, too. You can train, exercise, get drunk, get laid, and you still got lots of time; military life is boring when you're in the field, so I read; Lynch reads stroke books, I like history."

"You know what I do?" Kingsley asked. Here was a ranger monster as tough as Capeman; I couldn't imagine what he did in his spare time.

"I got a garden. I spend a lot of time working on it. It's really satisfying. Things grow because of you—me! It's your own world, something you can take care of and be responsible for. I like that. When things go bad, you can go out to your garden and forget about them. When you see things grow, you're watching the real world, and you understand that your problems don't matter."

The gardening monster shrugged. "I don't read, but I understand what Capeman's talking about. Everybody has to have something special in their life. It's what I'm going to do when I get my ranch." He glanced toward Moody. "That, and out-fart the cows."

Inadvertently, I looked to Moody, also. Surely next he was going to tell us what he did with his time, what was special to him. A history-nut frogman, a horticultural ranger—what would Ted Moody do? Knit? Bake cookies?

But then I saw the expression on his face—complete mystification. He sat in his corner, two hundred pounds, all muscle, head shaved, jaw squared, and I realized that Ted Moody did not read books, did not tend gardens, knit, or bake. For him, saving the world, doing his exercising, training, chasing women, and drinking took *all* his time.

It was at this moment that I realized how much I had bonded with these men, how we—all different in every way—had become a team. Colonel Brown would have been proud. I *cared* that Capeman loved history, and that Kingsley gardened, and I liked Moody for being a general badass. I also knew they cared about me and Jim, too. Jim had become a very special friend. I wanted so badly for us all to live.

We looked to Capeman to continue his story, but before we could prep him to go on, the convoy came to a sudden halt.

We hadn't broken out the crypto gear yet, so we just waited for Lee to bang on the hatch for a checkpoint inspection, but nothing happened.

As we waited nervously, we suddenly heard loud massive small-arms fire, accompanied by mortars and grenades. Through the open-air vents we saw muzzle flashes and the bright lights of flares.

Then we heard shouting and wounded men screaming.

Bullets pinged against our armor plating. We threw ourselves prone on the floor. Seeing the others pull sleeping bags and cover over their bodies, I wrapped my sleeping bag around me and shielded my head. We were under attack, though it seemed much more firepower was going out than coming in. Still, all it would take to incinerate us was one tank round or bazooka.

Sergeant Chou released his rifle safety and faced the hatch.

This was it, I figured. The enemy had discovered us. The radio signals must have given us away.

Then everything went quiet except for an occasional rifle report.

Torturous minutes passed. Finally Lieutenant Lee pounded on

the hatch. Chou opened it cautiously, and we saw Lee standing before us, a rifle in one hand, a bottle of rice wine in the other. He had tears in his eyes. Corporal Liu was with him.

"What happened?" Moody demanded, coming out from under his sleeping bag. I think he felt sheepish; hiding was not his way.

"Everything is fine," Lee assured us. "We were passing through a fortified Chinese checkpoint, a division perimeter. We didn't know it, but a Communist Chinese patrol had fallen in behind us. They must have been lost and didn't have the proper response to the perimeter guards' challenge. The guards thought the patrol was UN troops trying to infiltrate their lines. The guards opened up and there was a firefight. They ended up shooting one another; many Chinese were killed and wounded."

He laughed and handed us the bottle of rice wine.

Capeman took a swig and passed the bottle. We all laughed at the Communist blunder, but I noticed Lee motion Chou out of the vehicle. Liu replaced him and closed the hatch.

Capeman, Moody, and Kingsley celebrated with the wine while Jim and I declined; we had to keep our heads clear to encode the night's reports.

Thirty minutes later we stopped again, and Chou sent Liu out. Chou didn't say anything for a long time but he looked very somber as the convoy continued on. Something was wrong.

Chou waited until the bottle was drained; then he filled us in.

"Lieutenant Lee didn't want to tell you what really happened, but now he feels you should know."

We looked at him warily.

"The firefight was not between Chinese units."

"There was no lost patrol?" Capeman asked.

Chou shook his head. "It was a United Nations patrol."

"Oh, no," Kingsley murmured.

"We think a UN unit, probably American soldiers, tried to

rescue you. They didn't know about the Chinese checkpoint or that they were on a Communist division's perimeter. They opened up on the convoy and tried to rescue you from the convoy but were ambushed by the guards."

"Jesus, no," Moody moaned. "Our own guys?"

Chou nodded. "There was nothing we could do. The Americans thought we were holding you prisoners. We had to fire on them, too. If we didn't, the Communist road guards would have been suspicious."

"You killed our men?" Moody demanded.

Chou hung his head. "We lost five of our comrades and three were wounded. It is a terrible tragedy."

"Did any Americans get away?" Jim asked.

Chou sadly shook his head.

Capeman buried his head in his hands. When he looked up, there were tears in his eyes. "They died trying to save us."

This was the worst thing yet, and totally unexpected, just out of nowhere.

"But how did our troops know about us? Nobody was supposed to know about this mission," I said.

Moody offered an explanation. "Rangers and Marine recon units operate behind enemy lines. They have radios. They might have spotted us anywhere along the road. Yesterday we were all outside. They could have seen us, and alerted our forces that we were being held captive. So they staged a rescue mission."

Kingsley agreed. "We were all milling around in our flight suits yesterday, and the day before. Lee's men were standing guard. Someone with high-powered binoculars could have spotted us. Once he relayed the info, they had to try to rescue us. They weren't going to let us be taken to China."

"Jesus, Jesus," Capeman murmured.

Pearson had another explanation. "Remember that first

fighter-bomber that didn't unload on us? He might have spotted us at the last moment and pulled up. Most of us were outside and dove for cover. Maybe that's why the second pilot missed, also—a last-minute change in his aim. The pilots knew our exact coordinates and could have radioed the information, too."

"Either way, that rescue team was doomed," I said. "They had no idea what they were walking into. We're the only ones who know how many Chinese are out here. The reports I've sent out couldn't have had time to get back to our field commanders yet. That UN patrol didn't have a chance; nor would anybody who tries to take these guys on."

We all sat in glum silence, including Chou, who had lost five of his own comrades, and knew his men were partly responsible for killing ours.

"What if they try again?" Moody asked suddenly. "You think they're going to quit now? We gotta do something."

"What?" I asked. "The only person I can contact is the airborne operator. He can't give the forward units info about our whereabouts without authorization from Washington, and they won't do it."

"So we just let more guys walk into an ambush?" Kingsley asked.

I couldn't see a way out. There was nothing we could do.

All this was too much for Capeman; he could not accept that our own men had died trying to save him from mock captivity. "Maybe Lee got it wrong. Maybe it wasn't a rescue mission. Maybe it was a lost patrol after all. That happens all the time. One of their own recon patrols could have wandered off course and walked into an ambush."

The others picked up on that eagerly.

"Yeah," Moody agreed. "I've been lost often enough. I'll bet that's what happened."

But I knew he didn't believe it; none of us did.

We didn't say anything for a long time; each of us was tangled in our own grief and guilt. This tragedy was completely unexpected. We had more or less accepted something terrible could happen to us. We knew the risks; God knows, they had been told us often enough—we had cyanide capsules in our boots—but we never considered that other Americans could die trying to rescue us. No one had explained that to us.

The mission had turned tragic. We were alive, but awash in blood.

Even worse, I had an awful feeling that this incident was just a harbinger of events to come—but I kept this to myself.

As we inched along the frozen roadway, I couldn't get my thoughts off the men who had died; I could still hear their cries. I knew I shouldn't dwell on them, but I couldn't help it.

Who were they? Men my own age, probably even younger. They were here fighting for what they thought was right, only minutes ago filled with life and exuberance, now lying dead on frozen ground. It had all happened so fast. The finality overwhelmed me. They would not go home. They would not dream again, or hope, or love.

For once I wished I were religious. I wanted to pray for them, but that seemed alien to me, almost phony because I never prayed. It seemed wrong to turn to God in grief and need when I hadn't thanked him in joy and comfort.

I had never witnessed death; it seemed monumental, inexplicable, and cavernous. How could you be alive one moment and dead the next? Where did they go, these men who were here only minutes ago?

Just a while ago I was a little boy growing up in Texas. It was so clear in my mind—my house and my family. For some reason, I remembered a haircut.

We didn't have money for a barber. My mom used to clip my

curly hair and she loved it long. But the kids at school used to tease me—"Look at the sissy boy," they'd call in derision. So one day I stole fifteen cents from my mom and dad's grocery store cash register when no one was looking and went to the barbershop. I told the barber my mom was worried about lice at school and she wanted my hair cut short. He did it, but that night my dad whomped me good and my mother cried over my shorn locks. I didn't care; the kids stopped calling me names.

Where was that youth? I wondered. Where had the time gone?

Then memories flooded me. My mind was a kaleidoscope of images. Those hot Texas days and star-studded nights, sitting in school and hating to be there, playing football, racing and weaving my Harley down streets with the wind blowing through my hair, Nell and Lanny, that awful time when we lost our second baby.

Nell had had such a hard time, though she never complained. She was a petite woman, 5'1", weighing not even a hundred pounds, yet she bounded with energy, her long brown hair glistening off her shoulders in the sun. Even with little money, she managed to keep up with the latest fashions and cook meals that seemed far beyond my paltry lieutenant's salary.

She raised Lanny almost by herself because I was gone so often, and he was a handful—a boy with dark brown curly hair and blue eyes, tall for his age, fascinated by everything, especially my amateur radio gear. He'd twist the knobs and squeal with delight at voices that would mysteriously come out of the box. He liked to dial the telephone, too, and whenever he happened to make a connection, he'd babble happily to the voice on the other end.

Thinking of Nell and Lanny made me realize that every one of those men now dead in the field along the road had memories and stories, too, of their childhood, and perhaps of their own children; but now that was gone, just snatched away.

I looked at the guys with me. Would it happen to them? Or

me? Death came without warning, from nowhere, not with a knock or a whisper, just in an instant, with the speed of a bullet and no time to prepare or say good-bye.

Every mile put us farther from those fallen dead, but I knew I would carry them with me for the rest of my life, a burden that might never lighten.

I barely roused myself for the first stop of the night. When I took in the report at the second stop, Hinsley handed it to me without a word. There was nothing to say beyond the sad shake of his head.

Jim and I got out the crypto gear and set to work encoding further documentation of a massive enemy buildup behind the thirty-eighth parallel, but now all this had more meaning; the enemy soldiers were no longer numbers on a report, they were suddenly real and lethal.

The others fell mercifully asleep as Jim and I encoded the report, but I had trouble concentrating and Jim knew it, and knew what the problem was.

"Hey," he whispered, "you gotta get over this."

"I keep seeing those guys," I said.

He shook his head. "You can't think about it, Mike. You have to let it go. You'll tear yourself apart."

He put his hand on my arm. "Think about it later. It'll be with you a long time. Right now there's nothing you can do."

"There won't ever be a time I can do anything about it," I answered bitterly.

"True, but now it can only hurt you. Trust me, Mike; you can't let your mind go there. When I was in college, I studied philosophy. You could delve forever into what it all means and what life's all about. That's great when you're safe, fun games to play in a classroom or when you're drinking beer, but you can't do it here."

"So that's the lesson from Harvard—don't think?"

"The lesson is that there's a time to think, and a time not to."

He pointed to the others asleep in their corners. "Those guys know it instinctively."

He shook his head in admiration. "I didn't know men like them before this. You don't see guys like that at Harvard. But Capeman, Moody, Kingsley—they save the world, they kill and pillage, hell, they even read and garden. They're all action. That's good. I don't *want* Moody thinking. I don't want Capeman and Kingsley debating philosophical points. I want them to save my ass!"

He nodded toward Moody, Capeman, and Kingsley in their sleeping bags. "And you know what? They would, even a dipshit Harvard guy like me."

He looked doubtful. "I hope I can do the same for them."

Then he pointed to me. "You're thinking too much. Thinking can screw up your reflexes. It's the story of the centipede: as soon as he begins to think about his hundred legs, he can't move and someone squashes him. That's where we are here—we can't let anything get in the way of this mission. We have to keep our minds clear. So don't think. Or think about other things—your wife, and getting out of here."

Of course he was right; I hardly needed him to preach the obvious to me. But I knew, too, that knowing something and doing something about it are entirely different matters. "You're telling me you don't think about what happened?"

He smiled gently. "Of course I do, but I'm telling *you* not to think about it." Then he tried to distract me. "Tell me about your wife."

"We can't talk about personal stuff, you know that."

"I don't want her life history, just tell me what she looks like. Help me out with some fantasies here."

"Judy Garland," I said.

"She should be with me, then. Everybody tells me I look like Mickey Rooney."

"You're not *that* short. And you don't look a bit like Mickey Rooney, more like Quasimodo."

"Whoa," he said. "Mr. Literature, and you didn't even go to college."

"I saw the movie. So who does your girl look like, the one you're going to marry if you get out of here?"

"Rita Hayworth."

"Yeah, right."

"Seriously, red hair and built just like her. She's what keeps me going out here. If it wasn't for Barbara, I'd go nuts."

"So tell me about her; I could use some fantasies, too."

"Well, she's taller than I am."

"I certainly hope so." Then I felt bad. I started to apologize but he cut me off.

"Believe me, I'm used to it. I've been kidded since I was in grade school. After I joined the Air Force, one of my commanders asked the personnel officer, 'Who let the runt in? He could hide inside a trash can.' It's why I'm a navigator, not a pilot—I was too short."

Now I felt really awful.

"Barbara doesn't care that I'm short, and she's all that matters to me. She's gentle, soft as velvet, understanding, beautiful, and . . . you fill in the rest. We're going to have six kids."

"My wife is Nell," I ventured. "And our son is Lanny. He's five." I wanted to tell him much more about Nell and Lanny, but felt constrained.

"You're too young to have a kid, Baker. No wonder you didn't go to college, you obviously weren't studying when you should have been."

We finished encoding the report and sat on the floor next to each other, wrapped in bedrolls, waiting for the next one.

I pointed to the crypto machine. "This is much worse than I expected. I don't think anybody had an idea there were this many Chinese out here. How could we have screwed up so badly?"

He snorted derisively, "And how long have you been in the military?"

I sighed. "I know, but still . . . The scary part is that I plan to stay in. Hell, it's all I know. There's nothing waiting for me when I get out. You making the Air Force a career?"

He shook his head. "Just finishing my tour. I owed the government for college and navigation school. I have another year to do."

"Then?"

"Get married. This is no life for Barbara; she doesn't want to bounce around the world waiting for me to come back from some mission like this. Maybe I'll go back to school. Or teach. My family has a business; if all else fails, I can go home and get a job with my father."

"No regrets about joining the Air Force?"

"None," he said emphatically. "My grandfather came over from Europe. He changed his name because no one could pronounce a name with twelve letters, none of them vowels. He had nothing but his clothes when he came over. He worked as a longshoreman and put my dad through college. Dad got rich in the transportation industry. I had it made when I was born. I want to make a payback for all that America has done for my family."

His intensity was overwhelming. "I believe in what we're doing, Mike. This mission is more important than anything else I could do. When I was asked to volunteer for this, I jumped at the chance. It's an honor to serve on something like this."

It seemed a strange thing for a Harvard guy to say, emotional rather than intellectual, but his voice was filled with gratitude. "My country means more than my life."

His diversion had worked; I realized that I was over my

depression, for the time being, anyway. I grinned. "Too bad you only have one life to give, right?"

"Nathan Hale, huh? Actually, I understand that. But this mission is more like something out of the *Odyssey* or the *Aeneid*—you know, some perilous journey like Ulysses or Aeneas went on, overcoming obstacles to get the Golden Fleece, or to get back home to his wife."

Then Jim pursued the theme; I felt like I was listening to a Harvard lecture. "Strange, but a lot a great literature has to do with journeys—the *Iliad,* the *Odyssey,* the *Aeneid,* the *Decameron,* the *Canterbury Tales, Gulliver's Travels.* They're all about dangerous journeys and the things that happen along the way. Sort of like this mission."

Capeman had awakened; he was listening from his corner. "Golden Fleece my ass. We're just trying to get some information. And didn't all those guys die?"

Pearson smiled. "No, they were successful. They just had to go through a lot to finish, like we're doing—but they made it back."

"*Some* of them, but at least there were women on those trips."

"True, but they turned the men into pigs."

Capeman smelled his armpit. "We're already pigs."

Now Moody and Kingsley had awakened. "Who's a pig?" Kingsley asked.

But Jim didn't want to engage in a discussion of Homeric epics, and neither did I, what little I knew of them, though my memory seemed to recall that those journeys ended up pretty bad and I didn't want any comparisons with this one.

"So what happened tonight?" Moody wanted to know. "How many more millions of Chinese are out there?"

I didn't see any point in hiding the basics. Hell, the Chinese knew where they were; they didn't need to torture that information out of us.

"The last reports confirm seven People's Liberation armies

deployed from the Imjin River on the east to beyond Kaesong on the west, along with two North Korean divisions in the area around here. That's a half-million soldiers. Plus, there are two PLA armored battalions with Soviet T-34 tanks on the highway south of Kaesong and plenty of smaller units providing defense on the flanks."

"Glad I asked," Moody said.

We put away the crypto gear and prepared for the morning bivouac. We were on the coastal road between Yonan and Haeju. This was our fourth stop; it was January 14, 1952. It seemed like we had been traveling for months.

When the convoy pulled off the road to camouflage the vehicles, Lee told us to stay inside. He did not want us out from here on.

"We need to stretch our legs," Capeman said. I knew he really wanted to go out to exercise. There wasn't room inside, and without his physical outlet, Ted would become a nervous wreck; he'd probably never gone twenty-four hours without exercise.

"I need to take a crap," Moody added.

Lee shook his head. "Too dangerous. I cannot risk you being spotted again. You will have to use the inside latrine bucket from now on."

This was bad news. The compartment already reeked from our body odors; a deadly cloud of gas from Kingsley seemed to hover above us. The cold air was stuffy and fetid.

"At least let Dan out," Capeman pleaded. "It's worth the risk. I'd rather be bombed and napalmed."

Lee was adamant. "No one leaves the vehicle from now on."

The thought of two more days confined within this steel box was profoundly depressing, but of course we understood the sense of the order. We did not want another rescue attempt.

I stretched out on my bedroll and told the others to wake me at 1100. Maybe I could get a few hours' sleep before it was time to contact the airborne radio operator.

Chapter Thirteen
The End in Sight

Apparently I slept soundly, because the next thing I knew was being awakened by Ted Moody at precisely 1100. The guys were solicitous of me; it was like having protective big brothers watching out for you all the time. They knew the entire operation centered on the reports and that I was the only one who could rapidly transmit them.

After Moody woke me, he pointed to the latrine bucket. "It's all yours."

What I wanted to do was shave, but that was out of the question. There wasn't water to spare, and who cared how I looked, anyway?

By this time we all looked like shaggy bears, except for Pearson, who more resembled a badger. We were dirty and we stank, and while Capeman, Moody, and Kingsley were probably accustomed to this, it was new and uncomfortable for me. Jim didn't like it, either; he kept scratching at his beard.

I slapped myself alert with cold water and got out the communications gear. At 1130, I sent a signal that was immediately acknowledged. As promised, the airborne operator was ready. In fact, he stated that his aircraft had been flying in orbit and on station for a half hour.

It took several hours to complete the transmission, but by 1400 everything had been transmitted. So far sixteen reports detailing the massive Communist buildup had been sent and acknowledged. No one in their right mind would consider attacking against these odds, and I believed Truman was in his right mind.

Now there was nothing to do but wait for the final night's movement, and of course listen to the others bitch.

But this afternoon they seemed to have mellowed. Capeman wondered how Reed Lynch was doing in the other half-track. Although they had known each other for only a week, it was obvious that Tom missed his frogman buddy.

"I can't imagine being stuck with those Air Force pilots for a week," Moody said. "I'll bet Major Officers Club hasn't shut up the entire time." He was referring to Bill Robbins.

"He's not so bad," Pearson offered. "He's a good pilot, and funnier than hell. You just have to know him."

"I don't think he wants to know enlisted types," Kingsley threw in.

Pearson shook his head. "Pilots always act that way. They're just different. It's like with you guys; there's something special about what you do." He was trying to make rapport with the frogmen and rangers. "What you guys do is . . . well, I couldn't do it. I don't want to eat bugs or swim in butt-freezing water. But you have to understand about pilots. People like Robbins act a certain way because it's part of their mystique."

Capeman wasn't about to let that go by, even though of course he understood pilots were a different breed. "Mystique? Woo, French. There really is something about Air Force types."

Then he laughed to make sure Pearson understood he was kidding; Moody and Kingsley rode Jim pretty hard because of his size and education, but Tom had become solicitous of Jim, sort of looking after the runt.

"Puller seems all right, though," he said. "He looks like he played football in college—probably a running back. I think I could get along with him."

"Yeah, he's all right. For an officer," Moody grudgingly agreed.

"The CIA guys are the ones I'd have trouble spending a week with," I offered. "I bet Tyler hasn't said a word since we landed."

I hadn't meant anything by the remark; it just slipped out, but I saw the others look at one another.

"Well," said Kingsley, obviously wanting to go further with what I'd said. "He's CIA. Secret stuff."

"I've worked with those guys," Capeman said, shifting uncomfortably. It was apparent he wanted to talk, too. "Lots of times when frogmen go in on an op, it's a CIA snatch job. We go ashore and bring someone back for interrogation."

Moody, always to the point, never mincing words, looked to Pearson and me. "So what do you guys think about them?"

This I knew by now was standard military protocol. Capeman, Moody, and Kingsley were enlisted men; they wanted to talk frankly but wouldn't in front of officers, Jim and me, unless we signaled that it was all right.

Jim knew the game, too. "I think Jerry knows what he's doing. Look at the way he stood up to that submarine commander. Tyler? I don't know anything about him. He must be good—he speaks Chinese and Korean; he just doesn't have much personality."

"There's an understatement," I said. "I can't get anything out of him. It's like he's not really a part of the team."

"He's part of the team, all right," Moody said. "Just not a part like the rest of us."

"What do you mean?" He was hinting at what I suspected, but I hadn't thought anyone else shared my suspicion.

"You have to understand how the CIA works," Capeman said. "They don't trust anybody."

"So?" Pearson wasn't following this.

Kingsley had clearly thought this through and come to the same conclusion I had; or perhaps Capeman, Moody, and Kingsley had discussed it among themselves. He said in a matter-of-fact voice, "If you don't trust someone, they're threats to you. If they're threats, you have to consider taking them out."

Pearson was shocked. "What?"

Capeman looked at Jim as though he were obtuse. "Captain, somebody on this op has to be the bad guy. They gave us those cyanide capsules to take if we were captured. Under no circumstances do they want us to get captured. They are not going to risk us saying anything. So they have a real problem. What happens if we don't take the cyanide capsules?"

"Or we lose it," Moody offered. "Or if there isn't time to take it? Or it doesn't work? Lots of things could go wrong. That's why there has to be a fallback plan, a human cyanide capsule."

Exactly what I had been thinking. I had been proud of myself for figuring it out, but these guys had come up with the same thing long ago.

"Think about it," Kingsley pressed. "The operatives are backing each other up with overlapping intelligence; if one doesn't show, there's another to provide the same information. Everything on this op has a fallback plan. Every military op does."

Pearson was incredulous. "You think Tyler is the fallback plan to the cyanide?"

Capeman replied coolly, "Somebody has to be. It's not me, and I don't think it's you or Baker. I know it's not Robbins or Puller. Who does that leave?"

Pearson couldn't accept this. "I don't believe it."

Moody shrugged; he didn't seem to take it hard, that someone was designated to take him out. "That's the way things work—standard operating procedure in an op like this."

Pearson shook his head. "Our government wouldn't do anything like that."

Capeman laughed. "What do you think Ted and Dan, Lynch and I do for a living? We kill people—that's our military occupational specialty. We get medals for doing it. What do you do up in those airplanes when you unload tons of bombs? Kill people, and a lot of the time it happens to be civilians. You think those CIA guys are different? The only difference is who you kill. If what matters is the mission, it *doesn't* make any difference who you kill."

Moody agreed. "The mission is important, not the men on it. C'mon, Captain. You're supposed to be smart; you went to Harvard." There was no admiration in his voice. "I'll bet even Baker figured it out."

Even Baker? Here I thought I'd come up with an amazing insight, but these guys had been on to it immediately. What stunned me was that they accepted it as a given and weren't bothered by it. I was still troubled by the idea that someone on my own team had been designated to kill me if something went wrong, and Jim couldn't accept it at all.

"Relax," Capeman said. "It's just his job. He doesn't *want* to do it. You can't hold it against him; hell, if it weren't Tyler, it'd be somebody else."

This was a new and frightening concept to Pearson, something he hadn't encountered in college or the Air Force. It *did* make the world more dangerous and threatening; it also cast a different light on his view of a benevolent America.

"You'd let Tyler shoot you?" I asked Capeman.

"No, I'd take the cyanide capsule so he wouldn't have to."

"You guys have known this all along?" I continued.

Kingsley nodded. Actually he was offended. "Why do you think we were chosen for this mission? Because we got through other missions! And the way we did that was to figure out who were the bad guys."

Moody said simply, "We knew somebody had to be the hit man

on this op. We knew it wasn't us enlisted. We figured it wasn't Pearson—no offense, sir—and we didn't think it was you, Baker. That left the pilots, and we eliminated them, so that left the spooks. It couldn't be the guy in charge—Hinsley, so that left Tyler."

"Not that he's a bad guy," Capeman amended. "We just wanted to know, on this type of mission—on this op—who was the triggerman? There *always* is one."

"Yeah," Kingsley agreed. "We wanted to know so we could make sure he doesn't jump the gun. We don't want someone panicking and taking us out by accident or screwup. We've been watching him *real* carefully. Right now Lynch is keeping an eye on him." He shrugged. "He seems steady enough."

I laughed. The others looked at me curiously. "I thought I was the only one who had figured it out," I said sheepishly.

"*You* figured it out?" Pearson asked.

"Hey, I told you—I didn't go to college, either."

"You mean I'm the only dummy here?" Jim asked.

Moody opened his hands at the self-evidence.

Still, I was bothered. I felt offended that Brown had arranged this without telling us, though of course I saw why he couldn't. Nevertheless, to be targeted by your own government was unsettling. Talk about being expendable! However, what impressed me was that the other guys accepted this as part of the risk. Here were men not just willing to die *for* their country, but prepared to be killed *by* their country. To me it raised the idea of our sacrifice to another level entirely.

"Jesus Christ," was all that Pearson said.

Capeman tried to comfort him. "Don't worry about it. Nothing is going to go wrong; Tyler won't have to do anything. We're gonna be fine."

Moody jumped up. "I have to take a crap."

So much for this newly revealed threat we all faced. Kingsley,

Capeman, and Moody's composure in the face of death and disaster continually amazed me.

After we stowed the communications gear in its storage space, we camped down for the night, except it was early, and no one could sleep. Capeman decided it was time to resume his history lesson. No one objected. In fact, I think Pearson welcomed any diversion after what he'd learned about Tyler.

Capeman led off by informing us that everything had turned bad for Korea when Japan started to take an interest in the country. That was in the 1870s. Japan became militarily aggressive; they started to attack everybody, including China and then Russia.

When Kingsley wanted to know why, Capeman replied that maybe it went back to the samurais and their warlike nature, or maybe they needed more land. In any case, Japan invaded China, then Korea, but the Koreans held them off. Then Japan got into a war with Russia over some islands and kicked their ass in 1905. After that, they turned on Korea and conquered the country in 1910. They got rid of the king and took over completely. They treated the Koreans like slaves all the way until the end of World War II.

Moody, once again, had been drawn into the story. By that time, Capeman had become accustomed to Moody's interruptions. In fact, he seemed pleased when Moody butted in by asking, "So how'd we get into the pig fight?"

Capeman was up front, saying that that's where it gets tricky. Some Koreans who hated the Japanese went to China and Russia. They became Communists, and when World War II ended, they came back to Korea to take over the country. Some of those guys, including the leader Kim Il Sung, were real heroes in the fight against the Japanese. Other leaders went to the United States. When the war ended, they came back to Korea to take over the country, too.

I recall that basically that was the same thing that happened in

China that led to the Vietnam War—two groups fighting to run their country.

Moody popped up again by blurting, "But one group is Communist?" He wanted to have a clear understanding.

Capeman said, "Yeah." It became Mao in China, Ho Chi Minh in Vietnam, and Kim Il Sung in Korea.

Kingsley cut in by saying, "That's why we gotta help out; they're trying to take over the world."

Capeman shrugged and replied, "I'm here, aren't I? I'm just saying that what's going on here is pretty much a fight among Koreans."

In the discussion that followed, we all learned that the Chinese were in the fight to back their man.

When Capeman stopped his lecture, Moody leaned forward and said, "I see why you asked back in Japan during staging what the goal was, where we're going after we stop the bastards at the thirty-eighth parallel."

I was amazed; Moody had been listening? He remembered?

"So what's the answer?" Moody asked.

Capeman shrugged.

None of us had an answer.

Capeman lay back and closed his eyes; the story was over. He was bored, possibly because he saw no solution.

We settled down to get some sleep, but the artillery in the distance was too distracting. The war was being waged full bore only miles from us, a constant reminder of how close we were to the front line.

But we also were not far from Haeju, and everyone's spirits were on the rise. From here on we would be moving away from the battlefield; already the number of checkpoints had decreased. Our next stop would be Ongjin on the coast; that would be our last night with the convoy. From there we would be traveling even farther from the battlefield, going on to the rescue point, and then safety, and—for me—back home to Nell and Lanny.

But nobody wanted to talk about rescue yet; that was considered bad luck by Capeman, Moody, and Kingsley. They were very superstitious. I knew coaches who had winning hats they always wore and jocks who practiced personal rituals before their games, but men in combat were even more superstitious—probably because the stakes were higher: winning a game was important, but getting killed was on another plane. No one facing an enemy who was out to kill you wanted to add to the risk. That's why there were so many talismans and taboos.

If Capeman, Moody, and Kingsley thought that talking about rescue would anger the war gods, I was not about to upset them, either—you just never knew; better to play it safe. To be even safer, I tried not to even *think* about rescue. If the gods were napping, I didn't want to wake them.

At dusk we heard our soldiers preparing the convoy for departure. Before we left, Lieutenant Lee checked on us. When Chou opened the hatch, Lee couldn't disguise his reaction to the smell; it was awful.

Moody pointed to the guilty party, Kingsley. "Shoot him," he said. "Chou deserves a special medal for putting up with this. I hope you recommend him to Chiang Kai-shek for some Confucius medal of honor. I'm putting myself in for a Silver Star."

As usual, the humor escaped Lee. "There is no Confucius medal," he said seriously. Then he added somberly, "Tonight is dangerous."

"Every night is dangerous," Capeman noted in exasperation. "Last night we almost got killed by a United Nations military unit. What's so special tonight?" He held up his hands. "Never mind, don't tell me; I don't want to know."

Lee told him anyway. "We are going to Ongjin. That is near where the Communists first attacked in June 1950. They have many fortifications there, and besides that, there are many armored vehicles on the road; we may have to stop for them."

"But once we get to Ongjin, everything should be all right." It wasn't a question; Pearson wanted affirmation.

Lee wouldn't even give us that. "It will be all right only when you are on the rescue helicopter."

"And you guys?" Capeman was worried about our escorts.

"We will get out. There is a plan," Lee said confidently.

I realized he was not about to tell us *their* rescue plan; we could be captured and tortured for it.

Lee closed the hatch and we braced for the inevitable jarring of the half-track getting back on the road, but though the half-track engine roared to life, we didn't go anywhere. The convoy didn't move.

We heard a lot of noise, engines straining, and men calling out in frustration, then Lee banged on the hatch again.

"There is a problem," he announced.

"Already?" Moody asked.

"One of our vehicles will not start. The rotor in the engine distributor froze and broke. That truck was carrying fuel barrels but most were empty. We rolled them off the road and put the others on another truck."

"What happened to the broken truck?" I asked.

"We left it alongside the road. It is unfortunate, but not a big problem."

When he was gone, Moody said, "No problem, my ass. That's the longest explanation he's ever given us. Hell, he didn't even tell us when the UN patrol got clipped trying to save us; Chou told us. It's a *big* problem, isn't it?" He was looking at me.

"I don't like it. We're so close to the end that any screwup could be dangerous. A broken-down vehicle alongside the road—empty fuel barrels? If a Communist patrol finds them, and you know they will, they're bound to ask questions."

"But they already know about the convoy," Pearson pointed out.

"I know, it's just something that might raise questions. We don't need any more complications."

I thought the broken vehicle was a bad sign, but I was more worried about the radio signals; the two together could mean a lot of trouble. I had spent many more hours on the radio than I'd anticipated. Each transmission increased the risk—even if I did change frequencies often. The use of radio communications invited possible mission compromise.

The manner in which I keyed my transmitter, known by high-speed radio operators as "my fist," would raise suspicion by enemy intelligence. For an experienced operator, identification of an operator by his fist would be easy. It was his signature. Discerning that the same operator was keying the same transmitter during every transmission would be a dead giveaway.

In addition, the signal strength of transmissions received by the enemy would vary from day to day, indicating that the mysterious source of the radio transmission was on the move. Such suspicion would result in the use of radio signal triangulation by enemy COMINT units, thereby providing a geographical "fix" for each daily transmission while the convoy traveled along the road from Wonsan to Ongjin. Enemy intelligence could then conclude with certainty that a known convoy had to be the source of the transmissions.

An abandoned vehicle along a southerly, as opposed to a more direct, northerly route, would raise more suspicions. I didn't want to let on to the others, but I had a scary feeling about this.

"I'm sure it's nothing," I said, trying to dispel their concerns.

But all were jittery now, especially when we were stopped at a Chinese checkpoint only a few more miles down the road.

The stop was routine, except, to our relief, this guard was friendlier than any of others. He and Chou chatted for several minutes, then the guard patted him on the shoulder and left.

"We come from the same province in China; we were talking about that," Chou explained.

As we moved away from the battlefield, artillery fire faded.

Every mile brought us closer to rescue; every minute eased our anxieties and fed our hopes. The mood in the half-track lightened, especially when we contacted the last operatives. Twenty out of twenty-two expected reports had been received. One agent was reported killed by UN aircraft while standing near a bridge, but what happened to the second missing man was a mystery. He could have been killed, or captured, or he might have defected. That worried me, but I kept this to myself, not wanting to dampen the growing confidence of the others.

Even the CIA agents were upbeat. After they'd translated the reports and given them to Jim and me, they spent a few minutes with us. Hinsley told us we'd done a great job, and for the first time, John Tyler smiled. Maybe he's relieved, I thought; with the work almost done, he won't have to take us out. Even so, he didn't warm up that much, but then again, his job might not be completely finished; it wouldn't be over until we were rescued, or until he'd seen us take the cyanide.

Nevertheless, he gave us a pleasant good night, though Pearson didn't acknowledge it. I knew he wanted to question Tyler, but of course he didn't.

The reports this last night concentrated on the coast of the Yellow Sea from Ongjin to the Manchurian border. As with the east coast, mobile forces were set to deploy rapidly up and down the entire coast. Artillery batteries had been placed at possible landing locations to prevent another Inchon. Unlike the east coast, however, the west coast possessed a natural line of defense, with extensive mudflats reaching miles into the Korean Bay, able to impede conventional Landing Ship Tank (LST) and Landing Ship Infantry (LSI) craft.

Air defenses, too, had been significantly improved; fifty antiaircraft batteries ringed Pyongyang and others were dug in at every major bridge and military installation. Soviet MiGs based along the Manchurian border at Antung, Darien, and Port Arthur provided defense northwest of Pyongyang, an area dubbed "MiG Alley" by UN pilots.

North Korean units made up the bulk of the forces deployed there. Those along the coastline were more mobile than units entrenched along the main battle line near the thirty-eighth parallel. The North Koreans and Chinese had decided it was unnecessary to concentrate forces along the Korean Bay, although there were 250,000 Chinese troops in reserve north of the Yalu, capable of rapid deployment anywhere, including the western coastline.

The reports again confirmed an overwhelming enemy buildup—a million men and reserves, artillery, armor, tons of supplies and munitions. UN forces were no match for what lay in wait just across the battle line—a ferocious enemy ready to spring.

While everyone else slept, Pearson and I worked hectically to encode the reports; it took over five hours to complete them all. When we finished, just before we reached our daytime bivouac near Ongjin, we were exhausted.

Before we turned in, I slid my right hand down to the top of my flight boot. Locating the knotted cord, I pressed it between my fingers. I shivered, knowing a gentle tug on the cord would release the capsule. I told Jim that I hoped I'd be brave enough to take it if I had to. Jim didn't have any doubts about himself. "I'll do it," he said. "I'm sure not going to let that son of a bitch Tyler shoot me."

Then he looked over at me questioningly. "You really think that's his job?"

I nodded, but I didn't care anymore. All that was left for me to do was transmit the final reports to the airborne operator later in the morning.

Jim fell asleep immediately, but when I tried to nap until the time to transmit the reports, I couldn't; we were so close, and the whole situation felt too tense.

Remembering the Soviet air threat, I visualized atomic weapons loaded in the bomb bays of long-range bombers parked on Manchurian airfields—with MiG fighters, armed, fueled and waiting to escort them to their targets. Knowing that two thousand tons of supplies and ammunition were flowing into Korea from Manchuria each day, I pictured thousands of porters carrying munitions and supplies in A-frames on their backs, walking trails along mountain passes.

MacArthur had advised Truman that China could maintain only a 50,000-man army in Korea, but from the intelligence reports I knew that there were a million men within the enemy ranks, plus 250,000 North Korean regulars—in addition to a half-million men in reserve.

I couldn't cast the horror of atomic war from my mind; I kept seeing Nell and Lanny, and I was afraid for them. Maybe because of my fears, I felt almost sure something was going to go wrong, that we had been too lucky, and our luck was about to run out. I nestled in the corner of the compartment and tried to sleep, but I felt trapped inside the stinking, frozen steel box.

The war gods had wakened from their slumber. I felt their cold, malevolent eyes upon us.

Chapter Fourteen
Disaster

On that last morning, we woke in better spirits than ever. I'd managed to sleep a few hours at last and to feel revived, in fact almost exhilarated at the prospect of finishing the mission.

After five terrifying days, we were so close to safety and rescue that we began to feel we might even make it—even me, the eternal pessimist—though we were still careful not to challenge the war gods by talking about it.

We had breakfast—cereal and dried fruit along with coffee—and huddled close for warmth; little flames from slim candles of confidence and levity flickered, dispelling some of the gloom and fear that had blanketed us for days. Hope, something we hadn't allowed ourselves, had taken tenuous root.

The two Army rangers and the Navy frogman were in particularly good spirits. They bantered constantly. Talking about the empty fifty-gallon fuel drums from the abandoned truck that had been left on the road, Moody said he could have tossed one of the drums into the brush by himself; Kingsley said he could have tossed two. Capeman said there was no need to have abandoned the truck at all—he could have pushed it to the coast alone.

Jim Pearson, all 135 pounds of him, remained quiet, happy they were ignoring him for once. The constant butt of their jokes about his size, the Air Force, and, always, his Harvard education—he welcomed any respite from them.

Me they left pretty much alone, except for jibes about my youth, I guess because, as the communications guy, I was doing what they couldn't, no matter how muscular they were.

Kingsley with his ceaseless gas had become unbearably rank, even, at long last, to himself. This morning he said in disgust, "A bath is the first thing on my list when we get back."

Capeman and Moody frowned at this first mention of life beyond the mission; they didn't like to challenge the superstition.

Yet Moody agreed that a bath was the number-one priority for Kingsley, though not for himself. He cupped his groin. "A woman. That's first for me." Then he turned to Capeman. "What about you, sailor boy?"

Capeman was uncomfortable; I saw that he didn't want to further challenge the superstition and was debating internally whether or not to say anything. Finally he tossed an empty ration can at them and shook his head in derision. "You dumb grunts never get anything right. What's first is a bath *with* a woman."

That set off yet another ranger/frogman mock fight; they fell to jostling again, fake-punching one another, releasing the pent-up energy of physical men too fit to be confined in a steel box for six days. As they fell on one another, pummeling harmlessly, Pearson rolled his eyes at me. *Enlisted men,* I could see him thinking. But then Jim, at five foot five, was hardly a guy to wrestle rangers and a frogman; he was better off just rolling his eyes at them. Sergeant Chou completely ignored them, having decided they were simply boisterous, harmless children.

We were finishing breakfast, thinking about how to spend the next few hours, when we heard angry voices outside the half-track, the loudest of which was Lieutenant Lee's.

Talk this early in the morning was unusual, and Chou's

expression telegraphed that something was seriously wrong; we crowded around him to learn what was happening.

As the voices grow more heated, Chou translated. "Red Chinese officers," he said. "Very angry."

"Why?" Capeman asked anxiously. "What's going on?"

Chou whispered that a Chinese intelligence colonel was arguing with Lee about the convoy's authorization. "Colonel says he hadn't been notified that vehicles with American prisoners were passing through his area. He says it's not possible he wouldn't have been informed."

We heard Lee yelling louder, obviously trying to overpower the colonel by raising his voice, claiming that his orders were valid, but the colonel's equally loud response told us that he wasn't buying it.

"Colonel wants to know why we're on this road instead of taking safer, northern route to coast," Chou whispered. "He says this is more dangerous route, not direct and not safe. He says this is very suspicious."

We waited for Chou to translate Lee's answer.

"Lieutenant says U.S. Air Force bombed northern route. Roads not passable; he says we can't wait for roads and bridges to be repaired. He says his mission is to get Americans to Hosa-Dong as soon as possible; this is best route."

It made sense to us, but the Chinese colonel was not convinced; his voice grew louder and more demanding.

"Colonel wants Lee to go with him to headquarters to get confirmation."

We knew that would spell ruin; of course Lee knew it, too: there was no authorization, and no real prisoners, either. Even without understanding Chinese, we could tell Lee was refusing the order.

The exchange grew sharper. Then we heard men scuffling outside the vehicle and the familiar sound of rifle safeties unlocking.

We knew, as in the past, Lee must have surrounded himself with his men and called the colonel's bluff.

Beside us, Chou reached for his rifle and switched off his safety; until now he'd never gone this far. We'd reached a new level of confrontation.

This is it, I thought, we've been found out; it must have been the abandoned vehicle. Or maybe the radio signals; they must have triangulated them, fixed our position, and figured out that we were the source of those mysterious coded radio transmissions. Damn, damn, damn! I thought; it's my fault.

But after another tense moment, we heard the colonel yell an epithet and storm off. We looked to Chou.

"Colonel say he going to headquarters. He say we not hear last of this. He say he'll be back."

As soon as the Chinese officer was gone, Lee opened the back hatch and confirmed the bad news.

"He's on to us. Something or someone must have tipped him off," he said, betraying the first fear we'd seen in him. "This is not good." I saw him mentally debating what to do, and then he made a decision. "We will have to run for it."

In broad daylight, with American planes patrolling overhead and the Chinese in pursuit? We didn't stand a chance. But we also knew we couldn't stay where we were; we'd be no match for the Chinese when they came back.

"You mean this is really it?" I asked in disbelief.

He didn't answer; he didn't have to. I could see it in his eyes. But Moody wanted confirmation. "He's going to find out about us?"

Lee nodded. "Yes. Somehow he knows. When he gets to headquarters, they will check with higher headquarters and learn there is no official authorization for a convoy to transport captured American airmen. He will be back in a couple hours. We have to leave here."

Then, in a decision that was to haunt me for the rest of my life, I said, "I haven't sent the last three reports. I've got to transmit them before we go." I looked at my watch. "Maybe the airborne operator is already waiting."

Lee shook his head emphatically. He knew how perilous it was to remain here, but I pressed him. "I can't transmit on the road with the vehicle bouncing and jerking; I'd make terrible mistakes. I only have three more reports to send."

"Haven't you sent enough?" he asked. "It's not safe to stay here." He definitely wanted to leave.

"That's not the point. We were ordered to transmit *all* reports. That's why we're here."

Finally Capeman piped up, not accusingly, but pointedly. "Is there anything in these last three that's new; something different?"

"That's not for me to decide," I answered. "I'm just doing my job."

"The Nuremberg defense," Moody said under his breath.

"Screw it," I said. "I'll leave it to you guys. You decide what to do."

Capeman, Moody, and Kingsley looked at one another.

"How long will it take?" Capeman asked.

"I'll disregard SOI and contact the operator in the clear; if they're onto us, it won't make any difference if my contact is coded or not. It'll save time, but I'll still need two hours, maybe less."

"Fuck it," Moody said, plopping down in his corner. "If they're going to get us, they're going to get us—here or just farther down the road; they'd just radio ahead. Do the fucking reports."

Lee ran his hand through his close-cropped hair nervously. "All right. Two hours, but no more." He rushed off to tell the others.

It can't be true, I thought wildly. We were so close! I looked to the others. They'll make everything all right.

But all I saw in Moody, Kingsley, and Capeman was fear. I felt Moody and Kingsley could fight lions bare fisted, together take on a battalion of North Koreans, and that Tom Capeman could swim underwater from here to Japan and kill sharks on the way, but they were afraid and it showed. I felt my gut wrench; I saw mortality in their eyes. Suddenly I was terribly afraid, not just because they were afraid, but because I was afraid for them. I desperately didn't want anything to happen to them. They were my ticket out of North Korea.

Yet their fear passed quickly, replaced by anger. Fury swelled them so that they seemed even larger and more powerful.

As I looked at Jim, I visualized something not so much fear as sorrow; it was an intellectual response rather than a physical one. Jim's face was a tableau of loss—that he might never marry his love; that the future he had planned would not come about—but that passed quickly,. He jumped to action the same as the others. Pearson didn't show anger; I saw no hate in his eyes. I saw determination.

And in me? I don't know what the others saw. Fear, I'm sure, probably sorrow, but what I felt most was anger. I didn't want to die. I didn't hate anybody. I wanted *out.* I hadn't come this close just to die.

In any case, we all went into action.

Without a word, Kingsley and Moody jumped out of the half-track to help top off the fuel tanks. To this day I don't understand how these two rangers communicated; they just seemed to act simultaneously. Tom Capeman, so physical himself, responded to their body signals with his own antenna and leaped out to help ready the vehicle for departure, while Jim and I stayed in the half-track to get out the communications equipment.

Praying the airborne aircraft was in place, I commenced frantic calls. Even though I didn't know how, I prayed aloud as my fingers operated the high-speed code key. My heart literally jumped when the airborne operator acknowledged my earlier-than-scheduled call. Thankfully, for the second day in a row, the plane was in position early.

I immediately transmitted the SOI-coded confirmation and radioed in the clear that we were in serious trouble.

The airborne operator radioed his SOI-coded acknowledgement, followed by transmitting one word in clear text—"Go."

My fingers and right wrist become a blur as I keyed the transmitter and sent the encrypted reports. The adrenaline was flowing while thankfully my keying was virtually error-free.

I sensed the others growing frantic as I transmitted, but they knew the heart of the mission—more important than our lives—was the reports. We couldn't roll until I finished transmitting them. I could only imagine the panic of those in the second halftrack, who couldn't watch my progress.

No one said a word as they waited, knowing every second brought the possibility of death closer. Their eyes bored into me. After completing the first report, I glanced toward them and met Tom Capeman's stare. He sat rigid in his seat, waiting, knowing that his life was no longer in his own hands but in mine. I felt the intensity of his gaze, yet it wasn't demanding; it was patient, encouraging, even as the enemy closed in on the convoy.

Moody had gone into his own world; his face was grim but showed no fear. He was accustomed to danger. He looked as if he were steeling himself. He seemed to grow larger and fiercer as he sat in his corner, willing himself to get out of this.

But Kingsley! I remember his eyes most of all. They were deep blue and fixed on me while I transmitted. He sat across from me, six feet, 185 pounds, black crew cut, the most easygoing of us all, yet I knew he was worried—he would possibly die unless I got off these reports before the colonel returned. But then he did something that clued me in to ranger talk, that mysterious way he and Moody communicated without words. He shrugged, a sort of "screw them" shrug, as if we had all the time in the world and he couldn't care less about the danger. It was unbelievably calming and encouraging to me, and it worked; my fingers flew as I operated the high-speed Morse code key. In less than two hours the three reports had been transmitted.

The airborne operator acknowledged receipt in the clear. A total of twenty reports had been transmitted; only two hadn't made it.

When I finished, I shut down the radio equipment and secured it under the seat. I then strapped six Thermit bombs over the radio and crypto equipment, secured my top secret copy of the codebook and SOI between two bombs, and connected the timer-detonator cables. All that remained was to set and activate the six-minute timer.

Chou leaped out of the half-track to tell Lee that we were ready to go.

Within minutes we heard and felt the half-track roar to life. At the same time the engine of the lead T-34 tank kicked over.

Without time to brace ourselves, the half-track lurched forward, tossing us against one another, slamming us into the bulkheads as the convoy began to make a run for it.

We grabbed on to whatever we could.

The rumble of churning tracks under the compartment became deafening as the half-track hurtled down the narrow road in broad daylight.

What had happened? We were so close.

Accelerating even more, speeding far too fast for the icy roads, the convoy raced through Ongjin. We were able to hear the tank engine in front of us roaring at full throttle. When we hit a brief stretch of straight road, I grabbed an emergency medical bag from the front compartment and pitched it to Sergeant Chou while hanging on to a mounting bracket to keep from being hammered against a steel bulkhead. A moment later the half-track careened around turns again, tossing us helplessly from side to side.

Suddenly we heard tremendous explosions behind us, followed

by heavy-caliber automatic fire ricocheting off of our rear armor plating.

I had never been as afraid; it was perhaps even worse than when the Chinese general held a revolver to my head.

It couldn't be happening. Everything had been fine; now the convoy was being pursued and destroyed.

It played like a scene from a movie, but in a movie everyone is saved; at the last minute everything turns out all right, but this was different—it kept getting worse.

"Bastards!" Kingsley yelled as bullets slapped the armored plating.

We slowed, and within seconds our lead tank fired its main gun past us; the report rocked us as if the muzzle were inside our compartment. Our driver dropped back farther, giving room for the tank in front of us to aim and fire the main gun.

We had just resumed our speed when there was a tremendous explosion in front of us. By that time, our half-track had dropped a good distance behind our tank. The tank had been hit and secondary explosions were heard as shells exploded within the tank. As our half-track driver slowed while approaching the disabled tank, another deafening explosion jarred us, coming even closer. Then, within a few seconds, a concussion from a third explosion engulfed the half-track. We'd been hit. The half-track careened wildly to the right. It was as if an angry god had hurled a thunderbolt and struck us, deafening us with his fury, blinding us with lightning.

The half-track then veered back to the left on the narrow road. We grabbed on for our lives as the vehicle slipped out of control, hurtling off the road, crashing into a deep ditch, settling at a forty-five-degree angle on its left side.

Pearson's body had slammed against a bulkhead; he tried to get up but fell, crashing his head against the steel floor. He didn't move.

Automatic fire once more pounded against the rear plating.

We knew we had to get out even as bullets struck our hatch; it could only be seconds before a second tank round blew the half-track open, incinerating us.

Capeman screamed at us to get out; there was no panic in his voice, just furious insistence. But Jim lay on the floor motionless. Moody reached down and pulled him upright with one hand. Jim started coming around.

As the others clawed their way toward the hatch, I opened the seating compartment, checked the Thermit cable connections, and set the detonator timer, starting the six-minute countdown.

"Move," I yelled. "The timer is running. Get the rear hatch open. We gotta get out. Now!"

Sergeant Chou struggled to unlatch the heavy steel door, and he and Capeman pushed against it. Because the half-track was listing hard to the left, gravity took over, banging it hard against the left rear of the disabled vehicle. Smoke from the disabled tank engulfed our half-track. Outside, we could hear automatic fire. Bullets were hitting all around the half-track. The open hatch became a possible maw of death. A few rounds ripped through the hatch and ricocheted within the compartment.

I knew we were moving as fast as possible, but it felt like wading torturously through deep water; it seemed as if time had stopped. I sensed we would take a direct hit any second.

Chou grabbed his Browning automatic and jumped through the hatch as more automatic rounds slammed against the right side and back of our armor, sounding like someone pounding on metal with a jackhammer.

Ted Moody was next in line. His eyes were set, his body steeled—the eternal warrior into the breach. He glanced at us, a look rapacious for battle, almost exultant, and then he jumped.

Dan Kingsley stepped forward, just a foot from me, when suddenly the left side of his skull exploded. Brain tissue, skull fragments, and blood splattered over my flight suit. I gasped in horror as his body was thrown back into the compartment.

The left side of his face had been blown away; his left eye hung from what had been an eye socket. He'd been killed instantly.

Never having seen anything so grotesque, I was momentarily paralyzed with shock. Nothing could hurt Kingsley; he was invulnerable. But there he was, a crumpled, bloody corpse tossed and discarded. I stared at him in horror.

Beside me, Jim struggled to stand erect; he started to fall but I grabbed him. His eyes were glazed; he hadn't seen what had happened to Dan.

I tried to steady him. His face was battered, and mucus streamed from his nose. He tried to speak but all he mumbled was that he couldn't see well and that his head hurt.

I had to get him out of the vehicle; the Thermit timer continued to tick away. It felt as if we had been trapped in the vehicle for hours and it would detonate any second.

Pulling Pearson toward the hatch, I waited for Capeman to jump, but just as he started to exit, there was a sudden crack, a thump, and he grabbed his left shoulder. A round spun him around, ripping a long gash that spouted blood. I was gazing directly into his face.

He looked at the wound in disbelief; he didn't show pain as much as he did amazement and annoyance. Then he turned back to the hatch and jumped.

Knowing we'd need medical and rescue supplies, I searched for the emergency bag, but Kingsley's body had fallen over it. I struggled to roll Dan off, pushing on his corpse with all my strength to free the bag, and then I threw it out the hatch, grabbed Jim, and pushed him with bloody hands toward the opening.

I didn't know how much time had elapsed or how much longer we'd have before the Thermit detonated, turning the compartment into an inferno that would melt metal, but I knew there was nothing more I could do for Dan.

God forgive me but I left him, the sight of his bloody, battered head etched in eternal memory.

I shoved Jim through the hatch and jumped after him, landing near the lifeless body of Sergeant Chou. He lay face-down, his back a sea of blood, a huge wound in his side seeping intestines.

Moody had fallen across Chou's legs. He was on his back thrashing involuntarily, as though trying to swim.

I crawled to him but there was no expression on his face; his eyes were wide open, staring toward the sky; blood bubbled from his mouth.

"Ted, Ted," I screamed. "Don't go. Don't die," but there was no response.

I lifted his head and saw a gaping hole in the right side of his neck pouring blood. I tried to stop the rush with my hand but it flowed through the fingers of my flight glove. Then he stopped convulsing, and I knew he was dead.

I let him go, easing his head to the ground, and looked around. Suddenly the enemy fire had stopped.

Our disabled lead tank was but twenty yards in front of our half-track. Straddling the middle of the road, it was engulfed in flames, billowing smoke that provided a cover screen, yet before I had a chance to run, I heard a series of pops followed by a loud whoosh. The six Thermit bombs inside our half-track had ignited, causing the interior of the compartment to disappear in a fireball. Dan's body was instantly turned into ash. Small-arms rounds stowed in the half-track started to cook off like fire-crackers at a Fourth of July celebration.

Looking back, I saw the other half-track smashed against a bank on the right side of the road. The only sign of life in the whole convoy was Tom Capeman clutching his hemorrhaging shoulder after entering the haven of a ditch.

Then firing resumed, bullets striking the road, slashing gashes in its frozen surface. Through the intermittent smoke pouring from the tank, enemy soldiers caught sight of us and began firing. That's when I saw Jim, staggering zombielike on the road. He was walking directly into the enemy's line of fire.

"My God, Jim, stop," I screamed, but he continued on, mindless of my voice or of certain death within a few more steps.

I scrambled up and ran, making a flying tackle that knocked him to the ground. We hit the road as bullets slapped near us, sending chips of ice and pebbles into our faces. Then the firing slacked off. Grabbing Jim by the collar, I dragged him toward the ditch where Capeman was crouching, but I let go when I spotted Sergeant Chou's Browning automatic in the road. I scrambled to it, snatched it by the sling, and was about to go back to Jim when I remembered the emergency bag. It lay only a few feet away, but occasional automatic fire returned. Risking everything, knowing we needed the emergency kit to survive, I dove for it. Placing the sling of the rifle over my neck, I wrapped the kit around my left arm and started back for Jim.

But he wasn't where I'd left him. He had gotten to his feet and was again stumbling into the smoke and across the road toward enemy fire, as though in a trance.

"Jim!" I screamed, racing after him. Throwing myself against him, I once again knocked him to the ground. The impact seemed to jar sense into him, and for the first time his dazed look faded to comprehension.

"Jim, we gotta get out of here," I yelled, pulling him into the ditch where Capeman had taken cover.

We scampered past the burning half-track. Smoke choked us and burned our eyes. Small-arms rounds within the vehicle continued to cook off. Worst of all was the overwhelming, sickening stench of burning oil, paint, rubber, and human flesh—Kingsley's flesh.

After passing around the burning half-track under cover of the smoke, we reentered the ditch and managed to crawl until we put a few hundred yards between the half-track and ourselves. I glanced back and saw the half-track's driver's head hanging grotesquely from the cab window.

From our vantage point in the ditch, we had a view of the entire scene of carnage. Burning twisted vehicles were scattered along both sides of the road, which was littered with the bodies of convoy soldiers, some smoldering.

The firefight had been completely one-sided; Lee's men hadn't stood a chance. There were three Soviet T-34 tanks that had the tactical advantage of attacking from the rear, plus they were manned by crewmen who knew the "soft" spots on our own T-34. They were able to slow, aim, and direct accurate fire on the fleeing tanks and vehicles, massing white phosphorus and high explosive rounds on their targets. Our own weapons were forced to fire through friendly vehicles while on the roll. After our trail tank had been taken out, the rest of the convoy was knocked out—one vehicle at a time—until the enemy finally took out our lead tank, thereby blocking all other vehicles from any possible escape.

While we watched, one Soviet T-34 tank took a position in the middle of the road, while the other two T-34s pulled to flanking positions well off the road. All three fired continuous bursts from their turret-mounted machine guns.

Suddenly two men in Air Force flight suits leaped from the rear hatch of the burning second half-track. They raced toward a deep ditch, their uniforms in flames. I couldn't tell for certain, but I guessed that they were Lynch and Robbins. Their hands reached around for their backs as machine-gun fire ripped into their bodies; they stumbled to their knees, then fell forward, facedown on the road. Helplessly, we watched them die, cut to shreds, their bodies riddled again and again with bullets.

Then the firing stopped, but all was not quiet. The fuel tanks of the burning vehicles started to blow, sending fireballs into the sky; ammo was blowing up; but over that awful noise we could hear the cries of wounded men screaming for help.

While watching the horror, I was suddenly overcome with a childhood memory. As a boy I had played war with toy soldiers, tanks, trucks, and artillery. I would build make-believe forts of rocks and mud. One day my father backed his pickup truck into the yard over my wonderful fort, crushing everything I owned. I remembered weeping as I stood over my shattered toys, reciting the nursery rhyme "Humpty Dumpty." He sat on a wall, and all the king's horses and all the king's men couldn't put him back together again.

That childhood scene had become real. While lying in that frozen North Korean ditch, looking at the demolished vehicles and bodies strewn along the road, I dully whispered the nursery rhyme over and over. Realizing that all the king's horses and all the king's men couldn't restore the lives that had been lost, I started to cry. Tears cascaded down my face, weaving their way through Kingsley's splattered brain tissue and blood.

Capeman slapped me back to reality. He was yelling at me, but I didn't understand what he was saying. The automatic fire had started again with short bursts. As we watched, machine gunners took aim at the bodies on the road and fired bursts as though they were on a target range.

Other Chinese vehicles pulled up as the machine guns continued to rake the convoy. Then the enemy tank engines shut down, and we could see soldiers dismount from all the vehicles, automatic rifles at the ready. They were looking for survivors.

We had to get away immediately.

Taking quick stock, we saw how desperate our situation was. Tom's wound was bleeding profusely and Jim, though he had recovered somewhat, was still dazed; in a dull, dead voice, he said that his vision was blurred and his head throbbed. He kept shaking it.

Feeling a burning sensation in my leg, I noticed for the first time that I, too, had been hit; blood soaked my flight suit from my left knee to the ankle and was already beginning to freeze. Though I could tell the wound wasn't serious, a trail of blood had been left from both Capeman's and my wounds.

It would be only a matter of time before enemy soldiers picked it up and knew there were survivors.

Moving a few hundred yards farther down the road, we took cover within an outcropping of boulders. I opened the emergency kit and removed the medical supplies.

Hurrying to dress our wounds and get away before enemy troops discovered us, I cut away as much material as possible around Tom's wound with a pair of scissors. The round that had caught his upper left arm had ripped a deep gash almost four inches long, exposing muscle and flesh. I knew he was in horrible pain, but he didn't say a word as I cleaned the wound with a sterile swab, applied antibiotic powder, and placed a cotton bandage over it.

I wrapped his wound tightly with a gauze tape, then turned to my own injury. When I cut out a small circle of material from my flight suit, I saw only an entrance wound. Using two swabs, I gently pried the wound open and found a jagged piece of metal lodged in the anterior part of the muscle near the tibia, apparently a flattened ricochet round. I extracted it with a pair of medical tweezers, stuffed the wound with antibiotic powder and sterile gauze, then applied a pressure bandage. The bleeding stopped.

We were ready to go.

Tom took the lead when the smoke from the burning vehicles shifted, providing cover for us to move from our position. I put my arm under Jim's arm and guided him along. He continued to be dazed and unsteady on his feet.

We came to a curve in the road that turned left. Being out of enemy sight, we crouched and ran wildly, stumbling over brush and rocks.

Behind us, faint single rifle shots echoed. Rounds were possibly being fired into bodies along the road.

Then it hit me. Oh my God, my God, I repeated over and over. They're all dead. I couldn't get the sight of Dan and Ted out of my mind.

A wild thought startled me: Their bodies! We can't leave them. We have to get them. I had lost all sense of reality.

I turned and started back, but Capeman grabbed me.

"Their bodies," I cried. "We have to get them."

Then I understood how strong Capeman was. Wounded and bleeding, he pulled me down roughly with one hand and pressed me to the ground. His voice seethed. "They're dead! Leave them."

His eyes were steely. "Get ahold of yourself, Lieutenant. We have to get out of here—now!"

Chastened, I nodded meekly. He let go of me and we took off as fast as we could, three wounded men with one weapon among us, behind enemy lines, thirty miles from our rescue point.

Chapter Fifteen

Escape to the Sea

Stumbling wildly through dense frozen brush, Pearson, Capeman, and I finally stopped to rest when we believed we'd eluded the enemy soldiers, at least for a moment. We hadn't heard more shots or anyone following us, but we weren't paying much attention, we were just running.

Hiding behind another boulder formation, we dropped to the ground to tend to our wounds and take stock of the situation.

Pearson had regained some of his vision, but his head throbbed and he needed help maintaining his balance. He complained of nausea. There was no question he had suffered a bad concussion; he kept becoming confused or getting a dazed expression in his eyes. Jim also complained of having difficulty breathing. He had a raspy cough and was spitting up phlegm.

Capeman tried to keep him alert with questions.

But Tom had his own problem; his wound continued to ooze blood despite thick compresses, yet he waved me off when I tried to change his dressings. "I'm fine," he said with grim determination. "Don't worry about me."

My own leg injury was minor; the bleeding had stopped and it didn't hurt; or if it did, I'd gotten used to it.

What I couldn't get used to was the cold. This was the longest we'd been exposed outside and we had only our flight suits and jackets, which failed to protect us against a temperature that had to be close to zero—even without the windchill factor. The cold was so penetrating that it hurt, a pressing pain that reached into our bones and began to throb. Instinctively we huddled together. We had only one rifle, one magazine of ammunition, and no food except for spare provisions in the emergency kit, barely enough to last two men for a couple of days.

"It could be worse," Capeman said, hunching tightly into himself for warmth.

"How?" I wanted to know.

He rubbed his shoulder and grimaced. "I'll have to get back to you on that."

"We could be *dead,*" Pearson slowly pointed out, showing more alertness.

But none of us wanted to think about that. Dead were Kingsley, and Moody, and Chou. As were all the others. The horror was too overwhelming to contemplate; I was doing everything possible to not think of Dan's skull exploding or of Ted gasping his last breaths. Capeman was right; I must not give in to that.

For Capeman, this must have been the worst of all; he'd had to abandon his comrades, something alien to his very being. I knew he had to be thinking of Reed Lynch; he hadn't been able to save him; he'd had to abandon his buddy's body. Tom would rather have died than do this; he'd have given anything to save them, but to leave them scattered on the battlefield, massacred and mangled, was worse than death.

"What do you think happened?" he asked me.

"The Chinese colonel learned that the convoy was phony. We were doomed as soon as he went off for verification."

Pearson shook his head. "It could have been anything. Remember that operative who didn't show up? Maybe he was captured and tortured to give up information."

"It could have been the radio signals," I offered. "The Chinese might have made a fix on our position. Once they realized that the source of transmission was moving, it wouldn't be long before they connected it with the convoy. I was getting worried about the amount of time I'd spent on the radio. Or it could have been the abandoned truck that alerted them."

Capeman dropped his head into his hands. "Shit, shit," he moaned.

Seeing his pain, I had to get off my chest what troubled me—that perhaps *I* had been the cause of the disaster by insisting on finishing the last reports. "Maybe if we'd left immediately, we could have gotten away. It was my fault."

Capeman raised his head. He looked angrily at me. "Cut that shit out, Baker. The last thing we need is a crybaby beating himself up about this. Forget the martyr routine. Shit happens. Our job was to transmit the reports. That's what you did. We voted on it. I am *not* going to let you whine about this."

Pearson had no sympathy for me, either. In measured words, he added, "Mike, if they were on to us, they were going to nail us sooner or later. They could have radioed ahead to have another unit along the coast zap us. There was no way we were going to outrun them once they realized who we were. So drop the guilt trip. Tom's right, taking this on yourself is self-serving bullshit."

Maybe, I thought, but I couldn't get over it completely. We might have had a chance if we'd made a run for it immediately, but they were probably right again—we were dead men as soon as the colonel went for verification. Or maybe we were doomed from the moment we signed on for the mission.

Capeman had had enough. "We can't think about this anymore. We have to figure out how to get to the coast. Anybody have a clue where we are?"

Pearson pulled a map from his flight suit and spread it open on the ground. He smiled at Capeman in minor triumph. "Air Force types always carry spare maps; no navigator is ever without one." He had stashed a map of the area we were entering before we made a run for it.

Thank God for that, I thought. Kingsley and Moody were supposed to lead us to the rescue point. The rangers had memorized the maps and could have gotten us there without one, but we three were lost.

Capeman located our position almost immediately. Earlier, he had pored over the coastal maps with Dan and Ted. Of the three of us, he had the best feel for the terrain, though Pearson could read a map and I'd had enough training at OCS to read one as well.

We plotted that we were on North Korean Road 502, a two-lane, loose-gravel road that led to the western coast. Our approximate position was North Latitude 38 degrees, 09 minutes, 35 seconds, and East Longitude 125 degrees, 15 minutes, 00 seconds. We figured we were about two and a quarter miles south of a juncture with North Korean Road 52. The terrain features surrounding our site provided needed clues. Our location was between flat and hilly terrain, with overgrown trees mostly stripped barren and close brushwood. To our left, the highest hill peaked at 233 meters; to our right was a 207-meter hill. We were in the saddle between those two hills. Between those hills was frozen flatland that alternated between marsh and scrub grass. A confirming clue was a gentle curve in the road that turned toward the northwest.

We spent twenty minutes studying the map and decided to stay off the main roads and instead take a route following a trail that wound thirty miles through the mountains to the Yellow Sea. The entire area was, as far as we could tell, uninhabited; there were no cities and only one fishing village near the Yellow Sea marked on the map.

Thirty miles, I thought, in subfreezing temperatures through the mountains, wounded and pursued. What were our chances? Zero. Even if we managed to reach the planned rescue point, it would be too late. The airborne operator had to know that the convoy had been attacked. Probably our planes had already spotted the destroyed vehicles and seen the bodies. No one knew there were survivors. Would they even bother with a rescue attempt now? Probably we'd been written off as dead, and some cover story was already in progress.

But what choice did we have? All we could do was try for the coast and hope.

Before starting, I again cleaned Tom's wound and changed the compress. The area around the wound appeared to be reddened. Though I knew the pain must be unbearable, he clamped his jaws and bore it stoically. "I'm glad you paid attention to that medic," was all he said.

We got Pearson to his feet and headed off with Capeman leading the way, clutching his shoulder, a wounded monster on the run. Pearson shuffled behind him, and I brought up the rear, carrying the emergency kit and Browning automatic.

It was early afternoon on an overcast day through which the sun broke only intermittently, but even then it cast no warmth. At least it wasn't snowing, though that might have softened the hammering cold.

Our progress was torturously slow, yet that ended up being a blessing, because we didn't stumble into any enemy patrols. We had no idea if there were patrols sent out to look for us, or recon units simply patrolling the area, but we managed to hide in the brush off the road whenever an enemy patrol approached, easily heard since they made so much noise. I couldn't believe their lack of noise discipline. If we'd been going faster, or if they hadn't been talking and laughing, we might have walked right into them.

Hearing their voices, we had time to take cover until they passed, but that slowed us even more. We calculated we were traveling between two and three miles per hour; at that rate it would take us up to fifteen hours on the trail to get to the coast—if we didn't freeze or get lost, or get ambushed along the way.

Despite a mighty effort to keep from thinking back on the massacre, I could not drive those final minutes from my mind. The impact of the bullet exploding in Kingsley's skull echoed over and over, and the wash of his blood and brain tissue saturated my thoughts.

Once I must have stopped, paralyzed with these memories, because Capeman came back and shook me violently. He thrust his face into mine and seethed, "Stop it."

"I'm okay," I said.

He shook me harder. "No, you're not. You're thinking about what happened. Don't! There's nothing you can do about it; it's over. Let them go. You have got to keep your mind on getting out of here. I am not going to tell you again, Lieutenant. Keep this up and you're going to get us killed." He pointed to Pearson. "He's just hanging on. He may be a lot worse off than you think."

Then he gestured to his own shoulder. "I'm not worth shit either. This is all up to you now. Don't let us down, Baker. We've come this far; I am *not* going to let you fuck this up. You owe it to Jim and me, and to the others back there."

He let that sink in, then he said angrily, "I swear to God I'll clobber you if you stop again."

He meant it, too.

Tom brought me back to reality. I pointed to his wounded shoulder. "I could take you."

"No, you couldn't. Not if you had four arms and I didn't have any." Then he smiled, but not warmly. "Lieutenant. Sir." I'd had my final warning.

As the day wore on, we grew more tired, and as darkness surrounded us we couldn't go farther; we were starting to stumble and trip in the black ink of night. We needed rest; otherwise we'd wander off course and get lost. There were several side ravines that we could get trapped in and had to avoid. Jim continued to complain of a throbbing headache and dizziness. His nausea had led from throwing up to dry heaves. We all needed rest to recover our strength.

Capeman spotted a friendly outcrop of large boulders above the road. A flat place surrounded by boulders would protect us from the wind. After crawling through an opening, we dropped in exhaustion. Though we were out of the wind, it remained below freezing, and now that we weren't moving, the cold settled into our bones again with crushing pain.

Without blankets or bedrolls, we had only ourselves for warmth. We opened the emergency kit and let Capeman divide up the provisions. Though he was the junior man, Jim and I were happy to relinquish authority to him. We were in his domain.

"We'll eat a little tonight, have a bite in the morning, then save the rest for tomorrow night. After that . . . ?"

He let it ride. After that we would be rescued or trapped on the seacoast with no place to go, behind enemy lines, perhaps fifty miles from any friendly forces, with a half-million enemy soldiers in between. We didn't want to think about that possibility. Food was our last concern.

Jim remained nauseated and turned down his portion. After Tom and I had eaten our rations, we all hunched down for the night; there was no question about lighting a fire that could be seen. We huddled together like hibernating bears.

"Someone want to tell a bedtime story?" Capeman asked. "Or say a prayer? And I want to see everybody's hands at all times."

Pearson laughed for the first time, but it turned into a choked sob.

"Sorry," he said. He was quiet for a minute, then asked what I knew was on all our minds. "Do you think any of the others survived?"

Neither Tom nor I answered. No one had survived. No one had had a chance to take the cyanide capsules; it was over too fast. Maybe some of the Nationalist soldiers lived through the first attack, but they would have fought to the death because capture for them would have been even worse than for us. I didn't recall seeing Lieutenant Lee's recon vehicle, which was in front of the tank. I wondered if he and his driver had made it out, or if they had been killed or captured.

"What about Moody and Kingsley?" Pearson asked. I forgot he hadn't seen anything.

"They didn't know what hit them," Capeman said tonelessly.

"They didn't suffer?"

I remembered Ted gasping for breath, drowning in his own blood. "No."

He started to cry. Capeman put his arm around him. I wanted him to put his arms around me, too; I wanted him to make it all go away.

"It's a bloody place," Tom said at last; his voice sounded strained, almost far away, but at the time I didn't notice. "People have been fighting here for two thousand years."

"Everywhere," Jim murmured.

But Capeman knew better than to wallow in melancholy. Suddenly he brightened; I was stunned at his transformation, he was alive and animated. "Here's a question for you, Pearson. When was Harvard founded?"

Oh my God, I thought wildly; Tom's going to give us another history lesson. The idea seemed so ludicrous I almost laughed. But then I realized what Capeman was up to.

Jim, roused by the question, looked perplexed in the dim night light. He rubbed his head. "Harvard? What are you talking about?

We're on a mountain trail to nowhere. Everybody's dead. There are ten thousand Chinese out there! My head is killing me."

"C'mon, when was Harvard founded?"

"Jesus. I don't know, sometime back in the seventeenth century."

"Pearson, you went there, you ought to remember the date; wasn't it in your admission PR papers?"

Jim struggled to remember; Tom was drawing him in despite his reluctance, but it was working, just like it used to for Moody. His mind set to work, as Capeman had intended. "Okay, I got it—1636. Harvard was the first American university."

"Know when the first Korean college was founded?"

Of course he had no idea, and I certainly didn't, but Tom's font of Korean history and arcane information seemed endless. Again I was glad; his voice was calming and distracting, and I didn't care if what he said was true or not. I gave in to the spell he was weaving.

"Nine eighty-two!—650 years before Harvard. Confucian scholars started a university not far from where we are right now; they came from China, about fifteen hundred years after Confucius died."

"Are you making this up just to piss me off?" Pearson asked.

"It's true; I told you, I read about this place before I came over. The first university in Korea was founded in 982. That's almost a *hundred years* before the Norman conquest; there wasn't even an England then. People think they're barbarians over here, but they had their shit together a thousand years before there was an America, and the Chinese had it together a thousand years before that. Confucius lived six hundred years before Christ."

"You should have gone to college," Pearson said dryly.

"Why? You went and didn't learn anything. What would I have learned in college? Square roots and how to run a business I'll never own? Everything you need to know is in books. You don't have to go to college to read them."

Then Capeman's voice gradually turned strangely lifeless, fading almost to a whisper. I suddenly realized Tom hadn't been talking to distract Pearson, he had been talking to distract himself from his own pain.

I pulled out a flashlight from the emergency kit to check Capeman. He was deathly pale; his lips were tinged blue, and he was shivering. Though in incredible pain, Tom had carried off his history lesson so well that I had forgotten how badly wounded he was and how much blood he had lost. Here I'd wanted him to comfort me, but he was the one who hurt worst, and there wasn't anything I could do for him. Inwardly I kicked myself for eating some of the provisions; I didn't need them—Tom did. I promised myself I wouldn't eat anything more.

"So what else can you tell us?" I asked, trying to bring him back.

He looked at me blankly. "Huh?"

"What else did you read about Korea?" I prompted. If I could keep him talking and his mind off his pain, then maybe he would get through this.

But he just stared at me; I wasn't sure he had heard me. He had started to fade without me even realizing it.

Jim saw it, too. He sat up and put his hand on Capeman's forehead. "Jesus, you're burning up." He turned to me, "He's drenched. Isn't there anything in the emergency kit—aspirin, morphine?"

"Yeah, both." I grabbed the flashlight, fumbled in the kit, and pulled out a small bottle of aspirin, then got the syringe and morphine.

Capeman came around and shook his head. "No morphine. I don't hurt that badly yet. We may need it later."

"If it gets any worse," Pearson tried to joke, "we won't need morphine, we'll need the cyanide."

I opened the bottle and gave Tom six aspirin. With darkness

closing, he couldn't see anything, but managed a weak joke as he swallowed them. "You sure one of these isn't the cyanide?"

"No, Tom. Never," I promised. I handed the aspirin bottle to Pearson. "Maybe you should take a couple?"

He thrust the bottle back at me. "Jesus! You never give a guy with a concussion aspirin. What are you trying to do to me?" He looked at Capeman. "Maybe you guys got it wrong. Maybe Tyler wasn't the hit man, maybe Baker is."

Tom tried to laugh, but he couldn't. His shaking grew worse. Jim brought him into his arms and drew Capeman tightly to him. I got on the other side and wrapped my arms around him. We pressed against him until he finally began to settle.

"We have to keep him warm," Pearson said. He took off his woolen cap that was under his flight cap and placed it on Capeman's head.

"You need it," I said to Jim, taking off mine and handing it to him, but Jim refused it. "My head hurts too much; that cap feels like a boulder."

"What about Tom's shoulder wound?" I asked. "He can't lose any more blood. Maybe I should suture it."

"My ass you will," Capeman groaned, trying to sit up. "Then I'll know for sure we were wrong about Tyler. You are *not* going to operate on me, Baker."

"Relax," I said. "I can't do it in the dark anyway; I'll check the wound in the morning."

Capeman began to struggle to get up. He was slowly regaining his strength. "This is too much closeness for me. I'm getting hot; I don't want to get horny, too."

"In your dreams," Pearson laughed, but then he coughed and cried out in pain.

"What?" I asked nervously. "What's wrong?"

"My chest." He doubled over, struggling for breath.

Then I realized why he'd reacted in pain. Jim had pneumonia.

Pearson eased back. "Damn, breathing hurts."

Pearson's pain somehow revived Capeman. He sat up, ready to take over again. "We need to set up a watch schedule. They're out there; somebody's got to stay awake." He looked at Pearson. "Besides you. You're not going to sleep at all."

"I'm okay," Jim said through clenched teeth.

"Right now you are, but you can't tell with a concussion, and pneumonia makes it worse."

Tom was right, of course. Sometimes Jim seemed fine, but then he would fade. We couldn't let him sleep; he might slip into a coma and not wake up.

"I'll take first watch," Capeman said. "Try to get some sleep."

"I'm not sleepy," I responded.

"Go to sleep," he ordered. "I'll wake you in four hours."

"You sure?"

"Positive. Give me the rifle."

I handed it to him and eased back on the ground. I knew I wouldn't be able to sleep, but the next thing I knew was Capeman shaking me awake. "Your watch," he said. "I can't stay awake anymore."

"What time is it?"

"Three o'dark."

He had let me sleep five hours. I looked over at Pearson. "How're you doing?"

He was nodding, but awake. "Who could sleep with you snoring?"

"I suppose I talked in my sleep, too."

"Oh, yeah," Capeman said. "You really got to clean up your dreams, Baker. I feel sorry for your wife. Who's this Judy babe?"

"I can hardly wait to hear your dreams," I told him.

"Well, pay close attention. And remember them in case I

forget. I want to hear about them in the morning." He handed me the rifle.

"Anything happen?"

"Two patrols came by. I don't know if they were looking for us, but there was definite movement on the trail." He groaned and lay down, but before he slipped into sleep he pulled me close. "Check Pearson often. His labored breathing bothers me, and he can't get rid of his headache." Then he said something that really scared me. "He's losing ground. I don't think he'll make it."

Using the flashlight, I glanced over at Jim, who was not even aware that we were talking. He looked awful. They both did. I patted Tom gently. "Get some sleep."

I clutched the rifle and listened to Capeman begin to snore. Every few minutes I checked on Jim. Twice I heard movement along the trail, voices speaking in Chinese.

It was the longest, most miserable night of my life. To that point.

Chapter Sixteen

Death of a Patrol

Just before dawn, I shook Capeman awake. Pearson continued to hang on, though I couldn't tell if his weakness was more from injuries or exhaustion.

I handed Tom breakfast provisions, including what would have been my share—a chocolate bar, a can of banana bread, and cold instant coffee. As he ate, he looked at me suspiciously. "Where's yours?'

"I already ate. I was so hungry, I couldn't wait."

He didn't buy it, then put the chocolate bar and a can of banana bread in his flight suit. "For later," he said.

"Tom, you need the food; eat it. There's plenty left."

"I'll get fat," he said primly. "Food goes right to my ass." He looked at Pearson. "How're you doing?"

Jim was so groggy all he could mumble was, "Fine." But he wasn't; his cough and each spasm caused him to grimace in pain from his pneumonia. What worried me more was dried and frozen blood on his lips. I got out gauze from the emergency kit and gave it to him to put over his mouth to lessen the harsh effect of breathing in the near-zero air, and also to muffle the sound of his coughing.

"Great, now I look like a Chinese bandit," he attempted to joke.

"Better that than a U.S. pilot," I said, then turned to Capeman. "Let me take a look at your shoulder."

"Forget it, Florence. I'm all right."

In fact, he did appear stronger, though I knew most of it was an act. Still, I didn't relish the prospect of suturing his wound. God only knows what kind of mess I'd make; he was probably better off the way he was.

We got out the map and plotted the day's route. We had somewhere around fifteen miles left and estimated we could get to the coast by nightfall. We had moved onto higher ground, through mountains with an elevation of 1,447 meters, not quite a mile in the air. The mountains north of us reached elevations of 1,995 meters, well over a mile high. The mountains were wooded, with heavy scrub brush scattered among outcrops of boulders. The trail we followed was a virtual wind tunnel, with cold air whipping into our faces.

During the night I came up with a better way to use the Browning. I secured a cord from my right flight glove to the stock of the rifle, which was slung over my arm. I carried the BAR in front of me in a cradle position. Should I have to fire the weapon, all I had to do was slip my hand out of the glove, put my finger on the trigger, and squeeze. I figured this would save valuable seconds in firing.

We stumbled upright, hid the evidence of our stay among the boulders, and edged our way down to the trail. Just prior to dawn, very stiffly, we started off toward the coast. Jim was often confused and dizzy, complaining of occasional blurred vision that slowed our progress. I gave the emergency kit to Tom, but it was too much for him to carry; his shoulder hurt more than he wanted to let on, so Jim carried it, slowing us down even more.

As we walked, I practiced the act of slipping my hand out of the glove and putting my finger on the trigger. I got the maneuver down to less than two seconds.

About an hour down the narrow mountain trail, we heard

boisterous voices coming from in front of us. Leaping off the trail, we took cover in the thick, leafless scrub brush. Jim buried his face in the sleeve of his flight suit to muffle any cough, and I aimed the Browning at the trail. I had no idea when Capeman had stashed a bayonet inside his flight jacket, but out it came, and he held it tightly in his good hand.

A squad of a dozen Chinese soldiers came into view, walking from the direction of the coast, totally unaware of our presence. They were laughing, pushing, and joking with one another and passed within a few dozen yards of us. They were so confident, or perhaps so young and inexperienced, that they violated all noise discipline rules.

When they were gone, I dropped my head onto my own sleeve but recoiled instantly. Looking down, I saw frozen blood and brain fragments the length of my flight suit. Suppressing a desire to vomit, I tried to wipe off the particles, which extended from my neck to my knees, but they clung fast. Wiping more furiously, I lost control and started to beat at my clothing.

Capeman put a calming hand on me. "Let it go." He smiled faintly, "We're not on our way to a dance; nobody cares how you look, Baker."

Stumbling to his feet, Tom lost his footing in the brush and fell to the ground. Clutching his shoulder, he let out a painful moan. He had landed on his wound and almost lost consciousness. Pearson was struggling beside him.

"I'm dizzy and I can't get up; help me," Jim said.

Once again, seeing someone in worse shape, Capeman revived. He got up and with his good arm lifted Jim. I took the emergency kit from Jim and carried it across my back. We made it back to the trail and struggled on; all the while I continued slipping my hand out of the glove to clutch the trigger.

I walked in front of Jim and Tom. The trail rose gradually through the mountains. At one point, it widened. On the right side was sheer rock and on the left a cliff that dropped into a deep ravine.

Suddenly, from just around a curve in front of us, we heard voices and laughter. We had no place to take cover; nor could we turn tail and flee. We stopped dead in the middle of the trail. I stood in front of Jim and Tom.

I slipped my hand out of the glove, flicked the rifle safety off, brought the rifle into a firing position, and placed my finger on the trigger.

Five Communist Chinese soldiers came around the bend. The red star stood out on their fur caps. They were dressed in quilted winter uniforms, walking abreast at a fast pace, their rifles slung over their shoulders. They acted like they were on a school jaunt with not a care in the world, and certainly with no worry about any war going on.

When they saw me, they panicked; the last thing they expected to encounter this far north in their own territory was U.S. airmen. They tried frantically to remove their rifles from across their bodies. As they struggled, I took aim at the first soldier to my left; he was no more than fifty feet away.

Without another thought, my response completely rote, I squeezed hard on the trigger and the Browning erupted in an automatic burst from a full magazine.

As tracer rounds poured from the rifle, I raked the five men from left to right, back to the left and again to the right. Clothing and body pieces flew as the thirty-caliber rounds ripped through their bodies.

All five went down.

With the magazine empty, I stood stunned, unable to move; my finger continued to squeeze the trigger.

In all the movies I had watched, men who were shot fell and lay motionless, mercifully dead. But not now. An image of my father killing a chicken for Sunday dinner sprang to mind. After he chopped off the chicken's head, its body jumped and flopped around for a full minute, blood spurting from its severed neck.

The men before me reminded me of those chickens, thrashing and convulsing wildly, hands flaying in the air and struggling to their faces as if to push in air.

I walked over to the dying soldiers and stared down. They were so young, teenagers, perhaps no more than seventeen. Within a few minutes everyone stopped struggling except for the last soldier to my right; he was trying to sit up.

I was drawn to him and knelt beside him. He looked at me with pleading eyes, gasping for breath. I cradled his head in my hands and strained to hear him speak.

"Yen lean ne," he said, and then repeated it over and over. As I held him in my arms, he lost consciousness. Finally he convulsed for a final time and stopped breathing. I lowered him down gently.

After returning from the mission I learned that "Yen lean ne" simply meant "I forgive you." It is the last release from life of the dying Buddhist, forgiving those who have wronged him.

Staring down on those dead youths, I was overcome with remorse. The dead coalesced at my feet—Dan, Ted, Chou, all the others. Our own tragedy replicated, lay shattered, bloody, and motionless before me.

Then a powerful hand gripped my shoulder. Capeman stared at the dead soldier, then at me. I looked into his eyes but had no words. He had nothing to say, either. Then Jim joined us and looked down upon the dead.

"Mother of God," he whispered.

The three of us stood motionless over the dead. What had we become? We were ghouls standing over boys we had killed, sons of someone's mother.

I couldn't stand it. The horror of it broke in me and I began to sob. Then I bent double and started to heave. I had killed five men—boys, and I couldn't bear it. A minute ago they were alive, and now they were nothing.

Capeman let me go on until I began to choke, then he pulled me up. "We have to go. They could have heard that Browning for miles." It was a slight admonishment, but enough to bring me back to reality.

"I never killed anybody before," I said.

"They would have killed you," he answered simply. "And their buddies *will* kill us unless we get out of here."

Jim, seemingly in shock, turned away to head on down the road, but Capeman stopped him. "Help us," he said, bending down to strip off a quilt jacket from one of the soldiers. "Get one for yourselves," he directed us.

I couldn't bring myself to touch any of the soldiers, so Capeman removed a jacket for each of us. Then he grabbed three rifles and handed them to us; their magazines were full, and I hadn't realized that without these rifles we would be defenseless, because the Browning automatic was out of ammunition.

I tossed the empty rifle into the ravine.

Finally, Tom directed us to push their bodies off the trail. He couldn't do it himself, so I had to. I struggled to roll them to the ravine's edge, then pushed hard. I watched each body tumble into oblivion, the eternity to which I had sent them.

I watched for a long moment, until Capeman helped me put on the bloody quilt jacket, pulled me away, and we started once again along the trail through the mountains. In addition to providing added warmth, the quilted jackets would help to conceal our identities.

Though we were better armed than before, the added weight of the rifles and ammunition slowed us further. Jim could now barely stumble forward, and even Capeman started to slump with the rifle over his good shoulder. I took both rifles from them and tried to carry all three, but I, too, was exhausted.

"We gotta stop," I said. "I can't go on."

I couldn't help them and continue to carry the rifles, so I chucked the rifles into brush alongside the trail and continued to carry the emergency kit. They would have provided little defense, as both Jim and Tom were unable to use them, and one semiautomatic rifle against even a small patrol would have been suicide.

We found another small ravine and edged down its gradual slope to take cover. Capeman dug into his flight suit and handed me the chocolate bar and can of banana bread.

"I'll throw up if I eat anything," I said.

Tom unwrapped the bar, broke it in half, and handed a piece to Jim, then he took a bite out of his piece and thrust it at me. "Eat," he ordered.

I nibbled obediently, then realized how famished I was and gobbled the rest.

"Feel better?" he asked when it was gone.

I did but I didn't want to admit it. "No."

He opened the can and divided it into thirds. We devoured the bread without a word, shoving it into our mouths like animals, a small desperate remnant cut off from the pack, worn and beaten, exposed and isolated in an alien wilderness.

Jim didn't object; his nausea had passed.

"It ain't like the movies, is it?" Tom said, breaking the silence.

I looked at us, huddled close, wrapped in bloody enemy jackets, an empty tin of banana bread on the ground. It wasn't like the movies at all, nothing like what I had seen as a boy. Suddenly I was carried back; I saw that boy and the darkened theater where he had plunked down a treasured dime to be transported into another world.

"You know what the biggest shock was to me as a kid?" I asked.

"When you found out there wasn't a Santa Claus," Capeman offered.

"There isn't?" Jim said in mock surprise, revived by the chocolate and bread.

Capeman grinned. "Okay, Baker, I give up, what was your biggest shock—finding out that you're put together different than girls? That happens to every boy who reaches puberty!"

"Nope! T'weren't that. Truth is, cowboy movies were the biggest shock of my life. Going to those Saturday matinees; you know, Roy Rogers and Gene Autry and Hopalong Cassidy, with Flash Gordon serials. The bad guys would get killed, shot off their horses, or in a gunfight. I really believed it until it occurred to me that the same bad guys were getting killed over and over. I must have watched fifty movies before I realized I'd seen the same guy get killed last Saturday. I finally figured out they really weren't dead. It was just make-believe."

"And how old were you?"

I ignored him. "But that wasn't the real shock. The real shock was when I discovered I *wanted* it to be real; I wanted them dead. I felt cheated."

"So you joined the army."

"No. I thought there was something wrong with me for wanting them dead."

I reached down and picked up the empty can. The afternoon was gray and dismal, capturing just how I felt. "But now I don't want it to be real. I don't want them to be dead." I bowed my head. "I don't even want those guys back there to be dead." I looked up at Tom. "I don't like killing."

Capeman nodded. "Good. You shouldn't."

"You don't like it, either?"

He shook his head. "Mike, no one should like it. We do it, but we're not supposed to enjoy it."

"That's called sadism," Pearson said.

"It's called sick," Capeman said.

"What about Moody? You don't think he liked killing?"

Capeman was emphatic. "No. Ted was like Reed. You didn't get to know Lynch, but he was a lot like Moody; he acted tough, and he was tough. Mean. You definitely did not want to fuck with him. But being tough and doing your job is not the same as *enjoying* killing." He gestured behind him, far away down the road where the soldiers had died. "No one could like that. Those were kids doing what they were told to do. They died because they were stupid—talking and making noise and not paying attention. They were probably talking about girls or their families, or bitching about their officers, just like we do."

Capeman looked somber. "It's terrible that those men died, but you *had* to kill them. If you didn't, they would have killed you."

Pearson rose on wobbly legs; he'd heard enough and knew we had to get moving.

As Tom rose even more slowly, his teeth bit into his lower lip, and I realized he had fooled me again. Engaging me in conversation had distracted us completely; he was hurting badly, trying to rest longer without bringing attention to himself. I wanted to let on that I knew what he was doing but thought better of it; I didn't want to take that away from him. Besides, he needed all the confidence he could muster.

The rest of the afternoon was a grim, grinding struggle. By late afternoon Jim's cough had grown steadily worse, and with it came more discomfort from his pneumonia. More troublesome was his problem with balance and trying to remain alert; he should have been recovering from his concussion by now, but his head seemed to be bothering him more than ever. Tom and I began to worry that he might have suffered serious brain injury. By early evening, he had stopped talking and barely responded to our prodding. He was concentrating all his stamina on putting one foot in front of the other.

Capeman worried me even more. I knew the ferocious power he possessed, but by the end of the day it was failing. Each step looked like torture for him. Frost had formed on his beard and eyebrows, and he lacked the strength even to wipe his face. I kept urging him to rest, but he steadfastly refused; he must have known that if he stopped, he wouldn't be able to get up again, so he forced himself to trudge on.

I was exhausted from the weight of the emergency kit, but I felt guilty even thinking about my difficulties; Jim and Tom were so much worse off than I. I wasn't hurt; the least I could do was carry the kit without complaint. Nevertheless, if we had encountered another patrol, I doubted that we could get off the road, and if we did, I knew we could not have gotten back on.

Curiously, I did not think about Nell and Lanny as I struggled on; I thought only of Jim and Tom. It was then that I began to understand the mystique of combat—that what mattered most was the men with you, that a man actually would throw himself on a grenade for his buddies, risk his life and safety for others. Something rises from within, bigger than self, more important than life. It is *others*. It isn't a concept—country or religion, flag or God—but simply one another.

At one point, as dusk descended, Tom tripped and fell to the ground. I agonized to see him struggle to stand. He looked like a gored bull on his knees straining desperately to rise. Just as I went up to him, not wanting to because of his pride, he got to his feet and stumbled on. Then, just when I felt we couldn't go any farther, we rounded a bend in the road and Tom stopped in his tracks. His eyes lit up with relief.

While I helped Tom and Jim plant one foot in front of the other, Tom pointed ahead, and there, less than a mile away, was the sea.

Chapter Seventeen

A Night in Hell

That sea was the most beautiful sight I had ever beheld, but Jim couldn't see it. When we pointed to the coast he merely shook his head.

"Just get me there," he said.

The sea with its prospect of rescue jolted Tom and me. I couldn't believe we had trekked thirty miles and were almost there.

But right away Tom saw danger. Yongyon, a small fishing village connected by a road that followed Moktong Bay flats to the mainland, lay directly in front of us. We had to make a decision whether to go through Yongyon or walk around.

We took cover in the brush to discuss what to do.

A very weak Pearson had no opinion. "Just get me there," he repeated.

I thought it best to move around the village, but Capeman thought we should risk going through. "It's cold, it's getting dark; who's going to be outside to see us? Their hooches don't even have windows." He pointed to smoke curling out of chimneys. "They're all inside for the night. Even if there are guards, they're holed up. They don't like the cold any better than we do. I say we take our chances and walk through the village."

But I still worried. "What if someone comes out and sees us?"

"There can't be more than a hundred people in the village. What are they going to do? They don't have telephones; who could they call anyway? Even if they have a radio and managed to contact someone, we'll be long gone before anyone shows up. We should risk it; it'll save us over an hour."

I realized Tom was right as usual. Moreover, going off the trail to stumble around in darkness would be dangerous, as well as probably beyond our endurance. I nodded agreement. "Let's go for it."

We got to our feet and started toward the village. Please God, I prayed, don't let anyone come out. Let us make it all the way.

As we passed through the village it was eerily quiet, and no one seemed to see us.

Relieved, we picked up the pace and headed toward the coast on the road that led from the village. I was half-dragging both Jim and Tom, who were hanging on to my arms. I had no idea where my strength was coming from, but I felt stronger than I had in hours.

When we got to the coast, we turned onto a cliff trail and headed north along a bluff that overlooked the sea, some four hundred feet below. We couldn't risk observation by remaining where we were, so we looked for cover where we could camp for the night and signal the ship. I left Jim with Tom to scout for a place by the sea.

About a half mile from the trail I located a steep slope that led to a promontory. Below it was a long, narrow, rocky shelf running parallel to the sea.

When I brought Jim and Tom to the spot, Capeman said it was perfect. "We can flash the ship from out there and no one on shore will be able to see the signal." The hard part was getting onto the dangerous shelf, a drop of about four feet, without tumbling into the sea. Pearson couldn't make it by himself, so I had to lower him to Tom, who gingerly guided him onto the shelf. If he had weighed much more, I couldn't have managed.

We carefully edged along the shelf until we reached a wide ledge that jutted out over the sea. At the far end of the ledge we found a place that sheltered us from the wind whipping off the land, but it was intensely cold. Dropping in complete exhaustion, we rested for thirty minutes. I removed the emergency kit from my back. It was completely dark, shortly after 2100.

Reluctant to test the signal, almost afraid to attempt our last step toward rescue, not wanting our hopes dashed yet, we broke out the last of the provisions.

"It's going to be a long night," Capeman said, dividing the last candy bar and can of bread into thirds.

Jim was almost too weak to eat and I didn't want anything, but Capeman made us eat. "I'm going to feed you like a baby if you don't eat," he said to Jim, then to me, "You, I'll just cram it down your throat."

I ate what he gave me. I was too tired to resist; besides, I knew I needed energy to stay awake all night.

Though we had the quilt jackets over our flight suits and jackets, and were out of the wind, we were still freezing. Jim's cough had become much worse, his breathing more strained, and now I had developed a cough, too.

"What do you think about Jim?" I asked Capeman, as though Pearson wasn't even there, and for all intents and purposes, he wasn't; he was braced against the cliff wall, oblivious to us.

"Should we let him sleep?"

Tom studied Jim's features a moment, then nodded. "I don't think it makes any difference now. Rest would probably be the best thing; he's going to pass out in any case."

We eased Pearson onto the ground and faced him away from the sea. "Go to sleep," Tom ordered, but Jim didn't hear him; he was already out.

"If they don't rescue us tonight, he'll die," I said.

Tom was confident. “They’ll rescue us. They’re Navy.”

“Royal Navy,” I said.

“Navy is Navy. If this was an Air Force rescue, I’d jump off the cliff right now.” Then he shook his head, angry with himself, and said with immense sadness, “That’s wrong, Robbins would have saved us. He and Puller were all right.” He looked at me to make sure I understood. “We were just hassling them.”

“I know, Tom. They knew it, too.”

“Damn,” he said bitterly. “Damn, damn, damn!”

I put my hand on him; he was at the end of his endurance, too. “Get some sleep; I’ll take first watch.”

He ran his sleeve across his eyes. “We better check the signal light first.”

I removed the high-powered light from the emergency kit, a tripod-mounted, long collapsible tube capable of emitting a beam observable from five to eight miles, and placed it between us, aiming the lens toward the sea. Its design prevented the light from being seen from along the shoreline.

We both held our breath when I switched it on, and almost gasped when a bright light burst from the tube. “Thank God,” Capeman murmured.

Now all we needed was for the ship to be in position, someone to see the signal, and a helicopter to get to us before the Chinese found us or we froze. The odds were so overwhelmingly against us that I must have been punch-drunk from exhaustion, because I suddenly laughed.

“What?” Tom asked.

“I was calculating the odds of a chopper getting to us before the Chinese do.”

“Better than the odds of us having gotten this far,” he answered. “I thought we were finished yesterday when they blew up the convoy, then again when I got hit, and about six times after that. Finally, when I saw that five-man patrol and you standing there with your rifle facing them, I just hoped I could get the capsule out of my boot in time."

"Thanks."

He grinned. "You were great. I owe you. Jim and I are here only because of you."

"Bullshit. If Jim hadn't brought that map, we would probably have ended up in Moscow. And if you . . . if you hadn't been you, we wouldn't be here, Tom. You kept me going."

"Let's not get sentimental, princess," he grumped, in character to the end.

I laughed. "So how's your shoulder?"

He didn't say anything for a moment, then he admitted what I already knew. "In a couple more hours, I'm going to need that morphine."

For him to admit that, his pain had to be excruciating.

Within an hour Tom's words came more slowly, labored. "It's been oozing all day; I think it's infected. I'm damn weak. I didn't tell you because I didn't want you pulling your Red Cross act again."

"Maybe I should look at it."

It was as if Tom forced himself to keep talking. "And do what?" He shook his head. "Either I'm going to make it or I'm not. You looking at my shoulder won't make any difference. If the ship sees our signal and the chopper gets here, Pearson and I have a chance. If it doesn't, we're taking that cyanide and you're taking off to see if you can make it on your own."

"I am *not* going to leave you."

"Start thinking about it, Baker." He was serious. "Pearson won't last another twenty-four hours; he's barely conscious now. Pretty soon he won't even be able to take the capsule. You're going to have to give it to him. Or kill him. And I can't go much longer, either. That wound has been oozing blood for thirty-six hours. I've lost a lot of blood. I probably got gangrene. The minute I start to slip out of my mind, I'm taking that capsule. I mean it, I'm not going to wait until I get delirious and don't know what I'm doing. I'll put my life in your hands, but I won't put my death in them. So start thinking about how you're going to get out of here by yourself. You owe it to us, Baker."

"The chopper will get here," I said confidently. "It's Navy."

He groaned and lay back on the ground. "Yeah." He plainly didn't believe it.

As soon as he relaxed, I saw a transformation pass over him like a soothing hand. It was as though he had willed himself to talk, as though all force in him had been concentrated on getting this far, but now his energy had seeped away; he didn't even snore. He looked pale and lifeless, and I sensed he was at death's door.

Turning to the dark sea, I hit the oversize key on the signal light and it started to flash—dot dot dot—dash dash dash—dot dot dot: SOS.

I looked at my watch; it was 2200 hours.

God, it was the most lonely, forlorn place, a ledge overlooking the sea, staring into emptiness, with Pearson and Capeman expiring beside me.

Was anyone out there? A warship was supposed to be.

We were told that the Royal Navy patrolled from Ongjin Bay north to the Taedong Estuary. An assigned warship was scheduled to patrol along the coast on watch for our distress signal, which could come from one of six designated rescue points. The main rescue point was near Hosa-Dong to the north, but the ship was to sweep up and down the coast through the night, checking each rescue point. Though the three of us might have missed the designated rescue point, we were close enough that sailors on lookout could see our signal light and call in a rescue chopper, unless the mission had been scrubbed—and the chances of that were good. Who knew that any of us had survived?

Yet the ship could be out there. It had an assigned patrol station near the Taedong River. This was near major North Korean shipping lanes and ports along the Yellow Sea. To search for us, the Royal Navy ship had to leave her assigned station and travel south along the mainland to the southernmost rescue point near Ongjin Bay, then reverse her direction, steam north, returning to her designated patrol station. This round-trip took time—up to seven hours, depending upon the ship's speed. This would mean that the ship would likely pass our rescue point only twice during the night, but when? Waiting for that ship, I hunched forlornly over the signal light.

I felt like I was on the last outpost on Earth. Over and over I keyed the signal, sending a little beam into immense emptiness.

Blackness was the answer.

Chapter Eighteen
The Ledge

That night I was the smallest creature in the world, caught up in something so big—and all I could do was tap out a puny message—help me; save me. I don't recall being angry, just lost and forlorn. I was convinced that I would never see Nell and Lanny again; no one would know what had happened to me; I would simply disappear.

I thought about Nell and Lanny, my parents, my brothers and sisters, everything I had done—so little, all over and soon forgotten.

The dead—Moody, Kingsley, all the others, Robbins, Puller, Lynch, Chou, Liu—rushed at me all night, their ghosts flailing in the dark, struggling for recognition, and I saw the blood and horror again and again. I knew I shouldn't think of them; Capeman was right, there was nothing I could do, but I kept seeing Moody and Kingsley. I remembered jokes and laughter, Kingsley's terrible gas, Moody playing cards, and then their final minutes: Moody drowning in his own blood, and Kingsley at the moment of impact when the bullet exploded through his skull, spraying brain tissue in every direction. I couldn't bear it that their bodies would never be recovered.

Just as awful in memory were those soldiers I had killed only hours ago, now lying at the base of the ravine, and that young soldier crying out in my arms. I was wearing his jacket; his blood was mixed with that of Moody's and Kingsley's.

Dot dot dot—dash dash dash—dot dot dot.

I looked over at Tom and Jim, but I couldn't tell if they were breathing until I leaned over them and felt their breath. I didn't know how much longer I could stay awake, but I couldn't wake Tom. He desperately needed rest, and even if I woke him, I knew he couldn't remain conscious very long.

I tried every way imaginable to remain alert as I keyed the signal light throughout the night—I talked aloud, whistled, pounded on my shoulders, took off my cap and loosened my jacket to let cold air revive me, stood up, shifted positions, and repeated over and over that it was up to me to save Jim and Tom, that I had to stay awake to redeem the others, that if I fell asleep there would be no chance for rescue and the story of Broken Reed would die with me.

Every time I started to doze off I got mad at myself; I called myself names—coward! quitter!—and said I was letting everyone down, that Capeman, Moody, Kingsley, and the others wouldn't quit. They would never give up. Neither could I.

But it wasn't tiredness that finally overcame me, it was despair. No one was out there; it was all in vain—our torturous thirty-mile trip, the pain, everything we had endured. We were going to die like the others.

Our bodies would not be recovered; Nell would never know what had happened to me; my son would never know his father.

Did the others have wives and children? Surely some of them did. What about those young Chinese soldiers? They had parents, girls who loved them, lives they were going back to until I took their lives away. It was unspeakably sad, and I felt terrible remorse.

I would never know if what we had done had mattered. None of us would.

Less than an hour of darkness remained. I had been signaling for nearly eight hours. I was numb and sick. How could I wake Tom and Jim and tell them there had been no response, that we had been abandoned? That they were to die?

We couldn't stay on the ledge during daylight; we were totally exposed and could be seen by a patrol from up along the cliff trail. But neither Tom nor Jim could make it back up the slope. They would both die on this ledge. But how? What if Jim didn't wake up? What if he couldn't take the cyanide? That's what really frightened me. I couldn't leave him to freeze. I couldn't abandon him. But I couldn't kill him.

I grew sick thinking about the imminent daylight. I had never dreaded a dawn like this.

Worst of all was the thought of waking Tom. He would know that we were not going to be rescued, and I feared what he would do.

He would kill Jim. It would be a mercy killing. I couldn't let him do it, but I knew I wouldn't be able to stop him; I knew I shouldn't.

Then he would kill himself. He would do it so I wouldn't have to kill him. He would do it to spare me—it would be his final sacrifice.

All along I had wondered if I could swallow the capsule, if I would be brave enough to take it, but I had no doubt about Capeman. He would do it when I wasn't looking and there was no way I could stop him.

I stared into the darkness until my eyes started to play tricks on me. I saw lights that couldn't be there.

I closed my eyes, but when I opened them, far in the distance I saw a faint flashing light. It went away. I closed my eyes, yet when I opened them, there was the light again. It was coming from far out at sea, somewhere, I calculated, between Paengnyong Island and the North Korean mainland. I wasn't hallucinating; it was the signal light.

I shook Tom. He groaned.

"I see it," I yelled. "It's the light. Wake up."

While he struggled up, I flashed the signal, and in seconds a signal came.

"Jesus Christ," he said, rubbing his eyes in disbelief. "I see it, too."

Straining, we read the international Morse code signal together, WE . . . SEE . . . YOU. STAY . . . PUT. WE . . . SEE . . . YOU. STAY . . . PUT.

I immediately flashed back, ROGER. WILCO. OBR.

In another instant, the message was acknowledged.

As worn and exhausted as Tom and I were, we could barely contain ourselves.

"They're there," I kept repeating.

Re-aiming the signal light directly to where the ship appeared to be, I flipped a switch that sent out a continual flashing light to provide a beacon for a rescue helicopter.

Capeman raised Jim in his arms. "Wake up," he urged. "They're coming for us," he said. "The chopper is coming. We're going to be all right." Jim failed to respond.

I'm not sure Jim understood, but it didn't make any difference now. The only thing that mattered was for the rescue chopper to get to us before we were discovered. Dawn was breaking, and soon we could be seen by anyone along the trail. Besides, in daylight, anyone on shore could see a chopper approaching from the sea, or see the ship itself. We knew it would be a race now between the chopper and any unit still searching for us. All a patrol had to do was follow the flight of the chopper toward the ledge.

The wait was agonizing. The sun seemed to burst from the

horizon. Minutes passed, then thirty minutes. We could see the ship clearly. So could anyone else from shore.

Finally, far out at sea, we saw a speck on the horizon moving toward the warship. It passed directly over the ship's mast and dropped so low that it was flying only a few feet over the white-caps, heading directly toward us.

Then we could hear the chopper blades and saw the Sikorsky HS-1 looming larger.

A moment later, my heart froze. From another direction, I heard enemy soldiers shouting from a far distance to the east along the cliff trail. They had seen the ship and must have been following the chopper's flight.

It couldn't end like this, I thought, not this close to rescue.

The chopper and the soldiers both closed in on us.

The chopper must have been at full throttle, but then at the last moment it pulled up, barely missing the ledge. The noise was deafening, but suddenly bursting right above us was the chopper, on its side the wonderful word RESCUE.

Then everything was a blur. Hovering only a few feet over us, the chopper side door opened and two crewmen jumped out. They grabbed Pearson and literally threw him inside, then they shoved Capeman in, and, before I had a chance to climb on, they boosted me up and scrambled in afterward.

From the floor of the chopper I could see enemy soldiers racing down the trail about five hundred yards away; then I saw muzzle flashes.

The chopper immediately pulled away, banked to the port side, dropped swiftly toward the water, and headed to sea, gaining speed rapidly.

The crewmen worked on Jim for a moment. Their faces were grim, and then they turned to Capeman, lying on the floor, crumpled on his wounded shoulder. They rolled him over, opened his jacket, and unzipped his flight suit. There was a sea of blood. "Holy God," one of them mouthed.

Then they came to me. I wanted to tell them I was all right, but there were no words. They looked at the frozen blood and brain tissue on my flight suit, and the expressions on their faces said it all. One shook his head and went back to Pearson.

No, I wanted to cry out. I'm fine.

Chapter Nineteen

Safe at Last

I had a sensation of movement, but no recollection of anything until the chopper started to descend over land. I sat up and saw ambulances on an airstrip. For a moment I couldn't place where I was or what had happened, and then it rushed back to me. We had gotten out; we were safe. But then I looked around to the horror beside me.

Tom Capeman and Jim Pearson lay motionless on the deck of the chopper. Crewmen knelt above them. They looked at me curiously, as if they couldn't understand why I was still alive, then returned their attention to Tom and Jim.

Capeman was deathly pale except for his blue lips, and Pearson had stopped coughing; his eyes were open but sightless. I felt so drained that I lay back and just waited for whatever would happen.

The chopper landed gently, and we were taken off in stretchers. I saw the sign of the airfield—Kempo. We were near Seoul, South Korea.

As we waited to be loaded onto ambulances, a crewman called the chopper pilot over. He pointed to three bullet holes in the fuselage and said, "A few feet higher and they would have ripped through the control cables. A few feet lower and they would have gone through the compartment."

The pilot, reacting just as Robbins would have, shrugged nonchalantly. "Lousy shooting. Let's go get a beer."

I gestured to thank him, but he merely saluted me with two fingers and walked off—all in a day's work; now it was time to hit the officers' club.

A short while later at the field hospital, I got off my stretcher and walked over to Pearson and Capeman. I stared down at them, but no words came; they looked close to death. I reached out to touch their hands, then they were loaded into separate ambulances.

I had the awful feeling that I would never see them again.

"So what happened?" a corpsman asked as he led me to the third ambulance.

I tried to think of something flippant, some smart-ass pilot remark, but couldn't find any words.

"Where'd you guys get shot up?" he persisted.

I gestured behind me, somewhere out there, beyond understanding.

In the hospital, the doctor, an Army major, tried to be upbeat. "The first report we got on you was that you had a brain injury." He pointed to my flight suit. "That's brain tissue, but not yours. And if all that blood had been yours, you'd be in the morgue. Want to tell me about it?"

I shook my head. "I can't."

The major nodded. "Can't or won't?"

"Can't, sir."

His distaste slipped through. "Ah, one of those kinds of missions."

One of those kinds of missions that killed people, he seemed to be saying. One of those missions that struck at the core of his profession. How could he heal people when they kept getting wounded and killed?

"Well, let's take a look, airman. Get out of that flight suit and let me see the damage."

How about opening my head and taking a look there, I wanted to say, but instead went behind the screen he pointed to and stripped. I started to unlace my boots when I remembered the capsule. I pulled the knotted cord and let the tube drop into the palm of my hand. I put it on the changing table, took off my boots, and dropped them on my heap of clothes. Putting on a hospital gown, the first clean item I'd worn since the mission began, I dropped the capsule into a pocket and went back to the doctor.

He flipped open a chart. "Sergeant Mike Baker. Correct?"

How had he known that? I wondered. Who could have told him? Capeman and Pearson were in no condition to talk, and I hadn't told anybody who I was. Then I remembered my dog tags; they must have gotten the name from that, but dog togs revealed only my name, serial number, blood type, and religious preference; it didn't reveal rank. Where did he get that?

"Yes sir, Sergeant Mike Baker," I answered.

"Some colonel called the hospital and said three men would be coming in; he gave us your names and ranks."

It was Brown, of course. The chopper crew must have called in our names, and he had supplied our ranks.

The doctor gave me a cursory look, then pointed to another room. "You'll feel a lot better after you take a shower." He smiled. "You'll look better, too, and you'll certainly smell better. Take your time in there."

He left the room, and I hustled as fast as I could into the shower; hot water had never felt so good. I washed off the blood and stink, but the grief and pain remained.

When I returned, I fell asleep on the examination table waiting for the doctor. He was frowning when I woke; then he tried to look chipper.

"What about the other two men?" I asked. "How are they?"

He checked a note on his chart. "Captain Jim Pearson has pneumonia and is running a 104-degree temperature. He has a severe head injury, with possibly extradural hemorrhaging."

I had no idea what that was. "How bad is that?"

"They're prepping him for surgery; we have to relieve the pressure on his brain, but it's going to be tricky because of his pneumonia and high fever—not an ideal candidate for surgery."

"But he'll make it?"

The doctor gave one of those patented responses they must teach in med school. "We're doing everything we can. He's in excellent hands."

"What about Tom?"

"Sergeant Capeman?" Then a thought occurred to him. "Pearson is an Air Force officer. Capeman isn't in the Air Force; I don't care what's on his dog tags. And that man is definitely not a sergeant, no matter what that colonel said. He's too old and in much too good a shape. You're not in the Air Force, either, and I don't believe you're a sergeant. I've been around too long; I've seen way too many men pass through here."

He mulled it over a moment, looked at me suspiciously but didn't say anything, and then he went back to his chart. "Your friend Capeman has lost a dangerous amount of blood. He also has an infection that has entered his bloodstream. That is not good. He's also running a high fever."

I waited for another patented prognosis, but the doctor didn't add anything more, and I was too worried to ask.

"So let's look at you, Mr. Baker," he said, dropping any reference to rank. He wasn't about to go along with pretense; this was a medical problem involving lives, nothing else to him.

In the middle of the exam, after listening to my chest with a stethoscope, he stopped. "I don't like that cough. How long have you had it?"

When I hesitated, not wanting to tell him anything, he got annoyed and authoritative. "Look, Baker, I can't treat you if I don't know what's wrong with you. I don't give a damn about your mission, but I do care about your life. How long have you had that cough?"

"Maybe two days," I said meekly.

He called a corpsman and told him to take me for a chest X-ray. Then he pointed to my bandaged leg and ordered that X-rayed, also. He told the corpsman to put me on a stretcher and not let me off it, then he snapped the chart shut and headed out of the room. "I'll finish when you come back."

I must have slept while waiting at X-ray and for a good long time afterward, because when the doctor returned, he had the film from radiology.

"There's a small spot on your lung, probably frostbite from breathing subzero air. We're going to treat it with antibiotics. In the meantime, stay out of the cold air. I recommend Hawaii. Where are you from?"

"Texas, sir."

"That'll work, too." He held up the other set of X-rays. "Nothing broken and no shrapnel. So let me see what happened."

He unwrapped the bandages, still wet and soggy from the shower, discolored by blood. He examined the wound, nodded approvingly at the healing process, then asked what had caused a hole that size and so shallow. I told him I thought it was a ricochet round that was nearly spent by the time it went through my flight suit.

"Not a bad job of cleaning and dressing the wound," the doctor said. "There's no infection, and it won't require stitches. So who treated it? Don't tell me you had an Air Force surgeon on this secret mission along with everyone else?"

"No, sir."

"I didn't think so. Doctors have much better sense than to . . .

do whatever it was you were doing. So what else should I be looking for that might be wrong with you? Venereal diseases?"

I laughed. He had terrific bedside manner, coarse and humorous, as many military doctors develop after treating troops.

"No, sir, I guess I'm fine."

He stared at me a long minute, then gestured to the screen where my clothes lay. "Brains, bone fragments, blood." Then he motioned beyond the door. "Your comrades." He shook his head. "No, Mr. Baker, you're not fine. I don't think you're going to be fine for a very long time."

He tapped my head and said gently, "I wish I could write you a prescription to make it go away. Or operate and take it out, but I can't."

I closed my eyes tightly because I felt tears welling.

He raised my chin. "You're going to need to let those tears drop, Mr. Baker. I know you don't want to talk about it now. I'm sure you believe you *can't* talk about it." He shook his head in disgust, a man probably on his way back to private practice once the war was over.

"Stupid fucking military," he said. "But do me a favor. Do *yourself* a favor. Talk to somebody about what happened."

He put his hand on my head as if in benediction, and left the room.

A corpsman came in and wheeled me to a ward of wounded soldiers, all in casts and bandages. I looked about for Tom and Jim, but of course they weren't there. I was given pajamas and food, then left alone. Lying in the bed, safe and clean, I finally had a chance to think and reflect. At night the ward was quiet, and I was alone with the images of horror.

I had survived, I was alive. I would see Nell and Lanny. I would go home. But those thoughts did not counteract the overwhelming loss and pain I felt. My survival seemed a cheat on the others. How could I rejoice when the others were dead? How could I ever be happy when they lay mangled and abandoned? I knew I should not feel guilty for surviving, but neither could I feel joy or hope in the face of their deaths.

Sometime in the middle of the night I woke up screaming. A nurse rushed in to comfort me and gave me another injection to make the dead disappear and let me sleep.

In the morning I was embarrassed and apologized to the men on the ward.

"*Everyone* wakes screaming. We all have nightmares," one of them said.

Of course, I realized. Why did I think I was special? Was my ordeal any worse than what others suffered? They had lost arms and legs, lost their buddies, too; they had seen men die beside them and witnessed awful carnage. Of course they had nightmares, and those memories would haunt them for the rest of their lives, too.

When I went to the mess hall for breakfast, I put on a hospital robe and dropped the cyanide capsule in a pocket; it was the only tangible evidence I had of the mission; I was never going to let it go.

In the mess hall, I searched faces to find Tom and Jim, but they were nowhere to be seen. As I was eating, a corpsman came up and said a colonel was waiting for me in a conference room.

It had to be George Brown, and when the orderly led me to the room, I knocked. I heard his voice boom, "Come in."

I opened the door and saw him bent over a table studying papers, just like the first time I met him.

"Art," he enthused, moving toward me. "So good to see you."

I stood in the doorway. He came over, shut the door, and grabbed me in a bear hug. "All things considered, you don't look too bad, Art." Then he pointed to a chair. "Let's talk. Or rather, you talk; I'll listen."

"First I want to know about Tom and Jim."

He shook his head. "I can't tell you anything, you know that."

"Did they make it? Are they alive? You can tell me that."

He was emphatic. "I can tell you nothing. Put them out of your mind."

"No! I want to know if they're all right."

He didn't say anything for a moment, then he shook his head again. "I told you at the beginning not to form attachments."

"But . . ."

"But nothing! I am not going to talk about them, or any of the others on the mission. I know you've been through hell, but this topic is off-limits." His face was stern, very much the senior officer addressing a subordinate.

I bowed my head in submission.

He offered me a roll from a plate on the table; the mess hall must have sent them in. I wasn't hungry, but he grabbed one and took a bite. I watched him eat it.

Everything was back to normal; I found his manner insulting, but he was sending me a message—it was over: everything *is* back to normal.

"All right," he said, brushing off his hands, ready for business. "Tell me what happened."

I spoke for an hour; he had no questions. I teared up while describing the massacre. He waited patiently until I recovered. At the end, he simply nodded. "I'll check with your doctor, but I don't see any reason for you to stay here. If he approves, you and I will return to Japan tomorrow. We'll go through a detailed debriefing at Camp Drake, then you're going home."

"Tomorrow?" I whispered.

He stood up. The meeting was over. "There's nothing left for you here. Get some rest; I'll see you in the morning."

That was it. Dumbfounded by this anticlimax, I returned to the ward. Later in the afternoon, the doctor came in.

"I'm supposed to close your chart; apparently they need you for another special mission," he said disdainfully. He studied me closely. "It's up to me, Mr. Baker," he said, again avoiding any rank. "Tell me what you want. If you don't want to go, I will *gladly* keep you here. There are all kinds of tests I could run. Quite frankly you *should* stay here for observation. However, it's apparent they don't want you to stay, and that makes me very uncomfortable. So I'm leaving it to you."

"No, sir. I'm ready to go."

He grunted, and I think repeated under his breath, "Stupid fucking military." He signed his name in a few places, flipped the chart closed, and said simply, "Good luck, Mr. Baker."

As he was leaving, I stopped him. "Can you tell me about the other two men?"

He stood in the doorway, the charts in his hand, and seemed to be debating. He ran his hands over the charts that held the fates of Capeman and Pearson. Finally, he took a deep breath. "I was told you would ask. I have been ordered not to tell you a thing."

Surely this man would not feel any compunction to obey such an order. He debated with himself a moment longer, then he shook his head. "Maybe there's some reason I don't understand. I'm just a doctor." His voice was bitter. "Maybe this really is some national-security thing. I'm sorry, I can't say anything."

With that he left, unhappily.

That night I was given a sedative, and the next thing I knew it was morning and an Army fatigue uniform was on the bedside table. I put it on and stuffed the capsule in a breast pocket.

The doctor was making rounds on the ward as I was about to leave. He glanced up and met my eyes, but when I started over to thank him for what he'd done, he turned away and busied himself with another patient; he had washed his hands of me.

When I walked out of the hospital with Brown, I turned back

for a last look. I was leaving Capeman and Pearson. I couldn't! I couldn't leave them like we had left all the others.

I had an overpowering desire to rush back in and find them. Were they alive? On the intensive care unit? Or in the morgue?

Brown put his hand on my shoulder, not in restraint, but to steady me. It was the moment of truth. I bowed my head. I realized I would never know what happened to Jim and Tom. I would have to leave them.

With a final glance at the hospital, I turned away.

A few hours later I was on an airplane with Colonel Brown on my way back to where the nightmare had begun.

Chapter Twenty

Debriefing

We didn't talk much on the flight from Korea to Japan, nor on the sedan drive from Tachikawa to Camp Drake.

When we pulled onto the base in midafternoon of an overcast, drizzly day, I could hardly believe that only two weeks had passed since we had driven through these gates; it seemed a lifetime ago. For the other men, it was.

The staging area building was padlocked. There were no guards; the security was gone; it looked deserted.

Brown opened the padlock and we entered the staging building where we had prepared for the mission. No one was there.

The place was cavernous, empty, and dark. Brown did not turn on the lights. The folding chairs remained in a circle. The silence thundered in my ears. In a flash I saw them all looking up as we entered. Bill Robbins was grinning, and Tyler's eyes observed every movement; Moody folded his arms, and Tom Capeman rose back on his chair's rear legs. Jim Pearson pointed a finger in greeting.

I turned away.

Then I started to cry.

Brown pretended not to notice. In a moment I caught myself, looked again at the circle of chairs, and saw only emptiness.

"Let's go into my office," Brown said. He made coffee and, while it percolated, he got out a tablet of paper and a pen.

"I'm sorry we have to do this, but I have to go over everything again, in a lot more detail this time. This is the official and final debriefing. You will never be asked anything again about Broken Reed, and of course you won't talk about it again until after it is declassified in 1998."

He poured us cups of coffee. "Sugar? No, I remember you take it black like I do."

He smoothed open a page in a standard military-issue tablet. "So, let's start where I last saw you; you were getting into the launch to take you to the submarine. That was the morning of January 10. Hmm. Ten days ago exactly."

He wrote the date on the page, lifted his pen, and looked at me expectantly. "You got on the launch and headed out to the submarine. Pick it up from there."

Except for an occasional refill of coffee, I spoke in a monotone, answering his questions until it began to grow dark. He prodded for more detail here and there, but for the most part he just listened to my recitation.

When I finished, Brown wrapped it up with a few last questions. "You didn't see the others die—those in the other half-track?"

"No. Just the two men, I think Lynch and Robbins, gunned down as they ran."

"Could the others have been captured?"

I looked him square in the eyes. "John Tyler was still in the burning half-track with the other two." I waited for some kind of response—that he had been designated to take out anyone who balked—but nothing registered. He merely nodded and made a note.

"Your half-track with the communications equipment: That was destroyed. You're positive."

"Yes, along with Dan Kingsley's body still inside the half-track."

Still he registered nothing. "You did not see what happened to the Nationalist Chinese soldiers? You can't be sure all were killed."

"No. I know that Sergeant Chou was dead and the driver of our half-track, too. I cannot verify what happened to the others, though I saw the Communists rake the vehicles with automatic fire and hit them with tank rounds. Bodies were scattered all over the road."

He made a note. "The enemy patrol on the cliff that shot at the chopper—could they have been following you from the time the convoy was destroyed?"

"I don't know. It's possible. But they also could have been a coastal defense unit."

"You're not sure if the Red Chinese knew there were survivors?"

"No, though they probably found blood trails leading away from the convoy. Capeman and I left a bloody trail."

He made a final note, then closed the tablet. The room was almost completely dark, but he did not turn on the light.

He sat back in his chair. "I believe we're done."

"May I ask a few questions?"

He relaxed for the first time; his expression was friendly, even compassionate. "Of course, but I may not answer."

I lowered my head. "I know the promise I made when I signed on. I know we were never supposed to know the names of the other men. I understand the security, but can't you tell me who they were?"

"I cannot. I would be disobeying an order of the president of the United States. I know you want to know about Capeman and Pearson. Believe me, I understand. I am not a heartless man, but I cannot tell you anything."

"Just this one little thing," I begged.

His eyes were unrelenting. "If I told you they were dead, you would feel awful. If I told you they were alive, you would want to find them."

He shook his head. "I can't let you do that."

"But . . ." I started.

"No buts! I will go through this just one more time, then I am ordering you to forget it forever. So help me God, if you violate this order, I will personally see that you spend the rest of your life in Leavenworth federal prison."

He held up a finger. "Number one, I told you at the beginning that you would not know the real names of the other men, nor would they know yours. I will give you two words for that decision—national security. If you had known the names of the men and were captured, those names could have been tortured out of you. That information could have been used by the North Koreans or the Chinese Communists."

He held up a second finger. "Number two, any attempt by you to locate or identify the men on the mission, no matter how well-intentioned or innocent, could breach national security and leak classified information."

He let that sink in, and then he took a deep breath and released it as a sigh. "You must let this all go. You must let *them* go. This didn't end the way we hoped, but there is nothing that can be done. It's over. You must accept that."

"I don't think I can."

His face was sorrowful. "No, I don't think you can, either, but it would be better for you if you did. You don't want to carry this for the rest of your life. As far as military history goes, this operation did not take place. Every record of vessels and flights, including your rescue, will be erased, all files destroyed. No one will ever divulge anything about Broken Reed. There are no documents indicating the mission took place. That has been done on the orders of the president. He does not want any record of having gone over the heads of his military, civilian authorities, Congress, or without consulting United Nations allies."

He held up the tablet. "This is the *only* existing record. It will be destroyed shortly, by me personally. Your hospital stay, even our names on all flight manifests, have already been permanently deleted." He pointed around the room. "No logistical records for the operation remain. There are no medical records that reflect anything about you or your teammates. Everything will disappear."

He put down the tablet and turned it over emphatically. "This operation did not take place."

He leaned forward. "Even if you tried, which I know you won't, you will never find any evidence about Broken Reed."

"What about the men who died? What are you going to tell their families?"

He stared at me blankly. "What men?"

He did not smile. "That will be the official answer as soon as we leave this room."

Then he went on more gently, "However, I'll tell you how their deaths will be handled. The CIA agents' deaths will not be connected in any way to the Korean War. They will be reported as missing or killed in the line of duty at some other geographical location. In addition, the dates of their deaths will be delayed and altered. The details, along with notification of their next of kin, are being handled by the agency."

"And the others?"

"Several will be reported missing in action and presumed dead, carefully omitting any tie to an intelligence mission. Others will be reported killed in training accidents under circumstances that will ensure that the recovery of their bodies is impossible. Again, the circumstances and dates will be altered to prevent any tie to a common mission in Korea."

"And the Nationalist Chinese soldiers? Lieutenant Lee, Sergeant Chou, and the others?"

"The Nationalist government will avoid any association with this mission. They are not about to indicate their involvement in an operation against Red China. That would be disastrous, not just to the men's families, but to Chiang Kai-shek himself. The Nationalist government will *never* release any information tying itself to Broken Reed."

"So the only person who knows is myself? And maybe Pearson and Capeman."

He nodded.

Suddenly I felt cold. I might be the last survivor of this mission, the only one with personal knowledge of Broken Reed. What if I talked? What if I accidentally said something, let it slip somehow? Did they trust me to keep my mouth shut for the rest of my life, or until 1998, forty-six years from now? Every effort had been made to cover up this mission. I was the last tie to it.

John Tyler, at least some of us thought, had been assigned to take us out in order to prevent capture and disclosure of Broken Reed. Had someone else been assigned to make sure I would never talk? My God, did I have to live with this fear for the rest of my life? Or was I being paranoid?

The thought must have been transparent to Brown, for, as he had done so often in the past, he read my mind.

"I'm sending you home for twenty days' leave. This should give you time to recover, time to put your thoughts in order. If you need more, we'll authorize additional emergency leave. You can check into a hospital. I understand the trauma you've been through, and I'm fully aware that you'll have trouble adjusting. We want you to get over this and we know it won't be an overnight process."

He was silent a moment, letting the darkness enfold us. "I have another reason to ensure that you recover from this. It's personal."

He dropped his superior-to-subordinate role; he no longer spoke in his official capacity. He became my mentor again, a father figure; a friend. I felt he was genuine, and that his words were offered in understanding and friendship.

He spoke with great intensity. "I don't want this mission forgotten. I don't want these men to die unheralded. I *want* you to tell the story of Broken Reed someday. The men who died deserve to have their story told."

"After it's declassified."

"Yes. I probably won't be alive in 1998. My family is not long-lived. Forty-six more years? I won't count on it. You however, will not be that old. I know it seems a long time, but you won't even be seventy. You'll be surprised how time passes the older you get; it just starts to fly by."

To me it seemed like forever.

"I want you to tell people what went on. I want you to promise me that you'll tell the story someday."

That's my guarantee not to be killed? I thought. He's going to ensure my safety so that some fifty years hence I'll tell what happened? Who would care?

But, of course, I promised.

"Excellent," he said, standing up. He looked at his watch. It was after 1800. He placed a quick call, then said for me to follow him.

We walked through the great empty room to the lockers where we had stowed our gear before leaving ten days ago. I opened mine, and there was the Class A uniform I had worn when I left Germany, a shaving kit, and a small traveling bag with personal items.

"One final thing," Brown held out his hand. "I need the dog tags you're wearing; it's the last evidence of the mission."

So he doesn't know about the capsule, I thought. I pulled the tags over my head and handed them to him.

He clutched them in his palm. "That's the end of Sergeant Michael Baker." He pointed to my personal belongings. "Welcome back, Lieutenant Boyd, here's your tags."

He shook my hand. "I know this is meager reward, but congratulations on a job well done, Art. The information you men collected got to the president and I'm sure will have a great impact on his decisions."

He clasped my hand in his. "The mission was a success. Those men did not die in vain. Now, get dressed and meet me back in my office."

When he was gone, I stood a long time before my locker, then I looked to the other locked lockers. Inside were the last vestiges of the men who had been on Broken Reed. Or maybe their personal effects had already been cleared out, and nothing remained. I had no way of knowing. For me, the closed, sealed lockers symbolized the operation, and I realized I would never see any of them again, even if Jim and Tom were still alive.

I changed uniforms and transferred the capsule into a pocket, then I went back to Brown's office. He had turned on the lights and was sitting behind his desk.

"Your uniform looks a little loose, Art. You need to fatten up."

I had lost weight, but I didn't know when I'd get my appetite back; I didn't think I'd ever be hungry again.

He seemed to be waiting for something, and then the phone rang. "Why don't you answer?" he said to me.

I picked up the phone. "Lieutenant Boyd."

A familiar, flat, Midwestern voice that I had heard on the radio and in newsreels came on the line. "Lieutenant Boyd, I want to give you my personal and heartfelt thanks."

I just stared at the phone.

"Lieutenant Boyd?"

Finally I regained my voice. "Yes, sir."

"You and your team have helped save our nation and perhaps the world from a war no one could have won and that could have cost the lives of millions. I wish I could thank you personally, or give you a medal, but I can't. I am sure you understand."

"Yes, sir, I do. Thank you, sir."

"Now I want you to go back to your unit in Germany as if nothing happened."

"Yes, sir."

"One more thing, Lieutenant. I want you to know that you will never be released from the service without just cause, or until you decide to leave."

There was a short pause. "Do you have any questions for me?"

Still stunned, I merely said, "No, sir. Thank you, Mr. President."

"May God bless you, Lieutenant Boyd. And may God have mercy on the souls of those who gave their lives. On all of us."

The phone went dead.

Brown didn't say a word when I hung up. He stood, ushered me to the door, and locked his office. "I guess that wraps it up."

He walked through the room. I took a last look at the circle of empty chairs, then I left the building.

We got in the car and drove to the BOQ, where he dropped me off. "Get a good night's sleep, Art. I'll pick you up here at 0900. Your flight back to the States leaves at 1200."

On the ride from Camp Drake to Tokyo International in the morning, Brown and I spoke very little. Inside the terminal, he waited with me until my flight was called, then he walked me to the gate.

"When you board, you'll be on your own, Art. We will never see each other again." He put out his hand, then he grabbed me in a hug. Holding me close, he whispered, "Take care of yourself, Art, and your family."

He let me go, and his eyes were mournful. "God almighty—I wish this had ended differently!"

Tears flowed from my eyes without shame.

Brown stepped back and saluted. "It has been an honor to serve with you."

Unable to say a word, I returned the salute, executed a military about-face, and walked through the gate to whatever the future held.

Epilogue

President Truman did not escalate the war in Korea. Though pressed hard by many to combat the communist menace with more men and arms, Truman allowed the stalemate to continue along the thirty-eighth parallel. He believed, based on intelligence from Operation Broken Reed, that intensifying and enlarging the war would result in an atomic holocaust.

Armistice talks, which had started back in July 1951, continued with little progress. They were broken off numerous times and bogged down over many issues, including POWs. Nevertheless, combat continued unabated.

The communists, with a massive number of troops on the Korean peninsula, were in no hurry to concede anything; they felt time was on their side. Pressure on Truman to take decisive action increased relentlessly. UN allies wanted the war to end, but armistice talks dragged on and on.

Korea dominated events in the United States in 1952.

Dwight D. Eisenhower was nominated by the Republicans and won overwhelmingly in November; one of his campaign promises was to go to Korea.

He did, right after the election and before his inauguration in January 1953. Observing the military situation firsthand, he deemed it hopeless. It was entirely possible that President Truman had shared with Eisenhower what he had learned from the twenty intelligence reports received from Operation Broken Reed.

An armistice was signed at Panmunjom on July 27, 1953. The boundary between North and South Korea was established at the thirty-eighth parallel where the war had started three years earlier—exactly where it is today.

The war resulted in over 1,300,000 South Korean deaths, many of them civilians. The Chinese lost 1,000,000 and the North Koreans about 500,000. South Korean industry was severely damaged, and North Korea was devastated by U.S. bombing.

Since then, tensions in Korea have ebbed and flowed for more than fifty years.

In North Korea, Kim Il Sung ruled until his death in 1994. His son, Kim Jong Il, replaced him and is still in power. The Kim dynasty has ruled North Korea for fifty-seven years.

In South Korea, there has been a succession of leaders, one assassinated and several found guilty of corruption, but it has become a democracy.

Today, North Korea is a nuclear power, impoverished and erratic. South Korea has developed into a major industrial nation.

The Korean peninsula remains a trouble spot, almost literally a powder keg.

After Operation Broken Reed, I fell victim to post-traumatic stress disorder (PTSD) and suffered periods of anxiety and depression for more than half a century.

Flashbacks and nightmares haunted my days and nights; they still do. Nevertheless, because of my oath, I never spoke of, nor made reference to, Operation Broken Reed, for forty-seven years. Though I desperately wanted to know what had happened to Tom Capeman and Jim Pearson, I never looked them up. I couldn't. I didn't know who they really were.

When the mission was declassified in 1998, I did everything possible to uncover additional facts about Broken Reed and the fates of Capeman and Pearson. I petitioned the CIA, the Defense Department, the Truman Library, the Departments of the Army, Navy, and Air Force for possible records, even the British Navy, but I never learned anything. As Brown told me would happen, every record had been destroyed. Everywhere I went, I encountered a dead end.

Why such security? I always wondered. I have thought about this for fifty years and have come up with several reasons.

The first, of course, is that President Truman ordered that the mission be kept secret and all records be destroyed. Who would disobey a presidential order?

Yet why did Truman demand such secrecy? Most likely because he had circumvented civilian and military leaders. Specifically, he ignored top military leaders, members of his cabinet, members of Congress, the State Department, theater commanders and their staffs, field commanders, the CIA, and our UN allies. Had Broken Reed been compromised or revealed to those the president had bypassed, he would have incurred their wrath, or lost their loyalty and confidence. He was already on shaky ground with military and congressional leaders for having fired General MacArthur. Revelations would have inflamed his opposition.

A second reason why Truman might have ordered such security measures was to protect individuals. Many Chinese operatives were still behind enemy lines. Had there been any leak about Broken Reed or knowledge of their involvement, these men and their families would have been endangered for as long as they lived.

The Nationalist Chinese government had every reason to deny participation in Broken Reed, not just to protect those who had served, but to avoid conflict with the mainland. Had the Communist Korean government acknowledged such an operation, they would have had to admit an enemy unit had penetrated their lines and obtained critical information.

At the end of the mission, Brown had said, "Someone will watch over you throughout the balance of your military career." This promise was fulfilled, for despite the drop in my efficiency ratings as a result of my "prolonged sixty-eight-day emergency leave of absence" and my not having a college degree, which was required of all active-duty military officers, I was allowed to continue on active duty. I was promoted on a regular basis, although my service record designated me as an officer who should be released from active duty. I retired a lieutenant colonel of my own volition after twenty-two years of service.

I kept the cyanide capsule for forty-seven years, my only souvenir of Broken Reed. After the mission was declassified, I showed it to my wife, my son and daughter, two psychiatrists who were treating me, the Knoxville, Tennessee, Veterans Center team leader, and the Knoxville Veterans Affairs officer. Following the Knoxville Veterans Administration clinical psychiatrist's advice, I destroyed the deadly drug on the afternoon of August 4, 2000. The psychiatrist surmised that the act would help bring closure to a military mission that had held me captive for almost a half century, while at the same time removing the possibility that I might take the cyanide to end a life of mental suffering.

As I watched the 1,000 milligrams of potassium cyanide reduced to a harmless element, I felt a strange, warm feeling, but it was nothing like the release I felt when I completed the final rewrite of this manuscript, fulfilling a promise I had made over fifty-five years ago.

Because of the mission's national-security classification, no member of the intelligence team received any public or military acclaim for their act of service and bravery above and beyond the call of duty.

Afterword

The Korean Military Intelligence War

by Jay T. Young

This book describes a sensitive intelligence mission carried out behind enemy lines in January 1952, at the height of the Korean War. It was deployed at the personal insistence of President Harry S. Truman. At first reading, the details of Operation Broken Reed may appear difficult to believe; however, abundant historical and circumstantial evidence fully supports the authenticity of the mission. Retired Army Lieutenant Colonel Arthur L. Boyd, the mission's only known survivor, indicates in his account that only those individuals personally selected by President Harry S. Truman knew of the mission's existence in 1952. Broken Reed was a SAP, known as a "black" operation, directed by the president.

We still know relatively little about the role of U.S. and allied intelligence during the Korean War. In contrast to the vast outpouring of information about Allied signals intelligence (SIGINT) operations during World War II over the past quarter century, accounts of the role intelligence played in supporting both military operations and political decision making during the Korean War have been few and far between. One likely reason for this paucity of information is the ongoing tension on the Korean peninsula. Since North Korea remains a potential adversary of the United States, and one with a growing inventory of missile-delivery systems, large stocks of chemical and possibly biological weapons, and perhaps a small nuclear arsenal, Washington may still be reluctant to release details about how much and what kind of intelligence it obtained on North Korea and its Chinese and Soviet allies in the past.

General concepts of operations from that era, notably for special operations missions and perhaps SIGINT collection, may still have relevance for the Korean theater today. As is clear from the current debate over Pyongyang's nuclear capability, North Korea, the most closed and militarized society on earth, remains one of the "hardest" of intelligence targets. U.S. officials therefore may be reluctant to provide its ruthless leadership with insight into how we have gathered intelligence about them.

Scattered accounts over the past ten years have provided a small window into the world of Korean War–era intelligence and special operations. We know, for example, that the Allies supported extensive partisan operations behind Communist lines throughout the war. There was substantial opposition to the Pyongyang regime, especially in Hwanghae Province (located southwest of Pyongyang, near the thirty-eighth parallel). Large numbers of refugees from the north who fled south after the reinstallation at bayonet point of Kim Il Sung's regime in late 1950 provided the United States with eager sources of partisan recruits. This permitted our support of guerrilla operations deep into North Korea and aggressive attempts to retrieve the downed allied pilots whose capture the Communists so eagerly sought. (So it's no surprise that the organizers of Broken Reed decided to use the cover of a downed B-29 crew—highly prized by the Communists for possible intelligence on U.S. nuclear capabilities—for the phony convoy that would convey Broken Reed mission members and associated communications gear.) The Allies supported these operations with an extensive network of bases on islands off both Korean coasts and a small fleet of naval vessels (possibly including the HMS *Cardigan Bay,* which appears to have spotted Art Boyd's desperate signal following his convoy's destruction near the west coast of North Korea).

Moreover, one recent account reveals that the United States used bases in Taiwan and other islands off the coast of southeastern China to support Nationalist guerrilla operations against the Communist mainland regime, presumably to try to draw People's Republic of China (PRC) forces away from Korea. Note the important role played in Operation Broken Reed by Nationalist Chinese who posed as Communist troops guarding the supposed American POWs. Washington turned down Chiang Kai-shek's potentially incendiary offer of Nationalist Chinese regular forces for the Korean front, but clearly welcomed the use of Nationalist bases, partisans, and agents in aspects of the secret war.

We know only a limited amount about the role of SIGINT in the war. In recognition of the fiftieth anniversary of the Korean War, the National Security Agency (NSA) released a small number of brief assessments of SIGINT performance during the entire war, but these deal only with select junctures, such as the defense of the Pusan perimeter and the Chinese intervention. These brief synopses, two of them declassified from what appear to be larger studies, provide some tantalizing, but fragmentary, insight into SIGINT available to allied commanders during the war. It is clear, for example, that even with this sadly incomplete evidence, our access to Chinese civil communications permitted the monitoring of the Chinese troop buildup in Manchuria during the fall of 1950, prior to Beijing's move into North Korea.

Allied commanders, notably Major General Charles Willoughby, General MacArthur's inept and arrogant chief intelligence officer, preferred to believe that China would not intervene, and thus chose to ignore what warning information

SIGINT did provide. At an earlier crucial moment, when the North Korean Army was threatening to push the Allies back from their perimeter around the southern port city of Pusan, intercepts of North Korean communications by hastily assembled U.S. and South Korean signal teams provided U.S. general Walton Walker with timely and detailed information on North Korean plans and their army's growing logistical problems. Walker used this intelligence to blunt and ultimately defeat the North Korean assault.

Despite successes such as holding the Pusan perimeter, the bits of evidence we now have indicate that the effectiveness of Allied intelligence and special operations was highly uneven. The intelligence available to commanders in Korea seems paltry compared with what the Allies enjoyed during World War II, when Allied SIGINT efforts provided intelligence on Nazi and Japanese military operations and strategic decision making whose level of timeliness and detail made an incalculable contribution to the defeat of the Axis powers. Some attributed this situation in Korea to the decimation of the military after World War II. As Eighth Army commander General James Van Fleet noted in June 1952:

> It has become apparent . . . that during the between wars interim we have lost, through neglect, disinterest and possibly jealousy, much of the effectiveness in intelligence work that we acquired so painfully in World War II. Today, our intelligence operations in Korea have not yet approached the standards that we reached in the final year of the last war.

In addition to the problems caused by postwar spending cuts on intelligence, problems exacerbated by fierce interservice rivalries, the Allies in Korea also faced Communist adversaries highly skilled in intelligence and counterintelligence. Well-established masters of espionage, and blessed, as we now know, with high-level penetrations of the British and American governments (especially the British secret service), the Soviets probably had fairly detailed information about Allied intelligence-gathering capabilities that they could share with their North Korean and Chinese allies. In addition, since all three powers were totalitarian states, they had well-developed and effective internal security capabilities that made support for large-scale internal subversion by the United States extremely difficult.

The progress of the war and the physical nature of the Korean theater also constrained Allied intelligence effectiveness. By late 1951, as cease-fire negotiations began to accelerate, the fighting had settled into the static war of position that would characterize the Korean conflict through to the armistice, in July 1953. The ending of the mobile phase of the war had two important ramifications for Allied intelligence. First, as the Communist armies increasingly occupied fortified positions, they moved away from wireless to more secure landlines for communications. Although the Allied forces would, during this phase of the war, encounter some success in tapping into front-line Communist communications, which would provide them with some measure of tactical warning, they encountered great difficulty in determining broader Communist intentions and obtaining a timely and accurate "order of battle" (the overall number, location, and strength of enemy forces) for the entire Communist army. Second, as the war settled down into its static phase, the North Koreans could pay greater attention to their rear areas to guard against Allied-supported guerrilla activity. Such heightened security made it more difficult for the Allies not just to support partisan operations but even simply to insert, maintain contact with, and exfiltrate small reconnaissance teams and individual agents with valuable intelligenc[illegible] Such concerns undoubtedly helped form part of the rationale f[illegible] launching Broken Reed.

As is discussed in this narrative, the broader strategic situation facing President Truman in late 1951 was also part of the rationale for launching an operation as bloody and dangerous as Broken Reed. Scholars now recognize the crucial role played by the Korean War in changing the nature of the cold war. Many in the Truman administration, which had kept a tight rein on military expenditures, thought that the North Korean attack might be an attempt by the Soviets to start a third world war, which led the U.S. government to quickly launch a major military buildup designed to increase the size and readiness of U.S. forces worldwide. In fact, some saw Korea as a possible diversionary move to tie down Allied forces in northeast Asia while the Soviets launched major attacks in Western Europe or the Middle East. Moreover, intelligence in 1951 indicated that not only were the Soviets providing the Chinese and North Koreans with advanced equipment such as the MiG-15 jet fighter, but there were also clear signs that Soviet pilots were flying some of the aircraft.

U.S. strategists were greatly concerned about the large Soviet army and naval forces (especially the submarine fleet) stationed in the Soviet Far East, and nervously sought to determine if any Soviet ground forces had joined their Chinese and North Korean allies along the battlefront.

CIA assessments presented to President Truman and his advi-
in late 1951 presented a grim picture. One estimate published
gust 1951 noted that "[t]here have been many indications of
unist preparation for a new offensive, including troop
nt, logistical buildup, and reinforcement. . . . There have
unconfirmed reports of Soviet troop concentrations in
including locations along the Korean border. . . ." The
d that those Soviet forces in the Far East at the time
combat aircraft (albeit relatively few jets), 35 divi-
marines. In September 1951, the CIA provided

an assessment of the world situation over the next two years in which it stated, "The military strength-in-being of the Soviet orbit should further increase in the next few years. Of greatest significance is a probable improvement in Soviet capabilities for an atomic attack and for their defense against such attack, the further development of Chinese strengths, and continued growth of European satellite military powers." In short, in late 1951, President Truman was receiving grim assessments of the global strategic situation, which included reports of a possible major offensive in Korea by recently reinforced Communist armies and air forces.

Compounding Truman's uncertainty about the global strategic environment was his likely suspicion about the quality of the intelligence on Korean developments he was receiving. Truman was interested in improving the performance of U.S. intelligence. He is the father of the modern U.S. intelligence community. The CIA and NSA both were established during his presidency. But the performance of U.S. intelligence had been poor during the early stages of the Korean War. Ambiguous warnings by the CIA and others about a possible attack by North Korea had been followed by the unwillingness of MacArthur's intelligence officers even to consider the possibility of Chinese intervention, despite a number of warnings about possible PRC military action. Faced with an increasingly pessimistic view of Communist intentions and their strength by an intelligence community that appeared overly complacent, and that lacked consistent and reliable sources of information, Truman must have concluded that he needed independent verification of the true strength and disposition o Communist forces in Korea. Only with more detailed informatio than he now had, information held by sources on the ground w had little or no way to get their intelligence out of North Ko could the president hope to make a truly informed decision a what the Allies' next move needed to be. If he were to discover that reports of a new Communist offensive were true, and that Soviet forces were playing a major combat role, the United States might have had to consider the use of nuclear weapons to halt the Communist onslaught in Korea while retaining sufficient strength to blunt possible Soviet attacks elsewhere.

This is the strategic background behind the decision to launch Operation Broken Reed. The story of this mission, and what it accomplished at a time of extreme international tension, will rank as one of the most incredible of many secret cold war–era operations about which we are only now learning. Yet, Art Boyd's most fervent hope is that if readers take anything away from this account, it will be a sense of admiration and remembrance for the brave men of Broken Reed who gave their lives during a crucially important and highly dangerous mission over a half century ago.

—Jay T. Young

Jay T. Young has spent over twenty years working in intelligence in both the public and private sectors. A former senior military analyst at the Central Intelligence Agency, he specialized in military issues in Korea. Also a reserve officer in Naval Intelligence, he has served with S. Southern Command, Pacific Command, and the U.S. Seventh t. Currently Mr. Young is director of market and competitive intel- at Perot Systems in Plano, Texas. He has a BA in history from MA in War Studies from the University of London, and has all coursework for a doctorate in military history at The Ohio rsity.

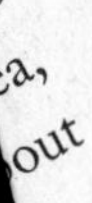

Index

Author's Note

Doubtless, there will be those who will question the authenticity of this story. To do so is understandable, for no official record remains to verify that such a military intelligence mission ever took place.

Indeed, the mission's authenticity has been questioned by an officer who was assigned to the South Korea Central Intelligence Agency station at the time of Broken Reed. Understandably, he expressed doubt that it had taken place. Neither he nor his station chief had been informed of the operation. President Harry S. Truman had ordered the entire Far East intelligence community cut out of the Broken Reed intelligence operation, reasoning that he did not want to risk having anyone interfere with, or possibly compromise, the mission.

Complete knowledge of the mission was held by only twenty-five individuals worldwide. Others who had a part in the operation were provided information limited to a "need-to-know" basis.

An overwhelming amount of circumstantial and historical evidence supports the mission as having taken place during the month of January 1952. Even so, the author fully comprehends and accepts the fact that many readers will express doubt that this unconventional and bizarre military intelligence operation ever took place.

On the other hand, it is possible that a reader will recognize that he or she played a vital part in Broken Reed. That person is exhorted to come forward in support of a story that honors seventy-five men who paid the supreme price while carrying out the mission.

Acknowledgments

Words are inadequate to express my deep and enduring gratitude to my wonderful and loving wife of sixty-two years, Nell. She stood by my side for over a half century as I continued to endure the hellish memories of Operation Broken Reed. Her enduring love brought me through the horror of flashbacks and nightmares. I would never have lived to complete this story without her presence in my life, for without her there is a certainty that I would have ended my life rather than continue to suffer mental torment in silence.

My son, Lanny, and daughter, Ranée, supported me with their love and continued to encourage me to finish the task, to tell a story that must be made known, to not walk away and give up in despair.

This story was written under the outstanding guidance and writing expertise of Michael Peterson, author of the best seller *A Time of War,* as well as many other books that became best sellers. Mike continued to assist in preparation of the final manuscript even while serving a life sentence without parole for a crime that he did not commit. He is one of the finest gentlemen that I have ever known.

My sincere thanks go to Al Zuckerman, my literary agent with

Writers House in New York City. His counsel, patience, and professionalism were instrumental in transforming "just another" war story into a tale of bravery and international intrigue, a story that demanded to be told.

I am grateful to Jay T. Young, a U.S. Navy Reserve officer who spent over twenty years working in intelligence within both public and private sectors. As a former senior military analyst with the Central Intelligence Agency, he specialized in military issues in Korea. Commander Young's enlightening research in support of *Operation Broken Reed* is reflected in his comments concerning this book.

My heartfelt gratitude goes to the following two gentlemen who were instrumental in the publication of the Broken Reed story. Initially, both encouraged me to write the story down as a therapeutic exercise. As the story unfolded over the years, both continued to urge me to have the story published, not only for my own benefit, but that others who might be struggling with a similar experience might derive help and solace.

Doctor Arvell S. Luttrell, a Knoxville, Tennessee, board-certified psychiatrist who specializes in combat-related post traumatic stress disorder (PTSD) psychiatric counseling, pressed me to reach deep into my memory, draw out, and deal with the painful, blood-soaked thoughts that have dominated my life for over fifty years.

Mr. Ronald Coffin, MSSW, team leader for the Knoxville, Tennessee, Veteran's Center, has worked with combat veterans with PTSD since 1981. Since my first meeting with him on February 25, 2000, Ron has provided insight and encouragement to face the hellish memories of Operation Broken Reed that I harbored for over fifty years. His continued prodding to "put the story in print" is a major causation for publication.

I owe a debt of gratitude to the following individuals and

organizations for their assistance while I endeavored to uncover corroborating evidence in support of the authenticity of Operation Broken Reed:

The Central Intelligence Agency
The U.S. Army Intelligence and Security Command
The U.S. Army Special Operations Command
The U.S. Army Declassification Agency
The U.S. Army Military History Institute
The U.S. Army Center of Military History
The Defense Technical Information Center
The National Archives and Records Administration
Donald C. Hakenson, Director for the Department of the Army Records Research Center
Colonel Daniel J. Baur, Director of Counterintelligence, Department of the Army Human Intelligence (HUMINT) and security
James A. Gilbert, Command Historian, Department of the Army Intelligence and Security Command
David A. Giodano, Modern Military Records, National Archives at College Park, Maryland
David D. Salvetti, Director, Center for the Study of Intelligence, Central Intelligence Agency
Dr. Kenneth Finlayson, Command Historian, U.S. Army Special Warfare Center, Fort Bragg, North Carolina
John J. Duncan, Congressional Representative from the Second Congressional District of Tennessee—who hand-carried a copy of an early Broken Reed manuscript to the White House
Ms. Carol Bryley, Classified Archivist, The Truman Library
The Harvard University Alumni Association—for their diligent search in an attempt to identify a member of the Broken Reed intelligence team

Colonel Ben S. Malcom—for assistance in making contact with the White Tigers, a Korean partisan organization that operated behind enemy lines in north Korea at the time of Broken Reed

William N. Naylor, Department of Defense Prisoner of War and Missing Personnel Office

Stephen Prince, Historian II, Ministry of Defence, British Naval Historical Branch, London, England

And to the more than fifty individuals who have read this manuscript—I extend my heartfelt thanks for their feedback and encouragement, which became instrumental in the publication of this story.